UNITY IN GREEK POETICS

UNITY IN
GREEK POETICS

GGGGGGGGGGGGGGGGGGGGGGGGGGGGGGGGGGGGGGGGGGGGGGGGGGGGGGGGGGGGGGG

M. HEATH

CLARENDON PRESS · OXFORD
1989

Oxford University Press, Walton Street, Oxford OX2 6DP

Oxford New York Toronto
Delhi Bombay Calcutta Madras Karachi
Petaling Jaya Singapore Hong Kong Tokyo
Nairobi Dar es Salaam Cape Town
Melbourne Auckland
and associated companies in
Berlin Ibadan

Oxford is a trade mark of Oxford University Press

Published in the United States
by Oxford University Press, New York

British Library Cataloguing in Publication Data
Heath, Malcolm
Unity in Greek poetics.
1. Poetry in Greek, to ca. 500—Critical studies
I. Title
881'. 01'09
ISBN 0-19-814059-2

Library of Congress Cataloging in Publication Data
Heath, Malcolm
Unity in Greek poetics / M. Heath
Bibliography. Includes indexes.
1. Greek poetry—History and criticism—Theory, etc.   2. Poetics.
I. Title.
PA3092.H43U55   1989   801'.95'0938—dc20   89-9223
ISBN 0-19-814059-2

Set by Latimer Trend & Company Ltd, Plymouth
Printed in Great Britain by
Courier International Ltd,
Tiptree, Essex

Preface

THIS book began life in a footnote written when I was a graduate
student of Wadham College, Oxford (see Heath 1987a, 105 n. 26);
work began in earnest while I was a Senior Scholar of Merton College
(1982–4); a Research Fellowship at Hertford College gave me the
opportunity to complete the research in substance (1984–7); and the
final revisions were made during a temporary lectureship in the
Department of Greek at the University of St Andrews (1987–8). I am
grateful to the many friends and colleagues who have helped in
making this nomadic phase of my career both enjoyable and acade-
mically fruitful— and who have helped also to bring it to a propitious
end.

Two kindnesses deserve particular mention. To Christopher Rowe
I am indebted for a prolonged discussion of the *Phaedrus*, from which
I have learnt much. Donald Russell commented on the text at two
stages of its evolution; his suggestions put me on the track of a good
deal of evidence that I would otherwise have missed, and did much to
improve the structure and presentation of the end product. I am
responsible, of course, for the errors, omissions, and obscurities which
remain.

M. H.

School of Classics, University of Leeds
November 1988

Contents

I

Introduction

WHEN someone speaks to us, we will generally try to make sense of what has been said. If the utterance consists of two apparently unrelated sentences, we are likely to infer that it is in some way pregnant; we will then find ourselves looking for a latent or unobvious connection between the two sentences, which might explain why they were uttered together. This attempt to find an integrated interpretation of an apparently incoherent utterance would provide one simple illustration of the phenomenon with which this book is primarily concerned. For what we would be doing in that case is assuming that the utterance was *unified*, and allowing ourselves to be guided by that assumption in interpreting what was said.

This is only one instance of a more general feature of interpretation. There are various things in respect of which an utterance may be well-formed or defective. For example, as well as being coherent in itself it should relate intelligibly to the context in which it is produced, and also to its addressee; there should be some point in saying this, to this person, here and now. Unity is therefore only one of the many criteria which we expect an utterance to satisfy if it is to be accepted as well-formed.

But the unity which we look for in any utterance is not always and everywhere of the same kind. If we are engaged in casual friendly conversation, we are likely to tolerate a degree of inconsequentiality in each other's remarks that we would find irritating in a serious discussion. But if we are reading poetry we will probably not be irritated; refusing to accept the apparent inconsequence at face value, we would try to reinterpret it as something more elusive and subtle. In a formal or literary context our expectations of well-formedness are stricter than in an informal or conversational context, but they are also less readily defeasible; we are prepared to work harder to find an interpretation in accordance with the criteria which we assume the work should satisfy. The recognized techniques of literary criticism provide us with a range of devices for eliciting

unified interpretations from apparent inconsequentiality; we are
familiar with concepts of ambiguity, irony, symbolism, and other
kinds of literary indirectness that help us to bring *prima facie* ill-
formed texts under proper control.

This variation of our expectations according to the kind of
utterance in hand corresponds broadly to the conventional notion of
genre in literary science; what we have been saying, therefore, is that
different criteria of adequacy and excellence are applicable to
different genres. But our expectations vary also according to the
person who is speaking; for example, when we are interpreting the
utterances of a known ironist we do not necessarily employ the same
techniques as we apply to things that are said by other speakers. This
point may be generalized to refer to classes or kinds of person.
Translating once again into terms of literary science, we may say that
genre is to be understood as a historical phenomenon, in terms of
historically and culturally specific traditions of literary practice; the
criteria of adequacy and excellence applied to texts of a given genre
vary from one nation and one period to another. If we are to make
sense of texts from a remote culture, therefore, we cannot afford to
take it for granted that our own expectations are applicable; we
should try instead to reconstruct the assumptions, about unity or
about any other aspect of a well-formed text, that are appropriate to
a text of that kind in that culture. We must become conscious both of
the content of our own systems of presupposition and preference, and
of their contingent nature; and we must learn to recognize the
distance between them and the presuppositions and preferences
which determined the composition and original reception of the texts
with which we are dealing.

By the term 'poetics' I understand primarily such a system of
presupposition and preference, a network of aesthetic and technical
principles underlying the literary production and reception of texts; a
secondary poetics is an attempt to articulate or to reflect explicitly on
such a primary system. My immediate concern is with Greek secondary poetics, with the literary theory and criticism of the ancient Greek
world; but I see this enquiry as a means of access to Greek primary
aesthetics. My ultimate aim is to uncover the assumptions which
Greek poets and writers of artistic prose shared with their audiences,
and to test the characteristic expectations and assumptions of modern
criticism of Greek literature against this reconstruction.

More specifically, I am concerned in this book with the concept of the 'unity' of the literary work. This is not an entirely satisfactory term; it seems to imply a quality that can be determined by simple enumeration, although the complex and inconclusive debates of literary criticism clearly involve a less tractable kind of metric. We would do better, perhaps, to use a term such as 'coherence'; for the underlying concern of discussions of 'unity' is, as I suggested initially, that texts should 'make sense as a whole'[1] or 'hang together' in some acceptable way. Clearly, different views may be held about what is acceptable if a text is to 'make sense as a whole'—different views have in fact been held; the notion of 'unity' is, as we have stated, subject to historical and cultural change. It follows that if we wish to understand Greek texts we need to reconstruct, among other things, the constraints and ideals of coherence which informed their composition. This is an urgent task. Appeals to an ideal of unity or coherence frequently play a decisive role in exegetical reasoning about ancient literature, but there is little sign that any systematic reconstruction of the relevant aesthetic is being undertaken—or even that the need for such a reconstructive effort has been adequately grasped.

An illustrative case may be helpful at this point; I shall take as my example recent discussion of Euripides' *Suppliants*. This is a useful instance, since the play does exhibit a number of problematic features in its construction—features, that is, that modern critics have tended to find problematic, although they are in fact recurrent and typical features in the Greek tragic corpus. This of itself suggests a discrepancy between the presuppositions of Greek poetic practice and those of modern exegetes, and invites us to explore the differences between them.

A brief summary will show why most recent critics have found the play's unity and coherence problematic. It begins with a speech in which Aethra, mother of Theseus, explains that Adrastus and the play's eponymous Chorus, the mothers of the 'Seven against Thebes', are seeking the assistance of her son in recovering the bodies of those who fell in the battle at Thebes; this is the initial situation from which the plot unfolds. First, the suppliants make their approach to Theseus; he replies in a lengthy moralizing discourse, which seems for the most part to have only a tangential bearing on the issue in hand. Theseus' first instinct is to refuse the supplication, but his mother persuades him to relent; this is her last contribution to the play.

---

[1] Young 1970, 2 n. 3; cf. Heath 1986b, 97–8.

Theseus goes to secure the consent of the Athenian people to his support for the suppliants, but as soon as he returns a Theban ultimatum arrives; this intervention has precisely no effect on the subsequent development of the plot, but—the Theban emissary being of an argumentative disposition—it does divert the play into an elaborate debate on the relative merits of democracy and autocracy. The next act begins with a Messenger's report of the hard-fought battle in which Theseus succeeds in asserting the suppliants' rights; but the incipient celebration of victory is curtailed by Adrastus' expressions of remorse and grief, and the subsequent act is devoted to lamentations over the recovered corpses, culminating in a funeral eulogy of the dead heroes spoken by Adrastus. The corpses are then removed for cremation, but their expected return is retarded: quite unexpectedly there appears Evadne (wife to one of the dead), soon followed by her aged father Iphis; despite his pathetic pleas she throws herself onto her husband's pyre—and is promptly forgotten. The ashes of the dead are brought back and there is further lamentation; the sons of the Seven anticipate vengeance. Theseus is on the point of handing the ashes over to them unconditionally, but Athene appears and checks him, so ensuring that Athens receives a just reward for its just endeavour; this theme is developed aetiologically, and a final prophecy foreshadows the success of the avenging expedition of which the sons have spoken.

The difficulties which a play so constructed presents to modern readers are, as I have already suggested, not so much isolated eccentricities as recurrent features in the extant tragedies.[2] First, the action of the play is pursued beyond the point of rest implied by the resolution of its initial situation; this feature is found also in, for example, *Ajax* (*PGT* 5. 42, 5. 63) and *Heracles*. In several plays it is combined with the technique of 'mobile focus' (*PGT* 3. 1); the tragedians are prone to displace prominent figures from the focal position which they have occupied for much, even most, of a play— Orestes in *Eumenides*, for example, Deianeira in *Trachiniae*, Antigone and Andromache in their respective plays. This particular tendency is less marked in *Suppliants*, since only relatively minor characters are treated in this way: Aethra disappears, Iphis and Evadne appear abruptly and disappear again, and the sons of the Seven achieve a belated and partly prospective prominence. Nevertheless, the general

---

[2] I presuppose the discussion in Heath 1987a, to which I refer in the text as *PGT* (references by chapter and section).

feature—the extended action—is obvious, and is closely connected with a second technique, the use of contrasting material. The suppliant action begins pathetically and shifts to a mood of patriotic enthusiasm (cf. *PGT* 2. 33), but there is no triumphant climax; instead, the poet juxtaposes a series of grief-laden scenes. This contrasting continuation has not been imposed by 'unfinished business', for very little actually happens in the extension (indeed, the most striking sequence of events, the intervention of Evadne and her father, is unprepared and without consequence); the contrast seems to have been contrived for its own sake. A third problematic technique is the use of digression; the debate between Theseus and the Herald is an obvious example—although this at least contributes to the encomium of Athens, and more radical excursions are to be found in other Euripidean plays (*PGT* 4. 22). Euripides' far-flung choral lyrics are also in question here (*PGT* 4. 23), although in this respect *Suppliants* displays considerable restraint.

In the face of these recurrent problems, three responses are possible. First, we might conclude, with regret, that the Greek tragedians were not as skilled at putting plays together as we might have hoped; this, however, is an unattractively patronizing conclusion to draw from mature works by the most highly regarded dramatists of the ancient world. A second option has found much wider favour among recent critics—the assimilation of the plays to modern standards. It is assumed that the problems are merely apparent; they exist only if we concentrate on superficial features of the texts, whereas at the less overt depths at which their real business is transacted the texts will be found entirely coherent. Confronted with the apparently diverging or 'centrifugal' elements of a text such as *Suppliants*, the critic responds 'centripetally', that is, by attempting to show that there is after all a single theme or purpose to which all those elements are subservient.[3] It might, for example, be argued that one element exists to cast an oblique light on another, or that both

---

[3] This is a wholly intelligible interpretative technique. To judge between interpretations one will naturally ask which gives the most comprehensive and economical account of the text, for that interpretation will be the most powerfully explanatory; and this may seem to place a premium on thematic integration. The a priori integrating tendency must, however, be controlled by a historical understanding of the kinds of interpretation appropriate and plausible in a given case; and this is the aim of my reconstructive poetics. I should perhaps add that I am not suggesting that strict thematic integration is the uniform and invariant practice of recent interpreters; but it is a widespread and influential tendency, as the examples cited in this and subsequent chapters should suffice to show.

reflect on a common (and more abstract) theme. Thus the apparent
diversity of the text turns out to be no more than the superficial
manifestation of an underlying and—in the teleological sense—more
final convergence. A brief survey will show how clearly recent work
on *Suppliants* exhibits this tendency.

R. B. Gamble, commenting on the play's 'apparent profusion of
interests' (note the reluctance to accept that this profusion may be
genuine), gives an unusually clear statement of the centripetal
assumption:[4]

Part of the trouble lies in the difficulty of discerning any definite line in the
play, running through it all and capable of accounting for the various scenes
and details satisfactorily. There is, of course, the obvious surface action
holding together the different scenes (or most of them) more or less
adequately: they are all in some way related to the return and burial of the
Argive dead. But within this outer framework of actual dramatic happpen-
ings, a large number of topics are touched upon which seem to bear little or
no relation to each other.

He concludes that the profusion of themes, each treated in an
ambivalent or equivocal way, is designed to reflect the ambivalence
and uncertainty that is 'a central problem in the life of man' (404)—
which thus becomes the integrating theme of the play.[5] This intellectualization of the play is built into Gamble's initial formulation of his
centripetal approach: 'What is the "meaning" of the whole, and how
do the several parts contribute to this? What insight, or intuition, or
"message" is represented by the complete thing?' (385). Intellectualization is present also in W. D. Smith's reading, according to which
'the *Suppliants* progresses not to the completion of an action which will
produce the tragic pleasure out of pity and fear, but rather to the
completion of the exposition of a human dilemma, which will
produce understanding primarily.'[6] This proposal enables Smith to

[4] Gamble 1970, 385. The dismissive attitude taken here to the 'more or less
adequate' surface action is reminiscent of the description of *Andr.* as 'merely a
dramatization of episodes ... linked together by a superficially adequate causal
connection' (P. T. Stevens 1971, 8); I comment on this view in Heath 1987a, 3. 2, and
will return to it in ch. 4 below.
[5] The one theme which Gamble thinks is not treated ambivalently is that of the
obligations imposed by common humanity; although he makes some justified criticisms
of Fitton's misrepresentation of fifth-century ethical assumptions, his own belief that
these obligations are not recognized in traditional ethics is quite wrong (see e.g.
Macleod 1982, Heath 1987a, 5. 1).
[6] Smith 1966, 154.

explain the 'complex form' of the play as a 'picture' of the complex forces affecting human decisions (152), and so to effect an integration: 'The external form of the *Suppliants* seems justified when one stops trying to explain it as a single action with addenda and sees it as two actions, differently structured, juxtaposed for contrast, but related as complementary aspects of the same picture' (152–3).[7]

This last remark reveals the concern felt by many over the play's extended action and the contrasting material which it contains. This concern is evident also in Kitto's discussion: 'The action seems to reach its proper conclusion at v. 975 at the latest ... and, besides being very scattered, it is very inconsistent in tone.'[8] Similarly, J. W. Fitton:[9]

By the end of the scene, the nominal solution of the initial dramatic problem is at hand: the retrieval of the heroes' bodies. The noble action of Athens has effected its purpose. If this were a simple patriotic play, we would expect a relieving of tension and a glorious close. In fact Adrastus and the Chorus are plunged into an even greater sorrow; and episode follows episode for nearly 500 lines.

Kitto, too, rejects the interpretation of the play (offered by the ancient hypothesis) as an 'encomium of Athens' on the grounds that it fails to account for the play's pessimistic parts (222). He does not consider the centrifugal possibility that the play is in part an encomium and in part something else. Fitton does consider this possibility, but summarily dismisses it: 'It fails to appreciate this drama with any aesthetic seriousness as an evolving and interdependent totality' (446)—an argument hard to resist in context, since Fitton supports his centripetal commitment with tendentiously derogatory descriptions of some possible subsidiary functions.

Fitton believes that the play expounds a 'central idea' (444); the play is 'a tragic satire showing how decent people ... are caught up in a vortex of human folly' (442). This reading, too, will strike some as partial; but recalcitrant elements of the play can easily be integrated by supposing that 'the ironical "idea" of the play is separate from its ostensible meaning' (443). Kitto does not resort to that universal

[7] Similarly Burian, who interpets the play as a 'dialectic of issues' (1985, 221 n. 63) argues that 'its complex structure corresponds to a complex vision' (155). More specifically, Burian reads the play in terms of the tension between Theseus' '*kosmos* of intellect' and the '*kosmos* of emotion' which overwhelms it in the latter part of the play.

[8] Kitto 1961, 221.

[9] Fitton 1961, 437.

solvent, irony; consequently he finds himself left with a few 'loosely appended passages' when he integrates the play as 'a coherent and well-designed presentation of a single theme', pacifism (227).[10] Zuntz takes a sterner view. He will not concede loose appendages: 'All these criticisms are conceived with no regard for . . . the drama as a whole. This is their sufficient refutation';[11] but he too thinks that 'this play centres.. upon the exposition of an argument' (6). In his view, it explores the question how man is to live in a godless world, and more specifically how he is to live in a *polis* (6); and thus the play is integrated once again.[12]

It cannot be denied that the techniques seen in these examples— techniques of 'thematic integration', as we might call them—are able to recover this and other texts for the centripetal aesthetic which these critics take for granted; indeed, we are offered an embarrass-ment of possibilities for their reclamation. But that is only to say that the texts *can* be so interpreted; it does not mean that the texts are *rightly* so interpreted—it leaves open the question of historical vali-dity. There is, in fact, a methodological price to pay if one takes this course.[13] When a text is apparently centrifugal in tendency, centripe-tal exegesis must argue that the real point of the text is to be found at a less overt level; it is a species of allegorical reading—although this may readily escape the notice of interpreters already committed to allegoresis by the currently dominant intellectualization of tragedy

[10] Cf. his comment on *Andr.* (1961, 228): 'Nowhere is it more evident that the unity of the play lies in its idea and not in its story' (cf. n. 4 above).

[11] Zuntz 1963, 3–4. But Burian says of Zuntz's reading in turn (1985, 218 n. 35): 'Apart from any other objections, this view denies any dynamic relation between the two main parts of the play, not to mention any serious reflection in the second part of the political themes that dominate the first.' Once again we may observe centripetal assumptions at work.

[12] M. H. Shaw (1982) accepts Zuntz's interpretation in substance, but argues that a more complete integration is possible if one shifts the emphasis to character: 'The first part of the play is not about the importance of pan-Hellenic law so much as it is about the traits of character which lead Theseus to act in accord with law; similarly, the second part is not about the upsetting of the order of existence and its consequences so much as it is about the traits of character which upset that balance' (4). Shaw, too, comments on the 'apparent double theme' of the play and its 'disparate mood' (3).

[13] It is usually impossible to refute interpretations of the kind surveyed here 'head on', since what we judge plausible depends to a large extent on the premises which govern the interpretative process; one must therefore reply indirectly—e.g. by appeal-ing to methodological considerations which may put the premises in question, or to contextual evidence of the kind with which this book is concerned. The point of my survey of recent interpretations, therefore, was not to 'refute' them, but to uncover their operative premises.

(see *PGT* 2).[14] But such a process will remain unnecessary, and therefore open to challenge as arbitrary and uneconomical, as long as the third of our three options remains open.

For we might, thirdly, conjecture that the tragedians, and those audiences and readers who admired them, had their own idea of how plays should be constructed—a distinctive concept of what is to count as skill in dramatic composition which, if we were able in some measure to reconstruct it, would dissolve the difficulties to which our alien preconceptions have given rise.[15] We still might dislike what they did; and we might (if we are very conceited) suppose that our own preferences are intrinsically superior to theirs. But we would at least have less difficulty in grasping what it was that they were doing, and why; and we might even be able to recognize that they were doing it, by their lights, very well. If in addition the range of our aesthetic appreciation were thereby extended, that would seem to me pure gain. The closure of this option cannot be achieved by any lightly dismissive gesture; it is by no means self-evident, when changes in other aesthetic preferences are so well documented, that a centripetal aesthetic should command universal acceptance. Therefore an interpreter sensitive to the historical mutability of taste should wish to explore the possibility that Greek literary practice worked with a concept of unity somewhat different from that at work in most modern criticism.

What evidence is there to support such a view? In an earlier approach to the problem (*PGT* 3. 2) I pointed to the relative lack of interest in the concept of unity in ancient criticism; where it does play an important role—notably, in Aristotle's *Poetics*—it was found that the criteria of unity applied were tolerant of centrifugal practices.[16]

---

[14] 'Allegorical', because the plays are not overtly expositions of abstract themes; to some this usage will perhaps seem objectionable, but Boeckh—a practitioner of the method—rightly took the point (1886, 88–93); for Boeckh as a forerunner of current centripetal intellectualization, see ch. 10 below.

[15] It is tacitly assumed in many recent discussions that to deny the unity of a poem according to some modern criterion of unity is to disparage the poet's artistic abilities. But the question of intent is obviously prior to the question of ability; it is always possible that the poet had little or no interest in the values defined by the modern criteria, and exercised his skill in some other direction.

[16] It is significant that 'unity' in modern discussion is most often used as a pruning implement, a weapon to turn against irrelevance and unnecessary decoration ('*mere* ornament' is a characteristic slur in the secondary literature). But in Aristotle's theory 'unified' implies 'single *and complete*'; a text must have all that it ought to have, as well as lacking what it ought not to have. Given rival aesthetics in which ornamental

Related to the tolerance of digression and similar techniques was an emphasis on diversity (ποικιλία); indeed, in much ancient criticism there is a far greater emphasis on diversity than on unity. This is sufficient grounds on which to conclude at least that the matter requires further investigation; and that is my present purpose. I shall argue in this study that we can reconstruct from Greek literary theory and criticism a concept of unity more liberally centrifugal than we are used to.

There is an obvious danger, of course, in arguing from Greek literary theory and criticism to the underlying principles of Greek literary practice—that is, from secondary to primary poetics. It is inevitably uncertain whether any given critic or theorist has correctly grasped the nature even of contemporary literary composition; and there is very little material that is strictly contempory. Virtually no secondary literature survives from before the fourth century BC; many of my sources are even later in date. But much of the literature to which I would wish to apply my conclusions (and certainly most of the Greek literature at present most highly regarded) belongs to the fifth century or earlier—and it would be absurd to deny that aesthetic preferences were mutable also within the ancient world. On the other hand, my point of departure for this whole enquiry was precisely the literary practice of the fifth century. I did not begin by trying to impose later categories on fifth-century practice; on the contrary, it was the attempt to account for recurrent techniques of fifth-century tragedy without recourse to the epicyclic expedients of centripetal interpretation that led me to adopt categories which I subsequently found I could exhibit from later theory. And it is not only tragedy that displays these characteristics. I have argued elsewhere that Aristophanic comedy lends itself to centrifugal reading; *Wasps*, for example, has disconcerted many modern readers by its thematic shift away from the legal system after the parabasis—and the parabasis itself is an essentially digressive device. We shall see further examples

---

digressions (for example) are respectively admired and despised, an ornamentally digressive poem will seem poorly unified to the despisers; but stripped of its ornament it would seem to the admirers incomplete and unsatisfying. Modern criticism is typically allied to the despisers; but we cannot know, independently of historical research, whether the Greeks were (in general or in particular cases) despisers or admirers—for either position is logically coherent.

in this book—Plato, Isocrates, the Hellenistic poets; and more could be said about (for example) Homer, Pindar or Herodotus.[17]

The convergence between ancient theory and apparent practice is not, of course, conclusive; no historical argument is. But it does have evidential value. There is more to be said for a theory that assumes a measure of continuity and understanding within the Greek literary tradition than for one that requires us to accept a coincidental harmony of modern critical preference with an ancient literary practice unrecorded in a body of critical writing far closer to it in time and cultural milieu. If it can be shown, as I believe it can, that *prima facie* centrifugal techniques appear in diverse authors and genres throughout Greek antiquity—from Homer, as it were, to Heliodorus[18]—and if, in so far as a secondary literature developed and has survived, it consistently supports readings that acquiesce in that centrifugal appearance, then it is reasonable to assume that we are dealing with a persistent tendency of Greek literary aesthetics.

---

[17] For fifth-century tragedy see Heath 1987a, chs. 3–4 (the scheme proposed in 3. 2 will be modified in ch. 11 below), and for comedy see the appendix to Heath 1987b. In two other preliminary studies I have attempted to illustrate the rise of centripetal assumptions in Pindaric criticism (1986b) and in the interpretation of Euripides' *Hecuba* (1987c); I shall develop this aspect of my argument a little further in ch. 10.

[18] Heliodorus is not, in fact, a very good example; he uses digressive techniques rather sparingly (note his restraint in passing over the crocodile in 6. 1; but he does treat the giraffe in 10. 27 more expansively), and in the Renaissance he was valued by some critics for precisely that reason as a model to oppose to the romance (Forcione 1970, 49–87; cf. ch. 10 below). Achilles Tatius would be a better example (e.g. the crocodile in 4. 19): see Hägg 1971, 103–11, 239–41, 326. But he does not alliterate so well.

2

Plato

THE earliest surviving discussion of unity in Greek criticism is to be found in Plato's *Phaedrus*; it is perhaps indicative of the differences between ancient and modern literary aesthetics that this work has itself been found problematic by modern interpreters, precisely because of its resistance to centripetal techniques of interpretation. Our discussion of the principles which Plato adopts must therefore go hand in hand with an interpretation of his practice in this and other dialogues.

The *Phaedrus* falls broadly into two parts. In the first part, there are three speeches about love. Phaedrus reads out one speech (he claims that it is by Lysias) which attempts to persuade a young man that he should grant sexual favours to the speaker, who admits that he is not in love with him, rather than to someone who is in love. Part of the argument, inevitably, is that the lover's attentions are harmful. Socrates makes some scathing remarks about the structure of this speech, and tries to do better; he too develops the idea that a lover's attentions are harmful to the beloved, although he significantly refrains from asserting positively that sexual favours ought to be given to the non-lover (241e5–7). However, even this limited case strikes him on reflection as offensive; if love, he says, is divine, how could it be harmful? So Socrates makes a second speech, a 'palinode' retracting his blasphemy. He still accepts that love as it is ordinarily understood is harmful; but he now maintains that this is a degenerate form of love, and that there is a purer, beneficial kind—that in which the beauty of the beloved triggers the lover's recollection of transcendent beauty, so that the purely physical passion is surpassed and the two together pursue the higher reality. Thus the exposition of the nature and destiny of the soul which constitutes the core of the palinode is not there primarily for its own sake, but serves to provide the necessary premises of the argument for a kind of erotic attachment that is beneficial rather than harmful (παιδεραστεῖν μετὰ φιλοσοφίας, 249a2).

In the second part of the dialogue these three speeches are quarried for illustrative purposes in a discussion of rhetoric. The question is raised whether, and on what conditions, discourse—whether written or spoken, poetry or prose—is a good and proper activity (258d7–11). Socrates proposes a number of criteria which this activity must satisfy if it is to be a genuinely scientific practice (τέχνη). In particular, it must be based on a proper understanding of its subject-matter; and a psychological understanding of different kinds of audience is needed, which will indicate when and how to apply in practice the technical devices which existing rhetorical theorists have catalogued in the mistaken belief that they constitute the science of rhetoric itself, rather than simply the preliminaries to it. Understanding, whether of the world or of the soul, is the province of the philosopher; so the truly scientific rhetorician must be a philosopher. But a philosopher, just because of his understanding of world and soul, will have relinquished, not only the technical deficiencies of existing rhetoric, but also its characteristic aims; for example (273e5–4a2):

The wise man will not exert himself to such an extent for the sake of speaking to or dealing with men, but so as to be able to speak what is pleasing to the gods and to act in all respects, so far as he is able, as would please them. The man of sense ... should not study to please his fellow slaves, unless incidentally, but his good and noble masters.

Specifically, the philosopher will be aware that the only fundamentally serious and important kind of discourse is oral discussion of philosophical questions (277e5–8b4: 'oral', because this part of the dialogue also gives a disparaging estimate of the usefulness of written texts in general). Thus Socrates' 'reformed' rhetoric is in practice hardly distinguishable from philosophy;[1] the reform amounts, on any reasonable view, to an abandonment of rhetoric.[2]

[1] In principle the situation is more complex. The philosopher may use his understanding to persuade the unphilosophical masses, although they cannot strictly be taught; this, although it is not philosophy, will be part of the reformed rhetoric (cf. 277c5–6). In *Statesman* 303e–4d Plato recognizes the social importance of this; but in *Phaedrus* he remains dismissive of discourse other than philosophical discussion and teaching. For a different view see Rowe 1986; I comment on his interpretation, and discuss various aspects of *Phaedrus* more fully, in Heath 1989 (accompanied by a response from Rowe).

[2] "'I should like balls infinitely better,'' she replied, ''if they were carried on in a different manner; but there is something insufferably tedious in the usual process of such a meeting. It would surely be more rational if conversation instead of dancing made the order of the day.'' ''Much more rational, my dear Caroline, I dare say but it would not be near so much like a ball.''' (Jane Austen, *Pride and Prejudice*, vol. 1, ch. 11.)

The distinctiveness of these two sections of the dialogue should not
be obscured by the use of vague labels to designate their supposedly
unitary theme. The first part is concerned with love; it argues that
erotic attraction is harmless, indeed beneficial, if and only if it is
taken up into a certain kind of philosophical activity. The second
part is concerned with rhetoric; it argues that rhetoric is a good and
proper activity if and only if it is philosophical. The answer in each
case is similar; the questions are different. And the second part makes
no attempt to present philosophy under its erotic aspect—whether
that aspect is understood as an aspiration for transcendent beauty or,
more specifically, as παιδεραστεῖν μετὰ φιλοσοφίας.³ It is true that the
discussion of love is applied in the latter part of the dialogue for
illustrative purposes, and it would in principle be possible to maintain
that this application was throughout its primary purpose; but this
does not seem to do sufficient justice to the philosophical seriousness
which the discussion has in its own right. It is more plausible to say
that the speeches have a dual role: the interest in rhetorical technique
is a guise for a serious investigation of genuine philosophical problems concerning love, and the investigation of that problem in turn
becomes (just because of its guise) the basis for a genuine enquiry into
rhetoric. Thus the dialogue as a whole has (at least) two distinct
themes; the sole—and sufficient—reason for their being brought
together, I shall argue, lies in the person of Phaedrus himself.

It may be helpful to ignore for a moment the philosophical
interests of the dialogue and concentrate on its form; that is to say, we
shall bracket out its material concerns and consider the dialogue
simply as a piece of dramatic narrative. From this point of view its
structure shows striking similarities to the techniques of Athenian
tragedy. The discussion between Phaedrus and Socrates develops in
an entirely plausible way, each stage arising naturally from what has
gone before; given these people in this situation, that is indeed what
they would do and say.⁴ Nevertheless, the end of the palinode

³ The first part of the dialogue does not argue that all philosophy involves
παιδεραστεῖν (and I do not believe that Plato would wish to assert this, despite 256e3–
7a2: cf. *Rep.* 403ab): only that παιδεραστεῖν is harmful unless philosophical; so the
argument is not a general one about philosophy or the philosophical life, but one
specifically concerned with a species of love.

⁴ οἷα ἂν γένοιτο, to use an Aristotelian phrase (*Poet.* 1451a37, b5, 8–9; cf. 54a33–6);
and *Phaedrus* satisfies Aristotle's criteria of unity for 'mimetic' (narrative and dramatic)
texts, a category in which he includes philosophical dialogues (*Poet.* 47b11, cf. fr. 72 of
De Poetis). Aristotle's treatment of narrative and dramatic unity is discussed in more
detail in ch. 4 below.

provides a natural point of rest; and the continuation of the discussion beyond that point involves an apparent shift of thematic focus—hitherto we have been concerned with love, but we now switch our attention to rhetoric. As we saw in Chapter 1, many plays in the dramatic corpus prolong the action beyond a point of rest implied in the play's starting-point, and switch attention from one major character or issue to another.

Not surprisingly, modern interpreters of *Phaedrus* have responded to its apparent duality of theme by seeking some measure of thematic integration. C. J. Rowe, noting the very partial use that is made of the content of Socrates' second speech in the ensuing discussion of rhetoric, suggests that this speech 'looks more like an exposition of substantive ideas for their own sake'; but he is reluctant to accept this interpretation, 'especially in the case of a work which makes unity a *sine qua non* of excellence in written compositions', and goes on to ask 'whether there is any way of interpreting the strategy of the *Phaedrus* which provides for the proper integration of Socrates' second speech into the strategy of the whole'.[5] Compare the approach of Hackforth; discussing the views of one recent interpreter Hackforth comments:[6]

Robin ... has convincingly shown that there are insuperable objections to regarding either Rhetoric or Love as the subject; but he seems to me less successful in explaining precisely how the apparent duality is resolved.

Note the assumption that the 'apparent' duality ought to be resolved; the characteristic modern preference for a single theme seems to be at work here. But does Hackforth achieve greater success? Rather than speaking of the 'subject' of the dialogue, he suggests that 'it is useful to ask for the purpose', and finds that 'there are three purposes, all important but one more important than the others' (9). This chief purpose, however, is not most important in the sense of being a hierarchical head, to which the others are functionally subordinate, for there is a competition between them; this results, in Hackforth's view, in a structural flaw. The overall economy of the dialogue is dictated by one of the subsidiary purposes, 'to announce a special method of philosophy' (9); Hackforth argues in his comments on 264e–6b (136):

---

[5] Rowe 1986, 107. Rowe takes Plato's statements of principle unanalysed as a premiss in his interpretation of Plato's practice, but—as we shall see—this is unsafe; Plato's principles are themselves in need of interpretation.

[6] Hackforth 1952, 9 n. 2.

There can, I think, be little doubt that the plan of the whole dialogue is centred upon the present section; for it is in the formulation of the new μέθοδος that the formal relevance of the three discourses . . . is alone to be discovered.

But, as he goes on to observe, 'formal relevance is not the same thing as intrinsic significance or value'; Socrates' second speech serves also a more important function: it is 'a contribution to what I have called the main purpose of the dialogue, the vindication of the pursuit of philosophy as the true nature of the soul.' This explains the length and magnificence of the speech—which is, however, disproportionate: 'Relatively to the formal structure of the whole, the great discourse is both too magnificent and too long; the balance of the dialogue is upset and the structural plan at least partially obscured.' Hackforth believes that 'it is . . . this *double* significance of the speeches which has always troubled readers amd made them feel a lack of unity in the work.' This feeling he regards as 'natural' but 'unjustified', but he does not explain why it is unjustified; in terms of the expectation of a single theme which he turns against Robin, a triple purpose, where the purposes, so far from being subordinate one to another, pull against each other in this way, would seem far from adequately unified.

The modern tendency to seek a unified thematic structure is remarked on by Guthrie, who refers to 'the search, which seems to obsess the scholarly world, for a single aim in each and every dialogue, a "chief object", "objet véritable", "fundamental purpose", "real subject", "Hauptzweck", "totius dialogi consilium" and so forth.'[7] Guthrie suggests that we should 'dispose of' this search; and I believe that his scepticism is justified. To see why, we must look more closely at Plato's discussion of the principles involved.

The first important passage comes early in the discussion of rhetoric which eventually issues into a repudiation of rhetoric as it is currently practised and understood; at this early stage in the discussion, however, we are still involved in preliminary criticisms. But as we have already seen, 'rhetoric' is an expansive concept for Plato, and his discussion aims to define the conditions of excellence governing all forms of composition whatsoever (258d7–11; cf. 278b7–d1). This

---

[7] Guthrie 1975, 130–1; he is discussing *Laches*, and offers a number of illustrations from modern scholarship, but he cross-refers to this comment in his discussion of *Phaedrus* (412).

discussion arises out of Socrates' criticisms of Lysias' speech. The speech itself is meant as a sophistic display-piece, exhibiting the speaker's skill and ingenuity in advancing a paradoxical thesis (cf. 227c3–8). Socrates calls the piece a 'juvenile display' (235a6–8), and is predictably unhappy about the thesis it maintains; but it is the critique of the speech's construction that most concerns us here: it is repetitive (235a4–5); it omits points that ought to have been included (235b1–d3); it does not begin, as a well-constructed speech should, by defining its subject-matter (262d8–4a4, cf. 237b7–c5)—in fact, its opening is more like a peroration (264a4–b2); and in general its arrangement seems random (264b3–8):

As for the rest, don't you think the material of his speech has been thrown out at random (χύδην)? Can you see any cogent reason why his second point must be placed second—or any of the points he makes where they are, for that matter? In my opinion—though I'm no expert—the writer has rather high-handedly said whatever occurred to him. Or do you know of any cogent technical reason why he has set down his remarks in that particular order?

In this respect, Socrates charges, Lysias' speech resembles a feeble epigram, the four end-stopped lines of which could be rearranged in any order without loss of sense, or indeed of artistic merit (264c7–e3).

So random arrangement is, for Socrates, unacceptable; for any part of a text, it ought to be possible to explain why, on technical grounds, it must come just where it does: we should be able to cite the ἀνάγκη λογογραφική (264b7) of its placement. That is to say (and here we come to the crucial passage), a well-constructed speech will resemble a living organism in respect of its physical embodiment; it will have all and only those parts which it ought to have, and it will have them in the right places (264c2–5):

I think you will agree with this point, at least: that every text should be constructed like a living organism with its own body; it must not lack head or feet, but must have its middle parts and its extremities, composed so as to fit appropriately with each other and the whole (πρέποντα ἀλλήλοις καὶ τῷ ὅλῳ γεγραμμένα).

This point is repeated a little later, without recourse to the organic analogy, in a discussion of tragedy.[8] The composition of a tragedy

---

[8] As we have mentioned, Plato is proposing principles to govern all forms of composition (258d7–11); in working up to that point he suggests that drawing up motions for the assembly is a species of rhetoric (258a1–c6), and dramatic composition is drawn in obliquely at that point by way of a metaphor (258b2–3).

does not consist in lumping together speeches of different kinds without regard for propriety; on the contrary, tragedy is precisely the ordered composition of such elements, their appropriate relative disposition (268c5–d5):

Socrates: What if someone went up to Sophocles or Euripides and said that he knew how to write very long speeches about trivial things and very short speeches about important things, and that he could make them pathetic when he wanted, or again fearful and menacing, and so on and so forth; what if he said that by teaching these things he would be transmitting the art of tragic composition?

Phaedrus: I think they would laugh, Socrates, at anyone who thought that tragedy is anything other than the appropriate disposition of those elements, relative both to each other and to the whole which they together form (τὴν τούτων σύστασιν πρέπουσαν ἀλλήλοις τε καὶ τῷ ὅλῳ συνισταμένην).

This remark about tragedy is one of a series of analogies which Socrates adduces to show that an art or science (τέχνη) is not constituted by the knowledge of its means or elements alone; that is necessary prior knowledge, but the art itself consists in the knowledge of when, where and how to apply those means to achieve the end of the art in question. A doctor must know when and how to apply his medicines so as to produce health (268a8–c4); a musician must know when and how to play notes so as to produce a tune (268d6–9a4). In the same way, Socrates argues, the technical manuals of the rhetoricians contain the prolegomena to rhetoric, classifying the devices and divisions of a speech, but do no more (266d5–8a7, 269a5–c5); the real art lies in the persuasive use of these elements, severally and in combination (τὸ ... ἕκαστα τούτων πιθανῶς λέγειν τε καὶ τὸ ὅλον συνίστασθαι, 269c2–4). This can only be determined on the basis of a scientific psychology, a science of the auditor's soul (ψυχή) which will disclose both what effects one ought to pursue and how in any given case they may be attained (269c6–274b5); only such a science will tell the speaker when best to employ his devices and when to refrain, their εὐκαιρία and ἀκαιρία (271e2–2a8).

One thing that may be noted in these passages is that Plato does not, in any of them, use the term 'unity' or any close equivalent; he speaks rather of completeness (requiring that a text have all and only the parts which it ought to have) and of coherence or appropriate order (those parts should be properly arranged). He does compare the text to a living organism, and this analogy has become a paradigmatic expression of the concept of artistic unity; but the metaphor has undergone many transformations in its long career (we shall see some of them in the course of this book), and we must be careful not to force later conceptions onto Plato's use of it. In fact Plato uses the analogy only to emphasize his point about appropriate order; as for any animal there is a natural complement of limbs and a proper order for their composition into a complete body, so a text should contain all and only those elements that are appropriate to it, and those elements should be appropriately ordered. Bielmeier (one out of many) will serve to illustrate the ways in which illegitimate inferences have been made from Plato's use of the image. Having remarked that its *tertium comparationis* is unclear, he discusses it briefly and concludes:[9]

> Through an argument *e contrario* we reach the conclusion that Plato's comparison of the speech with a ζῷον means that its sequence of thought must be constructed with the same inner necessity as the limbs of a ζῷον, which, despite their diverse functions, are held together by a unitary *Lebensprinzip*.

This *Lebensprinzip* is analogous to the text's 'unitary *Grundthema*', and so the image implies that a single theme is required. But where, one might ask, does this unitary principle come from? Plato says nothing about it; even granted that the appropriate disposition of an animal's limbs is determined by its biological functions (and so, in a sense, by a *Lebensprinzip*), the addition of 'unitary' is speculative; and to relate that to a *Grundthema* still more so. Bielmeier works a sleight-of-hand upon us to incorporate his theory into Plato's image.

The attempt to import a *Lebensprinzip* into *Phaedrus* 264c2–5 is gratuitous; it is only the external bodily form of the organism that is there in question, and there is no mention of its soul. When the soul of a text is mentioned in fourth-century sources (as in *Phdr.* 275d4–6 with 276a8–9; Alcidamas, *Soph.* 27–8) the point is a quite different one, the contrast between written and spoken discourse. As for the comparison with an animal's bodily form,[10] the 'headless' text

---

[9] Bielmeier 1930, 22–3. Bielmeier is defending the interpretation of Plato's theory of literary unity developed by the later Neoplatonists, which I discuss in ch. 9 below; for the background to his *Grundthema*, see the discussion of Boeckh in ch. 10 below.

[10] Gorgias, *Helen* 8, should not be dragged in here, as (e.g.) by Süss, 'der weittragende Vergleich mit einem lebendigen σῶμα' (1910, 51, cf. 51 n. 1, 74); there is no mention of a 'living body' here: Gorgias is pointing out the contrast between material *insubstantiality* of discourse and its great power. For justified criticism of Süss and others on this point, see Sicking 1963, 228–31 (the whole article is instructive for our present theme).

suggested in *Phaedrus*—incomplete and so ill-ordered—is something of a cliché in Plato; to supply the conclusion of a discussion is to add its head (*Phlb.* 66c10–d2, *Tim.* 69b1–2); if that precaution were to be omitted, the text would wander round without a head, looking very peculiar (*Gorg.* 505c10–d3, *Laws* 752a2–4). The idea is taken up by Aristotle with a neat pun: 'if the listener is of such a kind, then there is no need for a proem, except that one should state the subject in summary form (κεφαλαιωδῶς), so that the text has a head (κεφαλήν), just like a body' (*Rhet.* 1415b7–9). The term 'in the form of a body' (σωματοειδῶς) is used several times in the fourth-century *Rhetoric to Alexander* in the sense 'in one place, together', as opposed to 'piecemeal' (κατὰ μέρος). Thus the author contrasts at one point the preceding investigation of rhetorical devices individually and in isolation with the following discussion of their combination 'in bodily form' in whole speeches (*ad Alex.* 1436a27–31). Elsewhere (1438b14–29) the author lists three ways of handling the narrative of a forensic speech: if the facts are few and familiar, include them in the proem; if many and unfamiliar, treat them piecemeal (παρ' ἕκαστον), defending each part as one proceeds; if they are moderate in number but unfamiliar, the exposition can be placed after the proem in a body (σωματοειδῆ). The same distinction between narrative justified piecemeal (παρὰ τὰ μέρη) and delivered 'in bodily form' is made at 1442b28–33; Aristotle makes this distinction at *Rhet.* 1416b16–26, without referring to bodies (οὐκ ἐφεξῆς ἀλλὰ κατὰ μέρος). In this usage, clearly, there is no significant engagement of the organic analogy; and it may be observed that composition 'in the form of a body' is not a general ideal, but a particular technique, the use of which would in some circumstances be inappropriate.[11] But even where the analogy is engaged in the fourth century, there is no hint that it entails a unitary theme.[12]

---

[11] Note in these passages the contrasting use of the term ποικιλία. In *Rhet.* 1416b25 Aristotle uses it in the sense 'over-complex' (cf. *Poet.* 1459a34) in advising against the continuous presentation of material in some circumstances; *ad Alex.* 1438b21 praises discontinuous presentation in similar circumstances, using the same term in the sense 'varied'—and therefore likely to engage the audience's attention (ἀναλαμβάνειν, as at *Rhet.* 1354b32).

[12] A few additional references: in Ar. *Poet.* 1450b34–51a4 the animal is purely *exempli gratia* in making the point that any entity should be neither too large nor too small; *Poet.* 1459a20–1 compares text and animal as functional wholes—I return to this in ch. 4. One might also mention Pl. *Statesman* 277b7–c3, where the unfinished discourse is compared to a picture or statue of an animal roughed out but unfinished.

The cliché of the headless text does remind us, however, that completeness is an aspect of appropriate order; the text must have all and only the parts proper to it. So it would be wrong to press too hard the point that Plato does not use the term 'unity' in *Phaedrus*. A complete and ordered entity is a whole (ὅλον is a term which Plato does use freely in *Phaedrus*); and a whole is a unity. If an object lacks essential components or contains superfluous ones, or if a flawed disposition of its components makes it a mere aggregate of parts and not an ordered system, then it is not a single, complete entity; and it is therefore not a unity. But it must be emphasized that this is a purely conceptual point. Plato tells us that every text should have the right parts in the right order, and of course no one would deny that. But unless we know what order of what parts is in fact right, this point of principle has no practical application. But Plato does not tell us here what constitutes rightness in such matters, or how one would determine it; the substantive criteria which would enable us to apply Plato's conceptual point in critical practice are lacking. For example, Plato's principle is neutral between those who do and those who do not approve of digressive rhetoric in tragedy; for the question at issue between these two parties is not whether a text ought to be an appropriately ordered whole, but about what is appropriate in the ordering of tragedy. Plato does not offer a substantive theory of literary unity of the kind that might adjudicate such a dispute; so while we are at liberty to believe that every text ought to be—is appropriately ordered if and only if it is—thematically integrated, there are no grounds in *Phaedrus* for attributing that view to Plato himself.

It might be argued that Plato does give some hints about these substantive criteria in the commentary on Lysias' and Socrates' speeches; but these hints cannot be generalized in any straightforward way. For example, Lysias' speech is criticized because it does not begin with a definition of the disputed concept 'love'; that Socrates' pair of speeches does begin in this way is one of the points commended in them. But what about the *Phaedrus* itself? It does not begin with a definition, but it hardly follows from this that it is badly constructed. What is appropriate in an expository speech is not necessarily appropriate in an exploratory dialogue containing imitations of such speeches. Still more clearly, a dialogue which raises a question of definition, perhaps aporetically, cannot begin by stating the definition which it is seeking; definition does enter into the criteria of appropriate order for such a text, but in a distinctively different way.

To put this point in more general terms: the criteria of appropriateness that are needed to give substance to Plato's abstract principle are necessarily relative to genre. In a passage of the *Gorgias* about which we shall have more to say in due course, Socrates stresses that the excellence of any thing depends, not simply on its having order (κόσμος), but on its having the order proper (οἰκεῖος) to it (506e2–4). Hence the relativity to genre of criteria of appropriate order. In the same context (503e1–4a2) Socrates says that a craftsman consults his own function (ἔργον) in selecting and composing his materials—that is, his procedure is teleological. It would therefore be plausible to conjecture that what determines the criteria of appropriate order in each case is the function of the text or genre in question; the appropriate selection and distribution of elements in a text will depend on what that text (or a text of that kind) is or ought to be trying to achieve. But Plato still has not told us how to determine what they are in any given case. To throw further light on this question we shall have to look elsewhere in the Platonic corpus.

In *Theaetetus* 172de Plato claims that the philosopher is a free man, with leisure to consider whatever argument comes his way, and to move from one argument to another at will, without any concern about the length or brevity of the discussion so long as it hits on the truth. By contrast a forensic speaker is not free; he is constrained by the clock, and by his opponent's vigilance against speaking outside the terms of the charge (this is a frequent *topos* in extant forensic oratory, and in rhetorical theory).[13] The forensic speaker is a slave disputing with a fellow slave before a master whom he has to flatter; his character is consequently warped. We may note here the parallel to the contrast in *Phaedrus* between conventional rhetoric, which gratifies one's fellow-slaves, and true rhetoric; but we should also note that Plato's own conception of philosophical discourse provides apparent warrant for digression.

This passage in fact introduces a section in which Plato self-consciously (173b4–c6) exercises his freedom to suspend one discussion while pursuing another; he enlarges on the contrast between the philosophical and unphilosophical lives before breaking off: these, he

---

[13] See ch. 3 n.17 below. For an interesting discussion of the *Theaetetus* passage in conjunction with Pindar and Isocrates see Miller 1983.

says, are a sideshow (πάρεργα), and we should now return to our original discussion (177b7–c2).[14] The dialogue's main concern is with the definition of knowledge; Socrates subsequently declines to take up another topic that has arisen on the grounds that it would prevent them completing the investigation of knowledge (183e–4b). Its present concern is with the suggestion that knowledge is perception; Protagoras is introduced as a representative of this theory (152a). It has often been noted that the digression is implicitly a response to the application of Protagorean relativism to moral questions mentioned immediately before (172a); but Socrates' refutation of Protagoras does not need to respond to this point at all, since it turns solely on the theory's application to questions of advantage and to sense-perceptions. Andrew Barker concludes that this digression 'is entirely relevant to its context, even though Plato has clearly taken pleasure in developing its themes beyond what the context warrants';[15] it is not clear to me how, if it is developed beyond the requirements of the context, the digression can be 'entirely relevant'. It would be better to say that it is entirely *appropriate*—given criteria of appropriateness that allow the pursuit of a point of philosophical importance (which this clearly is) irrespective of its relevance to the theme which introduced it.

This is not the only apparently digressive passage in *Theaetetus*. At 201d Theaetetus suggests that knowledge is right belief μετὰ λόγου, adding that where no λόγος can be given of something it is unknowable. This theory is taken up in 206c and scrutinized, but in the mean while Socrates has mentioned that the proponents of this theory tend to identify knowables with composite and unknowables with elementary entities; and this theory is criticized at length even though, as Socrates eventually admits, its collapse leaves the theory of know-

---

[14] The introduction and conclusion of digressions are often apologetic in tone, but this is not because digression *as such* is in need of apology; the question is rather one of the right kind of digression—for it is of course possible to distinguish between legitimate digressions and illegitimate ones (e.g. those on trivial or generically inappropriate subjects, or those which have no adequate point of contact with their context). It is helpful to the reader to be told where a digression starts and stops, and self-deprecating expressions of concern lest the digression be of the wrong kind are a natural rhetorical strategy for conveying such signals. Isocrates handles this *topos* with particular subtlety; see ch. 3 below.

[15] Barker 1976, 461; cf. MacDowell 1973, 174: the digression is 'not wholly irrelevant', but it leads away from 'the original topic of perception' and in a modern book might have been relegated to an appendix.

ledge as right belief μετὰ λόγου unscathed—this being the question in hand (τὸ προκείμενον 206c2).

The structure of the *Republic* is a further case in point. The exposition of the just city is introduced in Book II to provide an analogy for the soul; at the end of Book IV Socrates, having successfully applied his analogy and produced a definition of justice in the soul, is about to face the question whether justice is advantageous. To this end he proposes a review of the different kinds of city and soul. This review is actually undertaken in Book VIII; at 543c4–6 Socrates says that they must now recall the point from which they 'turned aside' (πόθεν ἐξετραπόμεθα). In the intervening books the discussion ranges over such questions as the place of women in the city, its conduct of warfare, and the possibility of its realization; this last is a question which, as Socrates points out (472c), is immaterial to the paradigmatic role for which the city was first introduced into the argument, but it is nevertheless developed into an extended and complex enquiry. At the beginning of this digression Socrates expresses qualms about its probable length; the gathering wants to listen to discussion—in due measure (λόγων ἀκουσομένους . . . μετρίων γε). But Glaucon reassures him that the measure for such discussions is the whole of one's life (450a10–b7). This is somewhat similar to the point made about leisure in *Theaetetus*;[16] it also points towards a passage in *Statesman*, to which we should now turn.

At *Statesman* 283c the stranger expresses concern lest young Socrates should get the idea that their procedure in the examination of weaving was pointlessly circuitous. To prevent this misapprehension he makes some remarks on the nature of measurement. There are two kinds. If one calls something 'long', that must be either relative to some other thing that is shorter, or else relative to some norm. All arts depend on this concept of a norm—τὸ μέτριον; for it is by achieving a norm that an art produces its good results (284b1–2). Other terms relevant here are τὸ πρέπον, καιρός, and τὸ δέον (284e6–7). Consequently (286b7) any dissatisfaction with the length of the discussion of weaving—or, similarly, of the cosmological myth in *Statesman* or the discussion of non-being in *Sophist*—would be beside the point; the question is not whether such discussions are long or short relative to

---

[16] Cf. also *Rep.* 376d for 'leisure'; but the criterion applied there is a narrower one—relevance to the immediate question in hand.

some other discussion, but whether they achieve the norm—whether they are the *right* length. Indeed, the question is whether they achieve the *right norm*—not whether the length is suitable for giving pleasure or suitable for ease of understanding (these are secondary considerations), but whether it is suitable for promoting the discussants' abilities in dialectic (286c–7a).

From these passages we seem to be able to derive two principles. First, I think we have found some confirmation of the view that it is legitimate to digress from the original object of one's enquiry in order to examine other questions that are philosophically serious. Secondly, we find in *Statesman* the claim that the length at which any topic is to be treated must be determined by reference to the norm of improving the dialectical skills of the participants—that is, making them more philosophical. Although the question raised in *Statesman* is solely one of length, it is perhaps legitimate to generalize the principle to include whether and how and where a topic is to be treated.

Here it is relevant to compare what is said in the *Gorgias* about the 'good man speaking for the best' (503d6–7). He does not speak at random (εἰκῇ), but has some standard to which he refers (ἀποβλέπων πρός τι: 503d7–e1). In fact every craftsman looks to his own function (ἔργον), to the goal of his craft, for guidance in giving his product form; each composes his materials into an ordered whole, the parts fitting together appropriately (503e1–4a2, following Dodds's text):

In the same way all other craftsmen look each to his own function, not selecting at random whatever it may be that he makes use of, but so that his product will have its own form (εἶδος). Consider, for example, painters, builders, shipwrights—whoever you care to name, each of them arranges whatever it is that he arranges into a definite structure (εἰς τάξιν), and compels each thing to fit appropriately (πρέπον τε εἶναι καὶ ἁρμόττειν) with every other, until he has given the whole thing structure and order (ἕως ἂν τὸ ἅπαν συστήσεται τεταγμένον τε καὶ κεκοσμημένον πρᾶγμα).

For order (τάξις, κόσμος) is the condition of excellence in anything (504a8–9 etc.). We might expect this principle to be applied to the putting together of the component parts of the text itself; and I presume that Socrates would accept that the elements of a speech or other text do have to be ordered appropriately, just as he says in *Phaedrus*—for at *Gorg.* 506d5–e3 it is taken as a universal principle that the excellence of anything whatsoever resides in order and technical correctness (τάξει καὶ ὀρθότητι καὶ τέχνῃ). But although one could argue that the production of a well-ordered speech is the proximate end of rhetoric, it would still be true that what constitutes good order in a speech can only be judged by reference to the art's ultimate end, which is moral. For it is not in terms of an ordered and technically correct composition of textual components that Socrates is thinking in his account of 'the good man speaking for the best', but in terms of the ordering of the auditor's soul; thus at 504d5–e4: the true rhetorician looks to the virtues and applies his words (and indeed everything he does) with a view to instilling justice, temperance, and virtue in the souls of his fellow citizens and abolishing their opposites. This practitioner of the rhetorical art is doing what Socrates does as the only true practitioner of the political art; as in *Phaedrus*, therefore, true rhetoric is philosophical discourse. And we find once again that the criterion of appropriateness in the selection and arrangement of textual elements in philosophical discourse is determined by the function of that discourse, variously formulated as instilling virtues (*Gorgias*), improving dialectical ability (*Statesman*), or attaining truth (*Theaetetus*).

In *Phaedrus* the corresponding conception of the function of philosophical discourse is to 'sow seeds' in a 'suitable' soul (276e4–a4), or to 'write' on a soul about justice, beauty and virtue (278a2–4). On this account, there is no reason at all to expect a dialogue like *Phaedrus* to have a single theme. For Plato's conception of philosophical discourse is not dominated by the idea of exploring a given theme but (as we have seen) by that of achieving through a broader discussion which may range widely over different themes a certain end—instilling virtue or promoting philosophical understanding. In the *Phaedrus* above all, the conception of philosophical discourse centres on the interaction of the individuals participating in the discussion—the interaction of teacher and pupil for the latter's edification. Necessarily, therefore, what determines the course of the discussion is the teacher's perception of the pupil; this is the point of the psychological requirement. The appropriate structure of philosophical discussion is: whatever an ideally skilled teacher (Socrates) would say to such-and-such a person in order to instil virtue or promote understanding, as and how he would say it. The teacher takes some individual, with his particular preoccupations and needs, and works with those preoccupations and needs in order to point him towards or further into philosophy. If the individual's preoccupations and needs, the influences which tend to inhibit or can be used to promote his growth towards philosophical maturity, are diverse then necessarily the discussion with him will itself be thematically diverse; given Plato's conception of philosophical discourse it is the imposition of thematic unity which would in such circumstances amount to a violation of the dialogue's appropriate order.

3

Fourth-Century Rhetoric

WE have seen that in *Phaedrus* Plato does not specify substantive criteria of appropriate order to fill out his general statement of principle; had he done so, he would probably soon have found his preferences in conflict with those of his contemporaries. That Plato held idiosyncratic views on literary propriety needs no argument; and an unorthodox tendency can be discerned in his aesthetics at one point particularly germane to our present enquiry—I refer to his reserved attitude towards *poikilia* (ποικιλία), that is, towards variety and diversifying embellishment.[1]

Plato frequently rejects *poikilia* in musical style (e.g. *Rep.* 399c5–e11, 404d11–e5, *Laws* 812d4–e5). In *Menexenus* he remarks with ironical admiration on how orators can lend persuasive charm to their speeches by stylistic embellishment (κάλλιστά πως τοῖς περὶ ὀνόμασι ποικίλλοντες), whether or not what they say is true (καὶ τὰ προσόντα καὶ τὰ μὴ περὶ ἑκάστου λέγοντες: 234c4–5a2). In the *Republic* he argues that the representation of characters given to extreme emotional responses, though attractive by virtue of its variety, is morally harmful (603b9–5c5). Earlier in the same dialogue he rejected the free use of a 'mixed' style of narration (the kind which involves personation in addition to the narrative voice) on the grounds that it is incompatible with the specialisation of roles required of his citizens (the ability to impersonate diverse characters convincingly would imply an unhealthy versatility), and that it is

---

[1] According to Young 1983, 168, 'the concept of ornamentation—*even that of variety for variety's sake*—is wholly absent from the words ποικίλλειν, ποικιλία, and ποικίλος in the Classical period. They concern inherent complexity, elaborateness, or intricacy of essential argument, not decoration.' The examples cited in this chapter do not uphold this doctrinaire position (see e.g. Pl. *Menex.* 235a2, Isocr. 5. 27, 12. 2–4, 15. 47; and does Pindar really say, in *Ol.* 1. 27–32, that tales deceive when embellished with 'inherently complex' falsehoods?). Ornamentation is not the only, or indeed the primary, connotation of the term; but it can convey a wide range of implications—complexity, variety, elaboration and ornamentation are all possible renderings. Note '*mere* ornamentation . . . *mere* decoration' (168); it is essential to grasp that there is nothing 'mere' about decoration in Greek literary criticism.

liable to encourage in the narrator the bad traits that he assumes in personation (392d1–8b5); but he admits that the mixed style involves constant variety, and gives greater pleasure than pure narrative (397b6–c6, d6–9, 398a8–b4). He opts, therefore, for a restricted form of mixed narrative (396c5–e8), which he associates with Homer (396e4–5); in fact, it is not at all clear that Homer would pass his tests, and elsewhere Plato criticizes the unhealthy effects of Homeric personation on audiences (*Rep.* 605c10–d50). One can find passages in Plato to set against this general tendency: at *Laws* 665c5–7 he takes the more orthodox view that *poikilia* is desirable to avoid tedium and enhance pleasure; but this seems to be no more than a concession to the weakness of the audiences. In general it is clear that (in principle, if not in practice) Plato was profoundly suspicious on moral grounds of any departure from strict austerity and uniformity of presentation. The eccentricity of this view in its fourth-century context is evident both from the polemical tone of Plato's presentation of it and from the potential conflict with Homer, the most revered author of the literary canon, in respect of one of his most admired traits; in the more orthodox eyes of Aristotle, the free use of mixed narrative was one of Homer's glories (*Poet.* 1460a5–11).

Further evidence of the eccentricity of Plato's view of *poikilia* can be found in the work of his younger contemporary, Isocrates. For example, he apologizes for the relatively austere style of his *Philip*, which lacks (he says) the rhythmical and lexical embellishments (ταῖς περὶ τὴν λέξιν εὐρυθμίαις καὶ ποικιλίαις) of his earlier work, which do so much to make a speech pleasing and persuasive (5. 27). Likewise he begins the *Panathenaicus* by saying that he is too old to fill his speeches with such figures as antithesis and parisosis, and asks his audience not to make the unfavourable comparison of his present style with the *poikilia* of his youthful productions (12. 2, 4).[2] In the *Antidosis* he says that the epideictic manner resembles poetry more closely than it does forensic oratory, using a style 'more poetic and more embellished (ποικίλος)' as well as containing more elevated and original thought (15. 46–7). Elsewhere he contrasts the restricted stylistic resources

---

[2] But in 12. 246 he (or, more precisely, a pupil whose views on other points are admittedly open to question) implies that this speech is 'full of all kinds of *poikilia*'; and at 12. 270–1 Isocrates refuses to ask indulgence for the weaknesses of old age, emphasizing the care he has taken over the speech. So we should not take straightforwardly the professions of incapacity at the beginning of this speech and *Philip*. The 'old-age' ploy is one to which he frequently resorts: e.g. 5. 149; 8. 141, 145; 9. 73; 12. 38, 88; 15. 9.

available to the prose-writer (of whatever kind) with the wealth of exotic diction with which the poet may embellish and diversify (διαποικίλαι) his work, and which (together with the rhythm of the verse) make it enchanting (9. 9–11).

In these passages *poikilia* is seen as a valuable quality of style; that suffices to make the contrast with Plato, but our primary concern must be with broader levels of structure. To trace this theme in Isocrates we shall have to consider his treatment of digression; and the best approach to that topic is through the concept of *kairos* (καιρός), the time or place at which, or degree in which, something is appropriate (cf. Isocr. 15. 74, πρέπον ... τῷ παρόντι καιρῷ; compare Pl. *Phdr.* 272a3–8). Unorthodox though Plato's attitude to *poikilia* may have been, the general principle of appropriate order proposed in *Phaedrus* is firmly within the mainstream of fourth-century rhetorical theory, and is, in effect, a reformulation of the key notion of *kairos*. Already in the fifth century Gorgias had written on the subject—to little effect, our informant assures us.[3] The concept reappears in Alcidamas' treatise on the superiority of improvised to written speeches. He does not, of course, advocate speech with no prior thought, at random (εἰκῇ); the arguments and their disposition (τάξις) should be premeditated, but the verbal form of their expression should not be fixed beforehand (*Soph.* 33). This results admittedly in a loss of stylistic polish (ἀκρίβεια); but that is a questionable virtue in any case, according to Alcidamas, who points out that speakers deliberately avoid it in forensic oratory for fear of arousing the resentment and suspicions of the jury (12–13). At any rate, this loss of stylistic polish is more than compensated by the greater responsiveness to *kairos* (εὐκαιρία) which improvisation makes possible (33–4). This responsiveness includes an increased alertness to the needs of the immediate situation (9–11), to the reactions of an audience on a particular occasion (23), and to unforeseen moves of an opponent (24–5, cf. 14).

In Isocrates we find the jargon of *kairos* applied extensively to questions of structure (τάξις). In his attack on the sophists he criticizes them for teaching rhetoric as if it were a fixed technique (τέχνη), one which, like spelling, rested on the application of mechanical rules; in fact it requires attention to *kairos*, appropriateness, and inventiveness (τῶν καιρῶν καὶ τοῦ πρεπόντως καὶ τοῦ καινῶς

---

[3] Dionysius of Halicarnassus: see *Comp.* 12, II 45. 10–15 Usener-Radermacher.

ἔχειν: 13. 12–13). This requires a natural aptitude, and is not
reducible to a fixed technique (13. 14–15).[4] To learn the elements of
rhetoric may be like learning to spell; but learning to select, combine
and order those elements appropriately, to observe *kairos*, and to
adorn the speech with appropriate arguments and with a rhythmical
and melodious style—that is another matter (13. 16–17).[5] Elsewhere
Isocrates says that after preliminary training in the elements of
rhetoric students practise what they have learnt, and so bring their
opinions more into line with *kairos* (15. 183–4); 'opinions' (δόξαι) here
are at once explicitly contrasted with science (ἐπιστήμη); there can, in
Isocrates' view, be no science of rhetoric, and 'accurate opinion'—
sound judgement—is what constitutes skill (15. 271). The acquisition
of this skill is not easy. At the beginning of the *Panegyricus* he concedes
that the historical events to which he will refer are rhetorical
commonplaces, but observes that their opportune use (ἐν καιρῷ),
together with appropriate arguments and a good style, is a rare
accomplishment—which he, by implication, can promise in an
unusual degree (4. 9). In *Philip*, with more seeming modesty, he says
that he can guarantee the excellence of the advice he has given, while
leaving it to his audience to judge whether the speech has been
composed with due attention to *kairos* and to stylistic polish (τοῖς
καιροῖς καὶ ταῖς ἀκριβείαις: 5. 155, cf. 5. 11).

If *kairos* is important, there is a constant danger of missing it, if we
succumb to the temptation to neglect moderation (τὸ μετριάζειν);[6] as
Isocrates says in the *Antidosis* (15. 310–11):

We are all so insatiable in speaking that, though we praise observance of
kairos (εὐκαιρία) and say that nothing can compare with it, when we think we
have something worth saying we neglect moderation, and by adding point to
point little by little we entangle ourselves in the most extreme departures
from it (ἀκαιρίαι).

This is a *topos* which Isocrates frequently uses in connection with his
own work. For example, introducing Heracles into *Philip* he remarks

---

[4] Compare Dionysius' comments on Gorgias' treatment of *kairos* in the testimonium
cited above, n. 3.
[5] The argument here is similar to Plato's distinction in *Phdr.* between what is prior to
an art and the art itself, and displays the same emphasis on τὸ πρέπον. With the
following passage compare *Rhet. ad Alex.* 1436a23–31.
[6] As we saw in ch. 2, in *Statesman* 284e5–8 Plato includes *kairos*—with τὸ μέτριον, τὸ
πρέπον and the like—in the second kind of 'metric', that concerned with the relation of
a mid-point to extremes.

on the wealth of the material and on his own incapacity at an advanced age to do it justice;[7] and then he observes that exhaustive treatment would make the speech unduly long, so that it will in any case be best to select a single exploit apt to his theme and proportionate to the rest of his speech (προσήκουσα μὲν καὶ πρέπουσα τοῖς προειρημένοις, τὸν δὲ καιρὸν ἔχουσα μάλιστα σύμμετρον τοῖς νῦν λεγομένοις: 5. 110). Elsewhere he says that he has eschewed detailed exposition because the present *kairos* demands brevity (6. 24). In the first part of the *Panathenaicus* Isocrates uses the device of *aporia* to introduce, under the guise of reviewing the two options open to him (to reply to his critics or not to reply?), a number of jibes at his opponents (12. 22–3); he then decides that it would be inartistic to leave the debate unfinished: not to round off each point and make connections between one point and the next is like slovenly, random composition (ὅμοιος ... τοῖς εἰκῇ καὶ φορτικῶς καὶ χύδην ὅ τι ἂν ἐπέλθῃ λέγουσιν: 12. 24).[8] At the end of this polemical prologue, Isocrates introduces a *praeteritio* by appealing to what is proportionate and appropriate in a proem (συμμετρία, εὐκαιρία: 12. 33–4).[9] Later in the same speech he introduces his praise of the ancient constitution of Athens by saying that, though his discourse will seem unduly long to some (whose judgement he despises), a truly discerning audience will not find it annoying or inopportune, but proportionate and appropriate to what he has already said (οὔτ' ὀχληρὸς οὔτ' ἄκαιρος, ἀλλὰ σύμμετρος καὶ προσήκων τοῖς πρότερον εἰρημένοις: 12. 135–6).

Such questions arise with most urgency where Isocrates is, or appears to be, digressive. The most elaborate instance is again in the *Panathenaicus*, where the devices of *aporia* and *apologia* are used to embed the digression on Agamemnon into its context (12. 74):

I cannot see clearly, I am at a loss (ἀπορῶ) how to continue without making an error of judgement. I would be ashamed, having said so much already about Agamemnon's worth, to make no mention of his achievements; but I

---

[7] On old age see n. 2 above.

[8] In 15. 68–9 Isocrates introduces extracts from his early *To Nicocles* with an apology for its failure to fulfil the requirement of connectedness; he is evidently dissatisfied with its composition (see also 15. 11). The notion of 'random' composition is one we have met several times; compare in particular Pl. *Phdr.* 264b3–c5.

[9] Isocrates' polemical finesse here is admirable. Certain sophists have criticized me, he says, for setting little store by their discussions of poetry (12. 18–19); I could silence them, but do not have the opportunity now; I will return to the subject on another occasion—if I have nothing more worthwhile to discuss. The barbed disdain of the final words effectively contains the reply ostensibly passed over.

observe that to speak of things that lie outside of one's subject (ἔξω ... τῆς ὑποθέσεως) does not meet with approval, but is thought a sign of disorder (ταραχώδεις). There are many who misuse such digressions, and many more who condemn them.

Swayed by fellow-feeling (for Isocrates, like Agamemnon, has not received the honour he deserves: 12. 75), he accepts the risk and digresses. When the digression is drawing to its end he again observes that some will think he has spoken at undue length (12. 84). He stresses that he foresaw this criticism, and preferred to seem to some (for whose opinion he evidently has scant regard) to have neglected *kairos* rather than to omit what he ought to have said (τῶν ἐκείνῳ προσόντων ἀγαθῶν κἀμοὶ προσηκόντων εἰπεῖν: 12. 85); perceptive hearers, he continues, will admire him for showing more concern to do justice to his subject's merits than to maintain the balance (συμμετρία) of his speech, even though the resulting compositional fault (ἀκαιρία) would damage his reputation (12. 86).

All this is, of course, highly disingenuous. A writer really unconcerned about the lack of balance and propriety in question would hardly make such a parade of it, nor would one negligent of his own reputation (the last fault one could attribute to Isocrates) puff himself so lavishly. In fact, the contrast drawn in 12. 85 between *appearing* to some to neglect *kairos* and failing to say what it was (in fact) appropriate for him to say signals clearly, to perceptive readers, that the impression of artistic failure is a vulgar error into which neither he nor they need fall.[10] Isocrates is taking pains over his rhetorical *ethos*; he contrives to claim moral credit for an artistic negligence of which he simultaneously implies that he is not guilty. This ironical self-deprecation is carried on into the resumption of his main theme: he has inadvertently drifted too far from his subject, he says, and spoken (perhaps) at immoderate length; he can only ask his audience to indulge the weakness of old age (12. 88–9). Clearly, we are not to take these rhetorical figures literally; they are devices by which Isocrates works the digression into the continuous texture of his speech, effecting those artful transitions from point to point which he elsewhere declares necessary (12. 24; 15. 11, 68–9; see above), while at the same time engaging the complicity of the reader to whose superior artistic judgement implicit tribute is paid.[11]

[10] For the flattering address to perceptive readers, compare 12. 135.
[11] We saw other tactical uses of these figures in our discussion above of the speech's proem; the device of *aporia* is especially frequent: 7. 77; 10. 29; 15. 140, 310; 16. 39; cf.

Despite his professions of error and incapacity, therefore, Isocrates has, and wishes in this passage to be seen as having, full artistic control over the movement of his text. The same is true of his digression on Theseus in *Helen* (10. 18–38), where again he employs the figure of *aporia* and remarks on the risk of being carried beyond *kairos* (10. 29–30). But it does not follow from the recognition of artistic control in these sections that we should try to minimize their digressiveness. In fact Isocrates is speaking, as he claims, outside his subject (ἔξω τῆς ὑποθέσεως), and what is at issue in these articulatory passages is only the limits of propriety in so doing: what constitutes due measure in digression? In the case of the *Panathenaicus*, some have seen a covert reference to Philip in the figure of Agamemnon; that is doubtful, although the pan-Hellenic implications of the passage are clear; but neither Agamemnon nor Philip, nor even pan-Hellenism, is the subject of the speech (pan-Hellenism is a recurrent topic within it, but that is not the same thing). Its theme, as Isocrates says (12. 5, 35–41, 112–13), is an encomium of Athens, developed by means of a comparison with Athens' chief rival to glory, Sparta.[12]

Therefore the digression on Agamemnon is genuinely digressive. The digressiveness of the section on Theseus in *Helen* can be seen if one compares it with the subsequent treatment of Helen's rape by Paris. Much space is devoted to the explanation and defence of Paris' judgement—that is, to praise of Helen (10. 42–4, 48ff.)—and only a little to establishing his personal reliability as a judge (10. 45–8). The personal praise of Theseus is, by contrast, very extended (10. 21–38); this has, to be sure, a motivation related to the praise of Helen (10. 21–2, 38), but it is not clear that the length and detail of the digression (either the amount or the specific choice of detail) are adequately explained by that ostensible motivation; a centrifugal motivation is, by contrast, readily available in its appeal to the patriotism of an Athenian audience.[13]

Dem. 18. 129, 60. 15; Andocides 1. 8. On the rhetoric of this digression, see Race 1978 and 1980. Isocrates' technique is, I presume consciously, Pindaric.

[12] Cf. Buchner 1956. Eucken 1982 gives a useful survey of literature on the speech, and a discussion helpful in detail; I think, however, that his reading of it as a 'sozialphilosophische Betrachtung' (65) is mistaken (I would prefer to say that the encomium rests on social-philosophical assumptions, which are not themselves the theme of the speech) and leads him to exaggerate the thematic integration of the proem.

[13] Kennedy 1958 argues that the proem of *Helen* implies 'a serious and significant', probably political, speech, and that the pan-Hellenic statement in the speech's final

Some support for this reading of Isocrates' digressions can be found in the *Rhetoric* of Aristotle, Isocrates' contemporary and rival; here is expressed approval in principle of digression in appropriate circumstances. In *Rhet.* 1418a27–33 Aristotle remarks that political oratory is more difficult than forensic, in part because the forensic orator has many 'delays' (διατριβαί); the political speaker can, if all else fails, meet this problem by introducing passages of invective. The term which Aristotle uses here does not of itself imply digression, so much as dwelling on or elaborating a point (e.g. 1417a10–11 περὶ τὸ ὁμολογούμενον οὐ διατριπτέον); but it is not clear why a symbouleutic speaker should not have in the subject-matter of his speech points on which he can, indeed must, dwell. One suspects, therefore, that Aristotle has in mind the elaboration of a point beyond what is required for the exposition of the subject, which is, in effect, digression. For there are certainly tactical reasons why a speaker might wish to speak 'outside of the subject' in this sense; Aristotle observes, for example, that if one has a bad case one will wish to dwell (διατρίβειν) anywhere but on the question at issue (1415b22–3). The same need is met for the epideictic speaker by 'episodizing' his speech with praises (1418a33–8):

This is what Isocrates does; he is always bringing someone in. Gorgias' remark that he was never at a loss for something to say makes the same point; if he is speaking of Achilles, he praises Peleus and Aeacus and the god, and also courage, which does this or that and is of such and such a nature.

These 'praises' are, of course, not wholly unrelated to the subject-matter in hand; it is easy to see how those listed—Achilles' ancestry and his most characteristic quality—might naturally arise out of a speech about Achilles (with the praise of courage compare Isocrates' praise of beauty in *Helen*, 10. 54–60). But this is to say only (what should not surprise us) that the digression has a point of departure in the subject-matter; that does not mean that the elaboration of epideictic praises is not really digressive in relation to the task of

words is developed in the body of the speech: Helen 'stands for excellence and the right to the leadership of Greece', and the digression on Theseus indicates that Athens is worthy to take the hegemony from Sparta (81). This is a striking example of modern centripetal interpretation, and illustrates nicely its allegorical tendencies; it is subjected to devastating criticism by Heilbrunn 1977. Eucken 1983, 44–120 misconstrues the proem of *Helen* (see n. 15 below), but is otherwise very useful; he accepts that the Theseus excursus 'eine in wesentlichen eigenständige Thematik hat' (81).

expounding the speech's main subject (or subjects).[14] Aristotle's
recommendation, thus interpreted, agrees exactly with Isocrates'
practice, as we have deduced it from his digressions on Agamemnon
and Theseus.

Also relevant in this connection are Aristotle's comments on the
epideictic proem (*Rhet.* 1414b19–29), which he compares to the
practice of flautists. They begin by displaying their virtuosity in a free
prelude (προαύλιον), which is then linked to the introduction proper
(ἐνδόσιμον) of the composition itself. Similarly an epideictic orator
may begin by speaking on any theme that he chooses before
introducing his proper theme and embarking on the main part of the
speech. This, as Aristotle says, is what Isocrates does in his *Helen*. In
the first part of the proem the 'eristics' are attacked (10. 1–7), while
the second part is concerned with the composition of encomia (10. 8–
15); these are distinct parts, 'linked by the assertion that the
pecuniary success of the eristics encouraged others to enter the
market with encomia on paradoxical themes.'[15]

Thus we have the prelude and the introduction, with the smooth
link between them to which Aristotle here refers (συνάψαι, 1414b26),
and which, as we saw earlier, Isocrates regarded as a norm of
composition. This complex in turn leads into the encomium of Helen
(10. 14–15).[16] Similar preliminary sections are found in other Isocra-
tean speeches. It is worth noting that Aristotle gives as a reason for
this practice the avoidance of uniformity (τὸ ὁμοειδές); this is a
significant first encounter with a standard term for the literary vice
regularly opposed in later criticism to the virtue of *poikilia*.

As the technique of episodic praise is recommended specifically for
epideictic oratory, so it is only the epideictic proem that may be
'outside the subject'; Aristotle adds that the forensic proem, like the
prologues of epic and drama, is strictly expository (the dithyrambic
exordium is analogous to the epideictic): its proper function is to give

---

[14] The use of the term 'episode' is ambiguous evidence here, however, as will be seen
in the next chapter.

[15] Heilbrunn 1977, 157; his interpretation of the proem (154–9) is correct (despite
Eucken 1983, 65).

[16] When Aristotle adds in 1415a7–8 that rhetorical ἐνδόσιμα must be foreign (ξένα)
or germane (οἰκεῖα) to the speech, there seems to have been some terminological drift:
in the earlier passage it is the προαύλιον that need not be germane, and the ἐνδόσιμον,
introducing the main theme, would be germane by definition. But this is not sufficient
grounds for diagnosing interpolation, as does Buchheit (1960, 175–82); vagueness in
the use of terms is not untypical of Aristotle (we shall meet further examples in ch. 4).

a preliminary indication of the nature of the subject-matter itself
(1415a8–25). As we have seen, Aristotle does recognize tactical
reasons for speaking 'outside the subject' even in forensic oratory. But
in that context such devices may be seen as ethically dubious;[17] hence
the technique is not proper to forensic speaking as it is, in Aristotle's
view, to epideictic. Epideictic, which admits digression in at least two
forms, is composed at least in part for display; but the more severely
functional, and therefore ethically constrained, forensic genre,
excludes digression, or aspires to do so.[18] Therefore, while there may
in certain kinds of composition be ethical objections to digression,
there seems to be no fundamental aesthetic objection.

[17] Practising forensic orators frequently criticise their opponents for speaking
'outside the subject' in order to obfuscate the case and obstruct justice—or else they
defend themselves against this charge; see Aesch. 1. 166, 170, 175–6, 178–9; 3. 35–6,
193, 205–7; Dem. 18. 9, 34; 40. 50, 61; 57. 7, 33, 59–60, 63, 66; Isaeus 6. 57–9, 62;
Lycurgus 12–13; Lysias 3. 46; cf. Pl. *Laws* 949b, *Tht.* 172d9–e4; Arist. *Ath. Pol.* 67. 1.
Isocrates himself adopts this approach in the quasi-forensic *Antidosis* (15. 104), and is
similarly cautious in the mock-symbouleutic *Areopagiticus* (7. 63, 77); this contrasts with
his practice in epideictic speeches, as we have seen it.
[18] This is only one instance of Isocrates' recognition of the different norms
applicable to epideictic and forensic oratory: for the contrast of style, in particular, see
4. 11–12 (epideictic is composed ἀκριβῶς, not εἰκῇ), 12. 1–2, 15. 46–7; those
recommending forensic austerity must include Alcidamas, who also observes (see
above) that stylistic ἀκρίβεια is avoided in forensic oratory, and who has scathing
remarks about speeches written more like poems (*Soph.* 12–13, 34; cf., on conflicts
among fourth-century rhetoricians and philosophers, Coulter 1967 and Eucken 1983).
For other instances of generic thinking in Isocrates, see 10. 14–15, 12. 266, 15. 10. In
Ep. 2. 13 epistolary συμμετρία is contrasted with the length appropriate to a speech (cf.
Demetrius, *Style* 228); length will be a prominent feature of Aristotle's discussion of the
epic and tragic genres.

4

Aristotle

We distinguished in our discussion of Plato between the general principle of appropriate order and its substantive criteria; the latter, which make it possible to apply the general principle to particular texts, Plato did not discuss in detail. If we wish to make good this omission, the obvious place to look is in Aristotle's *Poetics*, where we do find an elaborate examination of the criteria of appropriate order and—as part of that—a famous and influential account of literary unity.[1] But the point which we made in our earlier discussion (and which the contrast between forensic and epideictic oratory in Chapter 3 has partially confirmed), that the criteria of appropriate order are relative to genre, is essential to a correct understanding of Aristotle's treatise. Aristotle does not profess to offer a universally applicable theory of literary unity; his concern is limited to unity in 'mimetic' genres, such as epic and drama, and he explicitly contrasts the criteria applicable to those genres with the standards appropriate to historiography.[2] It would be wrong, therefore, to draw conclusions too far-reaching from Aristotle's argument; but it is, even so, significant that the theory of unity he proposes is consistent with, and in some respects requires, a centrifugal aesthetic.

For Aristotle, a tragedy is the realization in textual form (in words, spoken or sung, and in visible stage-action) of a narrative—if I may use the term 'narrative' to render Aristotle's phrase 'imitation of an action' (μίμησις πράξεως). The *praxis*, or action, consists of the series of events (πράγματα) which the play is to narrate. The narrating text accounts for three of the six 'qualitative elements' which Aristotle discerns in tragedy—speech (λέξις), song (μέλος), and what is seen

---

[1] See Halliwell 1986, 286–323 for a useful survey of the *Nachleben* of the *Poetics*; I shall comment briefly on some stages in this theory's subsequent career in ch. 10 below.

[2] Halliwell's attempt (1986, 283–4) to infer Aristotle's attitudes to other genres is therefore misleading; cf. ch. 5 n. 3 below.

(ὄψις).³ Of the remaining three, character (ἦθος) and thought (διά-
νοια) are implicates of the third, plot or *muthos* (μῦθος), as Aristotle
observes (49b36–50a7, 50a20–2). *Muthos* is defined as the σύστασις or
σύνθεσις of the πράγματα, that is, as the ordering ready for textual
expression of the events which make up the *praxis* or action to be
narrated. Thus one might think of the *praxis* of Euripides' *Suppliants*
as containing the sequence of events 'departure-battle-return', which
has been reconceived in the *muthos* as the sequence of scenes 'depar-
ture-report-return'; both, though in different degrees, are abstrac-
tions from the dramatic text in which they are realized. But Aristotle
does not trouble to define precisely the distinction he would make
between *praxis* and *muthos*, and his use of the terms is not in fact
wholly consistent.⁴

It is *muthos* which, in Aristotle's view, is the most important of the
qualitative elements of tragedy (50a15–17): it is the element by which
tragedy achieves its end or *telos* (50a29–35), and therefore itself is a
telos relative to the other qualitative elements (50a20–3); it is that in
respect of which a poet is poet (47b13–20, 51b27–8, cf. 53b1–7). This
importance is reflected in the amount of attention which Aristotle
gives to *muthos*. One of the topics proposed for consideration at the
very beginning of the treatise is 'how plots should be constructed if
the work is to be successful' (47a9–10), and this becomes a recurrent
motif: so, in particular, 50b21–3, 52b28–30, 54a13–15. The phrase
'how plots should be constructed (συνίστασθαι)' is analogous to
Plato's requirement of 'appropriate order (σύστασις)', and the con-
ditional shows that Aristotle concurs with Plato in seeing this as a
prerequisite of literary excellence. Aristotle's subsequent remarks on
the failure of speeches, however well-written, to achieve the function
(ἔργον) of tragedy if they lack the order (σύστασις) of a well-
constructed plot (50a29–33), and on the insufficiency of 'random'

---

³ The last of these, however, is ὡς, not ἐν ᾧ (49b31–6, 50a10–11); that is, it is merely
a mode of presentation, not a medium of communication. This distinction reflects
Aristotle's underestimation of visual meaning (cf. 50b16–20, 53b7–8); see Heath
1987a, 4. 3, and Taplin 1977, 477–9, Janko 1984, 226–9, Halliwell 1986, 66–7, 337–43.
⁴ For example, a tragedy (49b24–5, 50a15–17) and its *muthos* (50a3–4, 51a31–2) are
both imitations of a *praxis*; on the other hand, the *muthos* itself is what a tragedy imitates
(50a11). This is a futher example of Aristotle's lack of terminological precision (cf. ch.
3 n. 16 below), but presents no serious difficulty: *muthos* is the imitation of an action by
contrast with the other qualitative parts, and tragedy is the imitation of an action *qua*
realization of that *muthos*. (For some hypercritical reflections on Aristole's use of *muthos*,
see Downing 1984.)

($\chi\acute{\nu}\delta\eta\nu$) arrangements (50b1–3), strikingly echo *Phaedrus* (264b3, 268c5–d5). But there is one crucial difference. The ordering in Aristotle's discussion is primarily the ordering of plot. His analysis of appropriate order does not focus directly on the arrangement of quantitative segments of the text, but on the underlying structure with which they are supplied by a single qualitative element; and the criteria of appropriate order for *muthos* are in turn expressed in terms of its own underlying structure, *praxis*. Aristotle's assumption seems to be that an appropriately ordered *praxis* confers appropriate order on the *muthos*, and this in turn on the text. We might formulate the contrast thus: Plato is concerned with the structure of the text which expresses some subject-matter, while Aristotle is concerned with the structure of the subject-matter which that text expresses. These two perspectives are of course complementary, but they are distinct; for example, the beginning, middle, and end of a narrative text need not correspond to the beginning, middle, and end of the plot, since the events of the plot may be narrated in some inverted order (as in the *Odyssey* and the *Aeneid*). This point will prove important.

In view of the crucial role which *muthos* plays in Aristotle's theory of tragedy, his shift of attention to the more abstract level is plausible; but in some respects it is misleading. First, it is quite possible for the dramatic realization of a narrative to give the impression that the *muthos* has been ordered in a certain way, even when an inapposite analytical approach would judge that impression ill-founded; consequently, no criteria for assessing plots in abstraction from the texts which realize them can claim to constitute necessary conditions of an appropriately ordered text.[5] More seriously, this shift of attention must leave the discussion of appropriate order thoroughly incomplete. Menander is reported to have claimed that, once the economy of the plot ($\delta\iota\acute{\alpha}\theta\epsilon\sigma\iota\varsigma$) is fixed, it is easy to write the lines (Plut. *Mor.* 347e–f); but even if this claim is conceded, there remain important questions of propriety in the process of linguistic and dramatic realization. Speeches without plot, as Plato and Aristotle say, will not make an appropriately ordered tragedy; but the best-ordered plot will be ruined if the speeches supplied are individually poor or collectively discordant. Aristotle is, of course, aware of this. In the

---

[5] I have discussed this point in Heath 1987a, 3. 2–3. In fairness to Aristotle I should concede that 60a11–b5 (in particular the treatment of $\check{\alpha}\lambda o\gamma a$) shows him more alert to the distinction between analytical plausibility and dramatic conviction than I there recognized.

passage in which he expresses most clearly the importance of tragedy's theatrical realization he makes this very point: in ordering the plot and supplying the words the poet should keep the performance in mind in order to discern what is appropriate (τὸ πρέπον, 55a22–6). He would presumably not wish, therefore, to deny that his account of appropriate order is incomplete, though he would probably continue to insist that it tackles the most fundamental and important aspects of the question; it is possible to suspect that his approach is, even so, not perfectly in balance.

Aristotle offers his criteria for the appropriately ordered *muthos* in two parts. One set of criteria defines the minimal conditions which a plot must satisfy if it is to be adequate at all (chapters 7–9); a second set of criteria defines the optimal plot among those which pass the test of minimal adequacy (chapters 13–14). We shall consider them in order.

In his formal definition Aristotle states that tragedy is (among other things) 'the imitation of a *praxis* that is complete and possesses magnitude' (49b24–5). These two points correspond to the two headings under which Aristotle goes on to discuss the minimal conditions of plothood (50b34–7):

> If it is to be excellent [or 'beautiful': καλόν], an animal (ζῷον) or any other entity composed of parts must not only have those parts in a definite order (τεταγμένα), but must also have the right magnitude. For excellence consists in magnitude and order.

This passage introduces the discussion of magnitude; 'order' (τάξις) looks back to the immediately preceding discussion of completeness—the first of the two qualifications of *praxis* from the formal definition that Aristotle takes up (50b23–34). 'Complete' is glossed as 'whole', which in turn is defined as 'possessing a beginning, a middle, and an end'. These terms are themselves explained by reference to causal dependence and interdependence, to whether or not an event is necessarily or probably consequent on or antecedent to some other event. The complete *praxis*, therefore, is defined in effect as a self-contained series of causally interdependent events. The closure of this series (its having a beginning and an end) is readily understood as an entailment of completeness.[6] It does, however, bring with it a slight

---

[6] Closure is seen as entailed by completeness at *Phys.* 207a7–14, *Met.* 1021b12–14, 1023b26–7; cf. 1024a1–3 on the possession of 'beginning, middle, and end' as a criterion of wholeness (thus also Pl. *Parm.* 137c7–8, d4–8, 145a5–b1, 153c1–2). At

difficulty. There are in fact no such closed causal sequences, cause
and effect ramifying indefinitely; if the definition were taken in a
strict sense, therefore, a well-ordered plot would be impossible.[7] This
is one point at which it is necessary to invoke the force of the plot's
textual realization: an audience can be prevented from feeling that a
chosen sequence is incomplete if their inclination to ask whence and
whither is deflected or controlled; and this a dramatist may contrive
to do. That the closed structure must be causal is not entailed by
completeness; as we shall see shortly, the structure of historiography is
defined as a chronological rather than as a causal sequence. This
criterion would therefore have to be defended by reference to
tragedy's *telos*, which for Aristotle is the excitation of a pleasurable
experience of fear and pity; Aristotle offers no specific discussion of
this point, although some incidental remarks (and especially 52a1–
11, where he argues that even an appearance of causal connection
enhances the emotional effect)[8] indicate how he might have responded.

As we observed in our discussion of *Phaedrus*, wholeness and unity
are intimately related ideas; when Aristotle introduces unity at the
beginning of chapter 8 (51a16), therefore, he is developing further
the criterion already established. More precisely, he is using it to
expose the defective unity of a particular kind of plot, that in which
the supposedly unifying factor is a single character. If the criterion of
unity is defined, as Aristotle has defined it, in terms of causal
sequence, such a plot is certainly inadequate. Many things happen to
a single individual in the course of his life that are not causally

---

1016b11–17 'unity' is related to wholeness, defined as possessing a single εἶδος, i.e. the
composition of elements appropriate to a thing of a given kind (e.g. a completed shoe
as opposed to the parts of a shoe not yet made).

[7] Aristotle would presumably have accepted that the dramatic plot is in fact
uncloseable: cf. ἔξω τοῦ μύθου (55b8) and related expressions.

[8] The contrast with chance or random happenings shows that when Aristotle says
here that the emotional effect is greatest 'when events occur unexpectedly because of
each other', he sees the 'because of each other' as contributing at least as much as the
unexpectedness to the emotional effect. For the importance of causal connection, see
also 52a18–21. That Aristotle in 52a4–10 is content with the appearance of causal
connection counts against Halliwell's insistence that he is concerned with the 'inherent
... intelligibility' of plots rather than their 'capacity to convince an audience' (1986,
103); thus also Aristotle's comments on Homeric 'problems' (esp. 60a22–6, 60b35–
61a1) and the comments on ἄλογα which Halliwell mentions (107)—which are in fact
as much concerned with the concealment as with the elimination of impossibilities (see
n. 5 above). Halliwell's discussion of 'unity' in the *Poetics* (96–108) is of great interest,
though misleading in several respects.

related; therefore a selection of interesting events from the career of Heracles or Theseus will not necessarily constitute a single *praxis* in the Aristotelian sense.[9] Conversely, we might add, concentration on a single individual not only fails to be a sufficient condition of unity; it is also not, on Aristotelian premisses, a necessary condition, since a series of events might have a rapid turnover of central figures and still form a closed and causally related sequence.[10] On this view, therefore, the technique of shifting focus in tragedy, on which we remarked in Chapter 1, ceases to be a problem. In the same way, the habit of continuing a play beyond the resolution of its initial situation is consistent with Aristotle's analysis if, as is evidently possible, the extension is causally consequent on the resolution; and a change in tone or thematic content between different parts of a play is likewise wholly compatible with the causal connectedness of the successive stages of the plot which those parts realize. Aristotle's analysis is also consistent with digression; but this is a complex and controversial point, to which we shall return after looking at the second minimal condition and the optimal conditions which Aristotle proposes.

The second minimal condition concerns magnitude (51a3–15).[11] Aristotle excludes from the discussion considerations, such as the playing-time available in a festival competition, which are accidental from the point of view of the poetic art, and looks for more intrinsic limits of magnitude. An upper limit is set by what can be taken in and held in the memory; to exceed that limit is to make it impossible for an observer to perceive an object as a unified whole (50b39–51a2). The lower limit is determined by the *telos* of tragedy; without a change of fortune a tragedy could not effect the 'appropriate pleasure' ($oἰκεία ἡδονή$) of fear and pity, and the necessity of including a causally consequential change of fortune is therefore a constraint on the minimum appropriate magnitude (51a11–15). Aristotle says here that, within these limits, the greater the magnitude, the better (51a10–11); but this seems to be a mistake, since he elsewhere suggests that tragedy is superior to epic because less extended (62a18–b3)—although this in turn sits uneasily with the view that extension is a desirable quality in epic (59b22–8). However

---

[9] This does not exclude the possibility that the career of a single individual might provide an adequate unifying structure for some other genre (e.g. biography), just as the chronological structure unsuitable for epic is proper to historiography.

[10] *Contra* Halliwell 1986, 217 (g).

[11] We noted this concern in Isocrates in ch. 3 n. 18.

that may be, epic no less than tragedy is subject to the upper limit
imposed by memory (59b18–20); yet tragedy ought to be of a lesser
magnitude than epic (56a10–19, 59b17–18), so that the optimal
magnitude for a tragedy must be considerably smaller than that
implied by the upper limit in the minimal conditions which Aristotle
here defines. But Aristotle does not attempt to resolve these difficulties.

Another possible source of confusion in Aristotle's remarks on
magnitude is the uncertainty whether it is the text or the plot which is
in question. In 51a5 he does speak explicitly of the length of *muthoi*,
and the criterion of change of fortune is most directly applicable to
plot; moreover 49b12–16 is absurd if applied to the length of a tragic
text or performance.[12] But the reference to playing-time in 51a7–8
applies to text. This is not the only instance of the slide: at 56a10–15
he argues that the greater length of its text enables epic to use more
extensive *muthoi* than are appropriate in tragedy; in 59b17–22 he
mentions the length of the epic plot (σύστασις), and at once refers to
the length of the text ('a single hearing'). The assumption is evidently
that there exists a close mutually constraining relation between the
magnitude of text and plot. This assumption is not wholly plausible;[13]
but in view of 59a32–4 and 62b5–7, we may perhaps infer that
Aristotle would have argued that the mutual constraint does obtain if
the events of the *praxis* are narrated at an appropriate pace, the
narrative being neither too compressed nor too 'watery'.

I do not propose to spend much time here on Aristotle's second set
of criteria, those concerned with the relative excellence of plots which
satisfy his minimal conditions. In an appendix to the first set of
criteria Aristotle distinguished simple from complex plots on the basis
of the role of recognition and reversal in their change of fortune
(chapters 10–11). The first relative condition is a preference for
complex over simple plots (52b30–2); this preference is not explained
or argued, although the element of surprise reinforcing the play's
emotional impact is presumably the kind of argument that Aristotle
would have offered (cf. 52a1–4, 54a4). The second criterion is
independent, in that it would apply equally to simple as to complex
plots.[14] It starts from the premiss that tragedy is an imitation of

[12] As is evident from Else's attempt to defend that interpretation (1963, 207–19).
[13] Cf. Else 1963, 209.
[14] 'Simple' in 53a12–13 is being used in a different opposition. It would be unfair to
cite this as an example of Aristotle's carelessness with terms; but in 55b32–56a32 *vs*
59b7–16, the confusion does not seem to be due solely to the crux in 56a2.

fearful and pitiful events (52b32–3; cf. 52b1, 53b8–14), and develops into a discussion of the kinds of events most evocative of those emotions (52b34–53a39). A supplementary discussion in 53b14–54a15 reaches incompatible conclusions.[15]

We have now completed our introductory survey of the basic principles of Aristotle's analysis of appropriate order; we must now examine some of its implications. I shall begin by comparing Aristotle's theory with the techniques of thematic integration introduced in Chapter 1, and then return to the question, postponed earlier, of digression.

Aristotle does not ever discuss the thematic structure of tragedy and epic; he apparently does not think (as many modern critics seem to do) that a tragedy is 'about' some philosophical or moral topic. If a tragedy is 'about' anything, in Aristotle's view it is about the events which make up the plot. We might, therefore, treat the plot as tragedy's theme; Aristotle himself describes it as the *telos* of tragedy. In this sense, Aristotle would certainly require thematic unity—although, as we have seen, Aristotle's conception of a single plot is a permissive one by some standards. But the plot is the *telos* of tragedy only relative to the other qualitative elements; in itself it is not the *telos* of tragedy, but the most important of the means for implementing a further *telos*, the emotional effect which is tragedy's appropriate pleasure (cf. 53b10–13). Emotional stimulus is not exactly a 'theme', but it is what tragedy aims at and what, in Aristotle's view, constitutes its success or failure. But at this level Aristotle imposes no requirement of unity. Just as Plato's *Phaedrus*, viewed as a narrative text, has a unified plot (for the conversation between Socrates and Phaedrus develops as a series of causally consequent events) and yet has diverse philosophical interests, so tragedies like *Eumenides* or Euripides' *Suppliants* have unified plots but build on them diversified patterns of emotional stimulus. This is wholly consistent with Aristotelian theory.

We must now consider further the question of digression. In 51a30–5 Aristotle makes a rigorous pronouncement: whatever can be removed or transposed without evident effect on the whole is not a part of the whole, and ought not to be there at all. It might be supposed that, since a tragedy is essentially the exposition of a *praxis*, and a digressive passage is by definition not concerned with the

---

[15] Discussed in Moles 1979, 82–92.

exposition of that *praxis*, a digressive passage cannot be part of the whole which a tragedy is (or ought to be). But this is to mistake the level on which Aristotle is arguing. The 'whole' in this passage is not the tragic text, but the plot which supplies its underlying structure. If a tragedy is essentially the exposition of a *praxis*, it follows that the *praxis* is of crucial importance to the narrative structure of the tragic text; it does not follow that the tragic text must be concerned exclusively with the realization of elements of that structure. A tragedy may be essentially without being solely the exposition of its *praxis*. As we have said, the *praxis* (or, more precisely, the *muthos*: but that is an 'imitation' of the *praxis*) is a *telos* relative to the other qualitative elements of tragedy; but it is itself subordinate to a further *telos*, the play's emotional effect. If this effect will be enhanced by a digression, or if (extending Aristotle's theory somewhat) in addition to the primary tragic pleasure one admits legitimate ancillary ends which may be achieved digressively, then an Aristotelian justification of digression at the level of the text is available.[16] It would therefore be possible to apply the principle of 51a30–5 restrictively at the level of the *praxis*, while taking a permissive view of digression from the *praxis* at the level of the text.

If this is correct, then Aristotle need have had no trouble with the suspension of the *praxis* of Old Comedy in the parabasis;[17] nor, in tragedy, need he have been troubled by causally inconsequential occurrences (such as the appearance of Evadne and Iphis in *Suppliants*) or by digressive rhetoric or lyric. His brief discussion of the Chorus in 56a25–32 is quite consistent with this. To understand this passage, one has to be clear that there are two points of contrast between 25–7 and 27ff.: not 'Sophocles handles the Chorus better than Euripides; the rest are unspeakably bad at it', but 'Sophocles handles the Chorus better than Euripides within the act; as to the rest, their treatment of act-dividing lyric is unspeakably bad.'[18] That 27ff. concern act-dividing lyric is clear from 'the songs (τὰ ᾀδόμενα)'; that 25–7 do not should be clear from 'regarding [the Chorus] as one of the actors (ἕνα ... ὑπολαμβάνειν τῶν ὑποκριτῶν)', a phrase which

[16] For primary and ancillary ends in tragedy, see Heath 1987a, 1. 2. The organic analogy (see n. 24 below) need not commit Aristotle to the assumption of a single *telos*: cf. *EN* 1097a28–30, and Ackrill 1974.

[17] I have argued for an Aristotelian view of unity in Aristophanes in the appendix to Heath 1987b.

[18] For this distinction in the Chorus' functions, see Heath 1987a, 4. 23, 4. 42.

would scarcely be intelligible applied outside the act.[19] Aristotle is saying, therefore, that within the scenes the Chorus ought to play an active role—it should not be the 'inactive attendant' (κηδευτὴς ἄπρακτος) of which the author of *Probl.* 922b26–8 speaks; but between the scenes one should eschew the modern practice of using ἐμβόλιμα, songs wholly unconnected with the play's *muthos* and therefore interchangeable at will.[20] This is not to be construed as a criticism of digressive lyrics, such as one might associate with Euripides; it permits digression with a point of departure in the *muthos*, and rejects only the more radical practice of Agathon and his successors.[21] In each case, such digressions could be accepted, if they were thought to promote the end, or an end, appropriate to the genre in question.

It is true that a principle analogous to that applied to *praxis* in 51a30–5 must be applied with equal rigour at the level of the text: if a digressive passage can be removed or transposed without making any apparent difference to the text as a whole, it is not genuinely part of that whole; it is for this very reason that I have stressed the need to defend digressions teleologically, in terms of a generically appropriate end. Precisely the same kind of defence is required for an extended action, a shift of focus or a tonal or thematic contrast. But this requirement is not peculiar to techniques with which modern criticism feels uneasy; any feature whatsoever of any text, including thematic integration, stands in need of such defence—only thus can Plato's requirement of appropriate order at the level of the text be fulfilled.[22] We cannot infer that Aristotle disapproved of those techniques which we find problematic from the fact that he does not explicitly construct defences for them (or provides only hints as to how, in the context of his theory of tragedy, such defences might be constructed); his silence is a consequence rather of the radical incompleteness of his account of appropriate order, on which we have already commented. It is no less true, of course, that his failure explicitly to exclude such defences affords no evidence that he did approve of these techniques. Opinions have differed on the defensibility of (for example) digression: some have held that digression may

[19] Contrast Halliwell 1986, 243–7.

[20] See Taplin 1976.

[21] But, for criticism of Euripides along these lines, see Σ Ar. *Ach.* 443, whose ἀκόλουθα . . . τῇ ὑποθέσει is paralleled by Horace *AP* 195, 'proposito conducat'.

[22] Cf. in particular Plato's remarks on the disposition of the elements in Lysias' speech and in the epigram to which he compares it (*Phdr.* 264a4–e3).

enhance a text, some that it is always distracting and impedes the effect. Further enquiry is necessary if we are to show that Aristotle inclined in one direction or another, and we may in the end have to leave the question unresolved for lack of evidence. The only point which I wish to make at present is that Aristotle's analysis of unity at the level of the plot does not foreclose the question.

That Aristotle is, quite explicitly, talking about the unified structure of *muthos* and *praxis* in this chapter may provide the solution to an apparent difficulty in his citation of the *Odyssey* as avoiding the defective single-person plot. This poem does not, he says, have a single-person plot in the vicious sense, since Homer has selected a single causal sequence from the manifold and various events of Odysseus' life. The problem is that the poem includes the wounding on Parnassus (19. 390–466), one of the events which Homer is praised for omitting (51a25–6); the solution would be that this incident is narrated digressively, and can therefore be disregarded when one is analysing the poem's unified and unifying *praxis*.[23] This is a point to which we shall return. Meanwhile, Aristotle's use of epic to illustrate his argument in this chapter permits us to mention at this point the later passage in which he discusses the unity of epic (59a17–29). Epic, like tragedy, should have a single—that is, a whole and complete— *praxis*, one having beginning, middle parts, and end; in this way it will be a functionally well-adapted whole, like a living organism.[24] Here the contrast is drawn not with single-person plots, but with single-period plots. A history must record whatever happened within a given span of time; but contemporary or temporally successive events are not necessarily causally interdependent, nor is there necessarily a common *telos* to which they tend, so that this chronological structure does not satisfy Aristotle's conditions of narrative unity.[25] The point is not that a history cannot be a whole—that completeness and unity are critically irrelevant standards to apply to historical writing;

[23] The objections to this interpretation in van der Eijk and van der Ben 1987 are not decisive; and I do not find their respective suggestions persuasive.

[24] The implication of 59a20–1 is obviously not that it is the function (ἔργον) of an animal to produce pleasure, but that an appropriately ordered whole of whatever kind is one which produces its proper *telos*, which in the case of tragedy and epic is to afford a particular kind of pleasure.

[25] Cf. his ch. 9 (51a36–b32) for a further, but related, contrast between historiography and narrative poetry: a causally integrated *praxis*, because its constituents are associated 'in accordance with necessity or probability', exemplifies universals in a way that the contingently coincident events of history may not; consequently, poetry is 'more serious and more philosophical' than history.

rather, what constitutes unity or wholeness in a history is different. The principle of appropriate order stands; but because the ends of historiography and those of narrative poetry are different, different substantive criteria of propriety apply.

The account that I have given of Aristotle's position is not wholly conventional; to find corroborative evidence for it we must look with some care at his use of the term *epeisodion* (ἐπεισόδιον). In later criticism this term unquestionably implies digressiveness; does it do so in Aristotle, and if it does, what view of such digressiveness is taken?[26] We need not trouble ourselves here over the sense of the term defined in 52b16, 20–1 (if this is indeed Aristotelian),[27] and used apparently in 49a28 and 56a31–2: that is, with *epeisodion* in a purely formal sense, as a quantitative segment of text;[28] our concern is rather with those passages in which the term is used in connection with the analysis of plot. Nor need we linger over 51b33–52a1, where *epeisodion* is applied to segments of plot,[29] but clearly does not imply digression; this passage criticizes 'episodic' plots, that is, defective plots which fail to satisfy the requirement of causal connectedness (cf. also 52a18–21, and *Met.* 1075b37–76a2, 1090b19–20). Aristotle is there concerned with plays in which the poet's preoccupation with competitive display (ἀγωνίσματα ποιοῦντες) has led to a failure to provide an adequate backbone of causally connected action; this would put a play like *Prometheus Bound* into question, but it would not preclude the legitimacy of digressive display in a tragedy which did possess an adequately connected *muthos*.

Crucial for the present question is the passage in chapter 23 which continues from Aristotle's discussion (examined above) of unity in epic (59a29–b7). Aristotle says that perhaps a majority (σχεδὸν οἱ πολλοί) of poets have composed epics with the defective chronological structure which he believes to be more suited to historiography than to narrative poetry. Homer displays his genius in this as in other

[26] For a discussion taking a view rather different from that advocated here see Nickau 1966; Nickau's position is criticized by Friedrich 1983, with whom I am in much closer agreement. (Tsagarakis 1973 contributes nothing of consequence to the discussion.) I discuss fifth-century uses of the term in app. A.

[27] Cf. Taplin 1979, 470–6, Janko 1984, 233–41.

[28] At 49a28 the whole context is about the historical development of certain formal features of the tragic text (but μέγεθος in 49a19 must mean 'grandeur', not 'magnitude', in view of 19–21); at 56a31–2 the parallel with ῥῆσις establishes the formal sense.

[29] *Muthos* and *praxis* are specified at 51b33; and the criterion of causal connectedness, cited in 51b35, applies to plots.

respects. He could have composed an *Iliad* embracing the whole Trojan War; this would have been an acceptably unified *praxis*, satisfying the conditions of closure and connectedness ('he did not try to make a poem of the war in its entirety, although it had a beginning and an end'): such a *praxis*, though unified, would have been unduly large or, if it had been compressed into a poem of moderate size, the result would have been excessively complex.[30] He has therefore taken an even better course; he has selected one part of the extended *praxis* which the Trojan War as a whole would have constituted, and has used other parts of it as *epeisodia* to interrupt (διαλαμβάνειν) the narrative.[31] Other poets have composed defective plots based on a single person or a single period; or at best they have composed non-defective plots of an inferior kind—the unified *praxis* of many parts (μίαν πρᾶξιν πολυμερῆ), such as the Trojan War would have been, by contrast with the single part (ἓν μέρος) which Homer actually chose.

I shall defend my interpretation of the crucial phrase ἄλλοις ἐπεισοδίοις διαλαμβάνει τὴν ποίησιν (59a36–7) shortly; first we should pause to consider a minor difficulty. In 59a2–5 Aristotle says that the *Iliad* and *Odyssey* are epics with a unified *praxis* consisting of a single part; therefore they provide material for only one or two plays, unlike the *Cypria* or the *Little Iliad*, which have a unified *praxis* of many parts, and so provide material for many plays. There is an apparent conflict here with 56a10–19, where the 'whole *muthos*' of the *Iliad* is described as containing many *muthoi* (πολύμυθος). To resolve the paradox of a single *muthos* containing many *muthoi*, we must understand Aristotle as meaning that a single epic plot contains many tragic plots; but then he is saying that the *Iliad* provides material for many plays—which in 59b2–5 he denies. This would be intelligible if Aristotle here has in mind also the poem's digressive expansions, the *epeisodia* of 59b35–7, as I understand that passage; but then the use of the term *muthos* is, to put it no more strongly, loose. (It may be in recognition of this error that Aristotle at once changes his example, and cites the *Iliou Persis* as the source of many tragedies.)[32] A similar confusion arises in 62b3–

---

[30] *Poikilia* is used here in a pejorative sense, as at *Rhet.* 1416b25 (cf. ch. 2 n. 11 above); μετριάζοντα is one of the *kairos* complex (Isocr. 15. 311, Pl. *Statesman* 284e5–8: cf. ch. 3 above).

[31] For διαλαμβάνειν in this sense, see (e.g.) Dem. 60. 13, Isocr. 12. 149, Alcidamas *Soph.* 21.

[32] Young 1983, following Else, believes that the reference in 56a13 is to 'the Iliad', not the *Iliad*—that is, to the story of Troy, and not Homer's poem; I find this unconvincing. Young's exposition of Aristotle's theory of unity is inadequate; e.g.

11; an epic makes several tragedies, and if one were to make an epic out of a single (sc. tragic) *muthos*, the poem would be too short for an epic—or, if the poem were long enough, the material would be spread too thinly. The *Iliad* and *Odyssey* are cited as if they were epics with a *praxis* of many parts; this must again include the expansive material by which these poems, despite having a *praxis* of a single part, attain an appropriate epic length without becoming 'watery'.[33]

My account of these difficult passages takes it for granted that *epeisodia* in 59a35–7 are digressive expansions; this view must now be defended. In favour of this interpretation is the example which Aristotle gives of such an *epeisodion*: the Catalogue of Ships in *Iliad* 2.[34] Considered in terms of the Aristotelian *praxis* of this poem, the Catalogue is digressive; it does not contribute to the advance of a series of causally related events, but is—to use a word noted in a similar connection in the *Rhetoric* (1418a27–33, cf. Chapter 3 above)—a 'delay' (διατριβή). There is a sense in which it could be said to be drawn from another part of the story of the whole war: such a review of the opposing forces might most logically have been placed at the beginning of that story. This is arguably true of the *teikhoskopia* in *Iliad* 3 (has Priam not learnt to recognize the Greek commanders in nine years of war?), and I think also of the combat between Menelaus and Paris into which the *teikhoskopia* has itself been inserted—for one might have expected the principals to have met in person at an earlier stage.[35] At any rate, this combat would certainly fall for Aristotle in

'Aristotle is allowing the epic poet in general his many μῦθοι, and the right to compose his "epic mass" as a whole, chronologically from beginning to end. Any other poet would have done just that, and that is just what other epic poets did with their own subjects' (165–6): not all other poets—'perhaps most' (59a29)—and this is precisely what Aristotle does not 'allow' the epic poets to do (59a18–30); 'Homer did to the epic what Aristotle says the tragedian should do to tragedy ... By choosing ἓν μέρος, he gave it unity' (166): but when Aristotle speaks of a 'unified *praxis* of many μέρη' (59b1) he meant just what he said—that one could have a unified *praxis* without choosing ἓν μέρος.

[33] Some think that the *Odyssey* does not succeed in this: e.g. Kirk 1962, 357–60.

[34] Nickau 1966 proposes to delete this phrase (κέχρηται ... ἐπεισοδίοις 59a35–6), recognizing that it is decisively against his interpretation. He cites its omission in the Arabic translation, but that omission can be explained palaeographically (as a leap from one occurrence of ἐπεισοδίοις to the next), and the text left is feeble (what, on this view, did Aristotle gain by adding ἐπεισοδίοις διαλαμβάνει τὴν ποίησιν?); moreover, the alleged interpolation is, as Nickau himself remarks, not very good Greek (his objection to the Greek of the paradosis is not decisive; Aristotle has not used the word πολυμερῆ yet, but he has it in mind, and this explains αὐτῶν).

[35] On the duel and *teikhoskopia* see Tsagarakis 1982. His argument does not give sufficient weight to Agamemnon's dream (which gives him as much reason for

the category of 'delay'; it is a self-contained incident, interesting in its own right, but not contributing causally to the advance of the *praxis*. Indeed, it is as inconsequential causally as, for example, the intervention of the Theban Herald in Euripides' *Suppliants* (see Chapter 1 above); it is only because single combat is tonally less obtrusive in heroic epic than sophistic debate in tragedy that its digressiveness (with respect to the Aristotelian *praxis*) is less immediately apparent.

This brings us to our second important passage, 55a34–b23; this discussion embraces tragedy as well as epic, but I believe that (confusingly enough) *epeisodion* is not used in quite the same sense in each case. First, tragedy. Aristotle recommends that the poet begin with a universalized abstract of his plot (ἐκτίθεσθαι καθόλου);[36] he should then particularize it by identifying the persons involved— 'adding names to the subject-matter', as Aristotle puts it (ὑποθέντα τὰ ὀνόματα);[37] and on the basis of that particularization he should work his plot into episodes (ἐπεισοδιοῦν). This last stage seems to involve the translation of the elements of the abstracted plot into a form suitable for dramatic representation by supplying circumstantial details appropriate to the persons involved. Thus in Aristotle's example, Euripides' *Iphigeneia in Tauris*, 'escape' in the abstract of the plot becomes 'escape by means of the purification' in its 'episodized' version; when the abstract 'brother' has been identified as Orestes, the poet is able to exploit his madness and its consequences to supply a mechanism for the escape appropriate to the particular situation. Clearly there is nothing in this to suggest digression; on the contrary, *epeisodion* is applied in 55b13 (as in 51b34–5) to segments of the plot

confidence as that which Tsagarakis thinks makes the duel inconceivable at the beginning of the war), and Agamemnon's uncompromising remarks which follow have to be read in the light of the breach of the treaty; even so, Tsagarakis's arguments against assigning these *epeisodia* to the early stages of the war must give us pause. Thuc. 1. 11, with its apparent reference to the building of the wall at the beginning of the war, perhaps reflects a theory of this kind; but see Davison 1965, 5–15 (a paper marred, however, like that of Tsagarakis, by the 'documentary fallacy'). It cannot be regarded as certain that Aristotle was thinking in this 'neo-analytic' manner (compare Kakridis 1949, 61–95 for similar ideas), rather than of the more explicit cross-references in the *Iliad* to other parts of the war; the later scholia emphasize that aspect (ch. 8 below).

[36] λόγοι here in the sense of 'plots', as at 60a27; I do not understand παρατείνειν.

[37] Aristotle does not use the term ὑπόθεσις of a dramatic plot, but he could have done so (as well as the present passage, cf. *Rhet.* 1404b15, with 1355a36 τὰ ὑποκείμενα πράγματα). It has been conjectured that Dicaearchus applied the term to dramatic plots, on the strength of fr. 78 Wehrli (see Pfeiffer 1968, 193; but this is disputed by Janko 1984, 113 n. 42); Philodemus certainly did so.

proper. There is undoubtedly some difference between these tragic *epeisodia* and those of epic; in tragedy, Aristotle says, *epeisodia* are concise, but in epic they are a means of extension. This might mean no more than that the events of the plot are narrated at greater length in epic than in tragedy; and it could plausibly be argued that the contrast is too lightly introduced for it to mean more than that. But we have found ample evidence that Aristotle was not always the most careful and helpful of writers; and if his audience were familiar with an established distinction between the tragic and epic applications of the term, this hint might have been sufficient for them to follow his train of thought. There is one clear indication that a stronger contrast is in question. Aristotle sketches the universalized abstract of the *Odyssey*, and adds: this much is integral (ἴδιον), the rest is *epeisodia*. It is difficult to see what sense could be made of that distinction if it were inserted into the discussion of *Iphigeneia*: if the escape is integral, what is not? The purification? But that is causally bound up with the escape; it is part of the specific form which the escape takes in Euripides' plot. Aristotle's meaning becomes clear if we apply to the *Odyssey* the same kind of reasoning which we have just applied to the *Iliad*. Many parts of the poem—Telemachus' journey, the story-telling in Phaeacia, the conversations in Eumaeus' hut—are not part of the *muthos*: for they make no contribution to its causal progress; they are (from an Aristotelian point of view) elaborate 'delays', by which the poem attains, despite a story that can be told so briefly, appropriate length. Thus the epic *epeisodion* is digressive, though the same term can be applied to tragedy in a non-digressive sense.

This in turn brings us to a third relevant passage (59b23–31). Aristotle has just been discussing the best length for an epic text, and goes on to observe that the possibility of narrating events that occur simultaneously in different places (not available to the tragedian, who is restricted to what happens on stage) is a means by which the length and grandeur (ὄγκος, μεγαλοπρέπεια) of epic can be increased. One great advantage which this gives the epic poet, he continues, is the opportunity to relieve the audience with variety (τὸ μεταβάλλειν τὸν ἀκούοντα);[38] by contrast, tragedy's more limited scope for diversification may result in artistic failure. Aristotle's phrase for the diversifying technique of epic is 'to episodize with dissimilar *epeisodia*'.

[38] Change is pleasant (*Rhet.* 1371a25–8). This may be due (as Plato maintained) to a deficiency of human nature: so *EN* 1154b20–31; but the deficiency exists, so variety is necessary.

Since the most elaborate example of this technique is the Telemachy, which requires the poet to keep in play three different theatres of action, and since this is, as we have remarked, a prime example of what is from Aristotle's point of view an *epeisodion* in the digressive sense, this passage is consistent with the interpretation given for epic *epeisodia* in the other two passages.[39] I incline to this view, but do not think the point can be demonstrated in this instance. Nor does it need to be; the two passages already discussed suffice to establish the general point at issue: that in connection with epic, at least, *epeisodion* may apply to digressive elements, and may do so without pejorative connotation; indeed, Aristotle sees such digressions as part of the order appropriate to epic. Digressions can be seen as helping a poem with a *praxis* of the optimally unified kind achieve the length (and grandeur) proper to epic; therefore digression is not, in Aristotle's view, incompatible with unity. In connection with tragedy, *epeisodion* does not imply digressiveness; but although Aristotle does not discuss diversity and digression in tragedy, the regret which he expresses in 59b28–31 at tragedy's inevitably greater uniformity suggests that he would wish to see such opportunity for diversification as does exist within the order appropriate to tragedy exploited to the full; and there is no reason to assume that he would have objected if this were done, within limits, digressively.

One final, but not unproblematic, reference to unity in the *Poetics* must be mentioned. In the last chapter Aristotle undertakes a critical comparison of epic and tragedy, arguing for the superiority of the latter. One of the points on which he comments is unity (62b3–11): epic is inferior because it is less unified, as can be seen from the fact that any epic provides material for many tragedies. Whether the epic deals with a single *praxis* of many parts, or with a single-part *praxis* diversified by digressive *epeisodia* to achieve the length appropriate to epic without becoming 'watery', the epic is (in the terms used at 56a12) πολύμυθος;[40] and it is therefore less unified than any one of the potential tragedies that could be made from it. There is a difficulty here. In 59b22–31 Aristotle argued not only that it is appropriate to

[39] The condition in 59b27–8 (the simultaneous events must be οἰκεῖα) might be counted against this, but is not decisive; οἰκεῖον is a vague word, and the Telemachy, though digressive, could qualify: it is the right kind of digression—not, for example, like an ἐμβόλιμον (see n. 20 above).

[40] One must understand 62b5–7: 'if an epic poet made a poem of one (sc. tragic) *muthos*, the poem would be either curtailed or watery.' For the argument concerning 'greater unity', cf. *Probl.* 917b8–13.

epic to be longer than tragedy, but also that this greater length is intimately connected with certain advantages which epic enjoys over tragedy: grandeur and diversity. It may still be true that the optimally unified tragedy is more unified than the optimally unified epic; but there are compensating factors which Aristotle recognizes elsewhere, but here ignores. This element of over-simplification in the comparison results in an adverse evaluation of the Homeric poems (which are, of course, the optimally unified epics in Aristotle's view), a consequence which Aristotle shows some sign of finding awkward. The difficulty should perhaps be set down to the artificiality of the whole exercise. Aristotle is not arguing on ground of his own choosing, but considering, almost as an afterthought, a question that others had raised; he is trying to show how a case could be made against those who assert the inferiority of tragedy, a case to which he is not necessarily committed without reservation.

However that may be, some conclusions can be stated. Aristotle's theory of unity (and his more general discussion of appropriate order) in epic and tragedy finds no difficulty with mobile focus or extended action, nor with the tonally or thematically contrasting exploitation of a plot; and it is compatible with—indeed, in epic it encourages—digression from the unifying *praxis* at the level of the text. The preference for single-part plots over plots that are unified but multipartite, and the preference for the greater unity of tragedy in the last chapter, suggest respectively that extended plots and digressive texts were not optimal for Aristotle; but this is no more than a relative preference, such as that for complex over simple plots, and does not imply that the less favoured structure is actually flawed.[41] Finally, nowhere in the *Poetics* can one find any hint of a centripetal or integrating approach to interpretation at a thematic level.

[41] It may be observed in passing that a complex plot must, in some sense, be 'less one' than a simple plot; this again points to the artificiality of the terms in which the comparison is conducted in ch. 26.

5

Epic after Aristotle

REDUCED to its barest essentials, Aristotle's prescription for an epic poem is that it should narrate a single, causally continuous action at substantial length, that action being 'serious'; at first sight these precepts are strikingly echoed in the opening lines of Callimachus' *Aetia*. The adversaries which Callimachus there cites (the 'Telchines', as he calls them) appear to have attacked him for the kind of poetry that he fails to write—poetry that is 'single and continuous' (ἓν ἄεισμα διηνεκές), long ('in many thousands of lines'), and concerned with kings and heroes (a πρᾶξις σπουδαίων, in Aristotelian terms). This apparent echo is, however, potentially treacherous. We insisted in the previous chapter that Aristotle does not talk so much of 'one poem' as of the 'one *muthos*' which underlies the appropriate order of a poem. Nor is it clear that 'one' in Callimachus means 'unified'—that is, that it has implications concerning structure or appropriate order; it might be a simple term of enumeration, 'single' as opposed to 'many'.

There is, in fact, much else that is obscure in these lines. It is conceivable, for example, that Callimachus is presenting the *Aetia* as themselves a refutation of his critics; in that case 'single and continuous' will be true of the *Aetia*, and must therefore have the sense 'formally connected' rather than 'possessing a unified subject-matter'. If, however, the *Aetia* are not meant to be, in the relevant sense, 'single and continuous', then the formula will imply some kind of underlying structure—perhaps a narrative structure of the kind of which Aristotle approved, but it is possible that Callimachus' critics would have been content with (for example) a chronological as distinct from an Aristotelian causal structure. This might be clearer if we could be certain which poems were approved and which rejected in lines 9–12, and if we knew more about their structure than we do; but these lines are very controversial.[1] There is one pointer to

---

[1] See Hollis 1978, Toechterle 1980, Bowie 1986, 28–30.

Callimachus' meaning. In line 16 he says that poems are 'sweeter thus'—that is, if they are not long (this seems to be the point of the images in the preceding lines; note the—possibly repeated—μακρόν). If the present work is meant to refute the charge that he cannot write long poems, then it is itself not 'sweeter'; and it is unlikely that Callimachus would have conceded this. If, on the other hand, the *Aetia* is 'sweeter', then Callimachus is inviting us to regard it not as a long poem, but as a collection of shorter pieces. On this view the phrase 'single and continuous' will not be applicable to the *Aetia*; and it will therefore mean not 'formally continuous' (which the *Aetia* are), but 'possessing a unified subject-matter' (which they do not).[2]

Though 'single and continuous' is obscure, we do clearly have references to two of the Aristotelian criteria for epic in the critics' demands—magnitude and the serious action. We should not suppose, however, that Callimachus is (or is alleging himself to be) under attack for failing to observe Aristotle's precepts as such; his critics are concerned, rather, with his failure to compose epic poetry in the traditional mould, and the convergence of their demands with those of Aristotle merely reflects the accuracy with which the latter had described the traditional form. But the failure to compose such a poem could not of itself have afforded material for polemic, since the tradition sanctioned other kinds of poetic composition; the Hesiodic corpus, for example, did not consist of epic poetry of the kind analysed by Aristotle.[3] Hesiod was an important model for Callimachus, and by no means a disreputable one; why, then, should Callimachus have been a figure of controversy?

The first, and less significant, point of contention lay, presumably, in the positive claims which Callimachus may have made for his own work. While the failure to write an epic was hardly in itself a poetic demerit, it might plausibly have been argued that a poet could not properly lay claim to greatness until his powers had been proven

[2] Dio Chrysostom (36.12) uses the phrase μακράν τινα καὶ συνεχῆ ποίησιν of continuous narrative in Homer (μίαν ἑξῆς διέξεισι μάχην), by contrast with Phocylides.
[3] Halliwell observes that Hesiod's didactic poems have a structure incompatible with 'the criterion of unity presented in the *Poetics*', and infers that Aristotle's theory is 'very inhospitable' to their genre (1986, 283). But if a text is not an 'imitation of an action', it cannot (logically) be faulted for failing to imitate a *unified* action; and Aristotle's judgement that such texts are not, in his technical sense, 'poetry' will not constitute an evaluation of them, but simply part of the delimitation of his field of enquiry. Similarly, when Aristotle denies that Empedocles is a poet (47b13–20), this is not to be construed as an adverse aesthetic judgement; see, to the contrary, fr. 70 (with Janko 1984, 121–4).

against the demands of the traditionally most prestigious form; but to maintain, as Callimachus does in his reply to the 'Telchines', that a poet's excellence (σοφίη) should be judged by his craftsmanship (τέχνη) and not by the quantity of his output, is to maintain the independence of poetic greatness from epic composition. That is implicitly to make a bolder claim about his own merits than a traditionalist would wish to allow—and is thus to provoke envy (φθόνος).[4] But Callimachus makes this point in a highly tendentious way; for his opponents would not—even on Callimachus' own presentation of their case—have wished to make out either that length was a sufficient condition of poetic excellence, or even that length simply *qua* length was a necessary condition. This mocking distortion reflects the other, and even more contentious, aspect of Callimachus' position. The alternative to his own non-epic composition is portrayed in extremely uncomplimentary terms—as the braying of an ass, appealing not at all to those of real discrimination (fr. 1. 29–32). Similarly, when Envy attempts to apply his crude quantitative measure of poetic excellence at the end of the *Hymn to Apollo*, the god—endorsing Callimachus' poetic—observes that a big river is likely to be polluted with much rubbish; the purity demanded by discriminating judges is only to be found in tiny springs (*H.* 2. 105–12).[5] So in addition to making provocative claims for his own work, Callimachus is making stronger and even more provocative claims about the poetic form he has chosen to avoid: that it is (under present conditions, at least, since one is bound to except Homer) exclusive of poetic excellence.

This position is reflected in the range of Callimachus' poetic activity: in the main, separate and relatively short poems in iambic, lyric, elegiac, or 'epic' (in the broader sense, hexameter) metres. Of

---

[4] 'Telchines' is glossed in Hesychius by βάσκανοι (cf. Call. fr. 1. 17) and φθονεροί; and note the appearance of Phthonos (Envy) at the end of the second *Hymn*. Cf. Walcot 1978, 78–9.

[5] We should not expect sane judgement or Callimachean subtlety of expression from Envy: on the contrary, the analogy of fr. 1 would lead us to expect a caricature; so Envy's remark probably means just what it says—that he dislikes poets whose poems are not immense, like the sea—and only in Apollo's reply are saner judgment and a more intricately figured mode of expression introduced. Bundy 1972 rightly sees the passage as an apologetic break-off device, securing the god's goodwill by pre-empting criticism; but the suggestion that the criticism is concerned specifically with omissions in this hymn fails to account for the generalizing terms of Envy's criticism and leaves Apollo's reply something of a *non sequitur*. There is a useful discussion (with which I do not wholly agree) by Köhnken 1981; note also Poliakoff 1980.

his two major works, the *Aetia* is, as we have said, not 'single and continuous'. There was no underlying structure of continuous narrative, but rather an aggregation of diverse stories loosely linked by their aetiological content; in the first two books a framework was supplied for the stories by the dialogue with the Muses, but even this element of formal continuity was abandoned in the third and fourth books, which are likely to have been compiled from poems originally issued separately.[6] *Hecale* did indeed have a continuous narrative structure: Theseus, having survived Medea's attempt on his life, is carefully guarded by his father, but manages to slip away to encounter and overcome the Marathonian bull. But the narrative emphasis of the poem evidently lay less on this 'serious action' than on the hero's meeting with the poverty-stricken old woman Hecale, on her hospitality, her history, her fate, and her guest's response; it is as if the heroic action of the *Odyssey* had been reduced to a narrative context for the conversations in Eumaeus' hut, in a poem the climax of which was the institution of posthumous honours for the swineherd. Thus even in composing a continuous narrative Callimachus has in effect evaded the 'kings or heroes' requirement of the 'Telchines';[7] and although the narrative was on a more generous scale than in the *Aetia*, the poem certainly did not exceed a single book, and was therefore not 'in many thousands of lines'.

Although the poem's fragmentary state leaves its structure in many respects obscure, it is clear that *Hecale* contained a number of formally digressive narrative inserts: accounts of Theseus' and Hecale's earlier lives, and in particular the crow's account of its own transformation after denouncing the daughters of Cecrops to Athene.[8] The technique of enfolding one story within another to make at least a formal digression becomes a mannerism of the short epos ('epyllion', for convenience) in the Callimachean tradition.[9] It is natural for centripetally minded criticism to search out and emphasize elements of resemblance or convergence between the enfolding

[6] Cf. Parsons 1977, 48–50.

[7] Cf. Zanker 1977 and 1987, 209–214; for the same technique in the *Victory of Berenice*, see Parsons 1977, Zanker 1987, 181–2.

[8] Presumably advising its companion against bringing the bad news of Hecale's death. See further Lloyd-Jones and Rea 1967.

[9] For the digressive enfolded narrative in short epic Hellenistic poets had a model in the Homeric *Hymn to Aphrodite*—which was not, however, much cited: cf. Janko 1982, 268 n. 1; some of his references are optimistic. The view that the hymn is itself Hellenistic is rightly dismissed by Janko (162–3).

and enfolded narratives, and to construe those elements as pointers to
the underlying purport of each poem; from a centrifugal point of
view, however, such a procedure may seem less convincing. Consider,
for example, Moschus' *Europa*. In this poem the insert takes the form
of a description of Europa's basket; its theme is Io. The points of
convergence are obvious: both the outer narrative and the inset
ekphrasis are concerned with stories of rape by Zeus involving a sea-
journey and a bovine metamorphosis; there is inversion, in that it is
the woman who is transformed in the inset, Zeus in the outer story—
but that is surely no objection. One should observe, however, how
much of his severely limited space Moschus has devoted to elements
of Io's story which have no bearing, direct or inverted, on that of
Europa: the land-based observers of the sea-borne cow (48–9); the
Nile and the restoration of Io's human form (50–4); Hermes, Argus,
and the origins of the peacock (55–61). The poet seems to dwell on
the picturesque aspects of the inset story, irrespective of their bearing
on the frame. The suspicion must arise, therefore, that the centripetal
approach places its emphases the wrong way round; for Moschus,
perhaps, the points of contact between the two stories were valued
less as the *telos* of the digression than as a point of departure for
decorative elaboration of a centrifugal kind.

In Catullus' *Marriage of Peleus and Thetis*, the insert again takes the
form of a description, this time of an embroidered coverlet displaying
the story of Ariadne. Ariadne's union with the god Dionysus is clearly
an inverted parallel to the union of Peleus with the goddess Thetis;
since both stories could serve as epithalamial exempla[10] the appropriateness of the embroidery to the occasion, and the digression's point
of departure in the outer story, are clear. But that is not the point
which receives emphasis in the digression as Catullus has developed
it; on the contrary, the union of mortal and god is not itself narrated,
but only prospectively suggested, and the emphasis falls rather on the
pathos of Ariadne's abandonment by Theseus and the tragedy that in
consequence attends Theseus' homecoming. Many recent critics
have, predictably, sought in this apparently centrifugal elaboration
of the inset some kind of covert commentary on the outer story;
typically, its pathetic and tragic elements may be seen as subversive of
the poem's ostensible celebration of the marriage and of the heroic
age—subversion confirmed, it is alleged, by the sinister epithalamium
of the Fates.[11] But this reading cannot, in my view, be sustained.

[10] See Menander Rhetor iii 400. 13–20 Spengel, with Russell and Wilson ad loc.
[11] E.g. Bramble 1970.

The coverlet, as the poet says, 'heroum . . . virtutes indicat'; that is,
it shows or brings to mind Theseus' conquest of the Minotaur and
Ariadne's union with Dionysus, which are things beyond the powers
of (in the Homeric phrase) 'mortals such as there are today'.[12] Since
no one ever supposed that what made the heroic age admirable was
the absence of error and misfortune, their presence in this digression
does not conflict with its celebration of the heroes (especially if, as a
number of scholars have concluded, Theseus' forgetfulness was
imposed by Dionysus out of love for Ariadne).[13] Ariadne's preceding
and strictly temporary distress does not negate her imminent felicity;
still less does it cast doubt on that of Peleus and Thetis. As to the song
of the Fates it is wrong to say that the poet endorses the facts given
but not the attitudes expressed in it,[14] for 'felicia . . . carmina' (382–3)
endorses the attitudes also; this is hardly surprising, since the heroes'
martial virtuosity is included among the glories of their age (394–6).
One would therefore have at least to postulate an 'unreliable
narrator' (in agreement with the Fates) distinct from the implicit and
ironical author; but what evidence is there to support such a move?
Essentially, that Achilles' career is described in terms that recognize
the grimness and tragic consequences of war. But in Homer (for
example, *Il.* 6. 480–1) one finds that martial prowess may be
admired, even though it brings destruction and distress, and may be
celebrated, even while the distress it brings is compassionately
understood; why should we not allow Catullus an equally complex
attitude? Apparently, on the grounds of attitudes reconstructed from
other poems; but that Catullus must express the same attitudes in
every poem, regardless of genre, is neither proven nor probable (the
whole procedure neglects the implications of Catullus 16). Vergil, in
the fourth *Eclogue*, sees the child of his Golden Age as a second
'magnus Achilles'. This is in the context of an epithalamion, alluding
to Catullus 64; the link made between his child and Catullus'
suggests that Vergil took a 'positive' view of his predecessor's meaning here.[15]
The ironical reading of the poem therefore fails, and we are left to
draw the simpler and (if centrifugal principles are entertained)
aesthetically unobjectionable conclusion that Catullus developed his

---

[12] Lines 397–408 are not about contemporary Rome, but about the time after the
age of the heroes; compare Hesiod, *WD* 156–201.

[13] See Giangrande 1972, 127; further references in Jenkyns 1982, 139–40.

[14] Jenkyns 1982, 143–4.

[15] Giangrande 1972 (see also 1981) has some helpful observations on these issues, as
well as some unhelpful (Rhianus is a red herring); Dee 1982 modifies and significantly
improves his case.

inset in the way he did in pursuit of *poikilia*: that is, because he
thought poems embracing diverse themes, moods, and modes of
presentation more interesting and aesthetically more rewarding than
those in which everything bears on a single point.[16]

In the fourth book of Vergil's *Georgics* (to cite one final example)
we find an 'epyllion' about Aristaeus' loss and recovery of his bees,
with Orpheus and Eurydice providing the enclosed narrative. The
outer story is motivated as the aetiology of the technique for securing
a spontaneous generation of bees described in the course of the book's
instruction in apiculture; within that aetiology the inset story is
motivated as explaining the causes of Aristaeus' loss of his bees (it is
put into the mouth of Proteus, whose advice Aristaeus seeks). But the
epyllion as a whole is curiously ill-constructed if one considers it
simply as an aetiology; the devising and first use of the *bougonia*
technique is handled relatively briefly (531–58) by comparison with
peripheral, but highly decorative, elements such as the nymphs and
their cave (334–73), and with the ostensibly explanatory narrative of
Orpheus: for that narrative, too, is developed away from its strictly
explanatory point, to dwell on the picturesque and pathetic aspects of
the story. On the face of it, therefore, the explanatory function in
each case is the point of departure for a narrative which, in the form
that has been given to us, is to a large extent not functionally integral
to the immediate or to the broader (technically or ideologically)
didactic context. It is always possible to assume that there must be
some covert integration of the narratives; but it will be clear by now
why I deny that that assumption is necessary and view with scepticism recent attempts to apply it.[17] Rather, I am inclined to believe

[16] For the centripetal presumption in recent criticism, see (e.g.) Putnam 1961, 165–
6: 'If *64* is . . . a series of narrative sections strung loosely together by means of the most
tenuous and superficial bonds, then we should certainly without further ado dismiss the
poem . . . There is no meaningless artificiality here. Rather, the whole is consciously
calculated and specifically pointed . . . toward a grand design'; further examples are
cited by Jenkyns 1982, 93–4. On *poikilia* in the poem, see Klingner 1964, 213–6; and, in
Hellenistic poetry in general, Deubner 1921.

[17] Observe the circularity in Griffin's approach (1985, 165): 'This is one of the most
beautiful things in ancient poetry, and here as strongly as anywhere in Vergil's work
we must feel that more is meant than meets the ear. He will not lightly have put at the
end of a long poem a strikingly melodious and pathetic conclusion, whose connection
with what precedes, and whose position in his work as a whole, he has made merely
mysterious. We are entitled to expect that the poet did not end his poem with so
complex and unexpected an episode, and one whose interpretation has proved so
difficult, if he had not had something complex to say; but also something to which he
attached importance.' But will the connection be found mysterious, and the episode

that Vergil, seeking a suitably splendid finale to his poem, chose to
develop an artistically wrought narrative in the neoteric manner, and
(in accordance with that manner) to enclose within it a thematically,
emotionally, and stylistically contrasting panel; and I see no reason to
suppose that he felt constrained by centripetal scruples in so doing.

If we wish to test this line of approach against an approximately
contemporary theoretical position, we must turn to Horace's *Ars
Poetica*. Horace, despite his familiarity with and evident admiration
for the Hellenistic poet, is not adopting a Callimachean standpoint in
this treatise (on the contrary, he prescribes for the kind of traditional
long epic that Callimachus had declined to write: 73–4, 131–52).
However, my argument is precisely that the Callimachean and
neoteric use of digressive insets is not peculiar to that tradition, but is
simply one (distinctive) manifestation of the centrifugal tendency
characteristic of Greek literary aesthetics in general. If that is right,
Horace's precepts should not conflict with the centrifugal principle;
yet he begins the poem with a satire on grotesque conflations and a
demand for unity. Does this beginning in fact entail what we have
termed a centripetal aesthetic?

It is, we should note, *grotesque* conflations to which Horace objects:
he begins by comparing a text of which the parts do not constitute a
unity (indeed, an 'organic' unity; 8–9: 'ut nec pes nec caput uni
reddatur formae') to a painting in which the head of a beautiful
woman is attached by way of a horse's neck and a random collection
of (variously feathered) limbs to a fish's tail (1–5); and having freely
conceded the retort that painter and poet enjoy a licence 'quidlibet
audendi' (9–11), he adds that this does not extend to combining the
flatly incompatible—the lamb lying down with the tiger (12–13).
Such incongruities are, for Horace, the antithesis of unity (23:
'simplex . . . et unum'), and it derives from the unskilful pursuit of the
artistic virtue of *poikilia* (29, 'variare'), just as (for example) the vice
of obscurity often attends the pursuit of the virtue brevity (24–31).[18]

therefore difficult to interpret, if one does not presuppose what Griffin is trying to
establish—that the epyllion has a covert, indeed allegorical, bearing on the themes of
the rest of the poem? (The poem 'is not made of the same stuff throughout, but on the
contrary very varied, in tone, scope, pace, and degree of relevance to the professed
subject-matter': Griffin 1981, 32.)

[18] Brink (1971, 104) is right to equate 'simplex' with the Greek ἁπλοῦς, but I think
oversimplifies when he says that this is the opposite of ποικίλος; Horace, after all, says
that a text should be 'simplex', but also implies that *poikilia* is a virtue. As in D. S. 20. 1. 5
(see ch. 6 below), ἁπλοῦς admits and entails an appropriate degree of *poikilia*.

It is not clear that Horace has any objection to digression as such; on the contrary, his approval of *poikilia* could be taken as implicitly condoning digression. His insistence on unity is concerned rather with the permissible limits of the pursuit of *poikilia*. To use another Greek term, his concern is with *kairos*—indeed, that is the sense of Horace's 'locus': 'sed nunc non erat his locus' (19) implies that in some places 'purple passages' are appropriate and should be inserted;[19] one can only judge what is appropriate in any given context by looking to the structure and purpose of the whole ('totum', 34) and asking whether one's proposed insert would be disruptive and produce monstrous incongruity. This general principle is familiar from material already examined, and it will recur in later chapters also. From it we cannot deduce whether Horace would have found (for example) the Ariadne digression in Catullus 64 out of place, for he does not state any specific critical standards in this passage—that is to say, like Plato he does not offer substantive criteria of appropriate construction (and we may reasonably suppose that neoteric ways of achieving *poikilia* were diversely valued by contemporaries). But that very fact shows that Horace's poem does not entail, and cannot legitimately be assumed to adopt, a centripetal aesthetic; no centripetal commitment is in evidence, and Horace says nothing that would allow us to conjecture one.[20]

That Horace prescribes for epic poetry of a traditional kind should remind us that Callimachean purism with regard to epic was not standard, either in his own day (hence its controversial reception) or when taken over by the Roman neoterics (who imitated Callimachus' polemical postures).[21] There is abundant evidence for the widespread

[19] The phrase 'purpureus pannus' is somewhat obscure, but is most plausibly explained as referring to the ornamental *segmenta* (see Brink ad loc., and Marquardt and Mau 1886, 548–9). In that case it does not suggest something aesthetically offensive in itself; on the contrary, the ornaments themselves were valued—though not always appropriate. Note Servius' interpretation of this passage in his note to *Aen.* 10. 653: 'Descriptio per παρέκβασιν facta ... has autem descriptiones esse aptas et raras convenit, sicut Horatius docet in arte poetica ... : sunt enim ornatui.'

[20] 'Polemic against digressive style has its parallel in Aristotle's condemnations of "episodic plots"' (Brink 1971, 94). But Aristotle's 'episodic plots' are not plots from which the text digresses, and (I have argued) Aristotle too is prepared to admit and admire digression ἐν καιρῷ; nor is Horace talking about the Aristotelian plot (the causal structure underlying a narrative text) at all: a point which Brink himself makes several times (e.g. 117), although he persists in referring to Aristotle at every opportunity. Horace is not, in fact, polemicizing against 'digressive style' as such, but against *inopportune* digression. Brink also sees the requirement of unity in *AP* 151–2 (1971, 224); but this is concerned only with consistency of invention (cf. 125–7).

[21] See e.g. Cat. 95; on the term 'neoteric', see in particular Lyne 1978.

composition of large-scale epic in the Hellenistic era.[22] Little of this output has survived—fortunately, perhaps; for the most part we have only titles or isolated fragments, which give us no guidance in questions of structure and unity. In the case of the third-century poet Rhianus we are a little better served: in addition to citations of his *Heracleia* (probably in fourteen books),[23] *Achaica* (not less than four), *Eliaca* (not less than three), *Thessalica* (not less than sixteen), and *Messeniaca* (not less than six), we have some evidence for the last-mentioned poem in Pausanias' account of the Messenian war, for which it was used as a source; but even so, we can say little more than that Rhianus' hero Aristomenes was comparable to Homer's Achilles (Paus. 4. 6. 3), and that his plot spanned a period of eleven years (4. 17. 10–11)—at best, then, in Aristotelian terms, a 'single action consisting of many parts'.[24]

The same description would apply to the one Hellenistic epic that has survived complete, the *Argonautica* of Apollonius of Rhodes; but it is a matter of dispute precisely how this work relates to Callimachean principles, a dispute that has been complicated by the (mutually inconsistent) traditions of the poet's quarrel with Callimachus.[25] In fact, the poem does satisfy the demands of the 'Telchines': it is a continuous narrative about heroes in many thousands of lines. Of these points, the last is not in dispute; the poem falls a little short of six thousand lines.[26] Continuity is a little more controversial, but the poem's plot does constitute a single Aristotelian *praxis*: it has a *telos*, the winning of the fleece and its return to Greece, which is stated (1. 4) and concisely explained (1. 5–17) at the outset, and which is eventually achieved, the incidents *en route* advancing or obstructing the heroes' progress to that goal. Working within that broad structure Apollonius has sought to emphasize the continuity by frequent cross-reference. This is sometimes achieved by means of prophecy: Idmon's death is foretold at 1. 140–1 and 1. 440–7, and occurs at 2. 815–50;

[22] See Ziegler 1966, Lloyd-Jones 1984, 58.

[23] See Jacoby's note to *FGrH* 265 F 47–54; the alternative is four books.

[24] Koster 1970, 122 cites Ar. *Poet.* 1459a35 (ἐν μέρος ἀπολαβών) in connection with Paus. 4. 6. 2 (Rhianus did not narrate the whole war): ingenious, but implausible.

[25] The 'quarrel' is irrelevant in any case, since we could not know (e.g.) how much allowance to make for personal factors. For a sceptical (perhaps indiscriminately so) handling of the evidence, see Lefkowitz 1980; cf. Lloyd-Jones 1984, 58–60. I would note that the analogy with Pindar is double-edged, since Callimachus himself (like other Hellenistic scholars) would probably have read Pindar biographically.

[26] That this approximates to the optimum length for an epic proposed by Aristotle (1459b20–2) has often been observed.

Phineus prophesies the course of the voyage, in an incomplete and
open-ended way, at 2. 311–425, and this prophecy is recalled at 2.
617–8, 646–7, 1051, 1090ff. (where a gap is filled in), 1135, 3. 549–56,
943, 4. 253–6. Sometimes Apollonius uses other kinds of retrospective
allusion: the stay at Lemnos is recalled a number of times by
references to gifts given there to the heroes (2. 32, 3. 1204–6, 4. 423–
8); Lemnos and Phineus both figure in the general review of the
voyage given to Lycus (2. 762–71), who himself has reason to take
particular interest in the defeat of Amycus and the Bebrycians at the
beginning of the book (2. 752–61, 792–800; cf. 2. 138–41). Moreover,
Apollonius links many of the incidents *en route* in more extended
causal sequences. At the beginning of the voyage Heracles is
acclaimed by the heroes as their leader, but defers to Jason (1. 341–
50); this adds plausibility to the suspicions of an envious plot against
him when he disappears (1. 1290–5), especially since he has repea-
tedly distinguished himself in the course of the book—instigating the
departure from Lemnos (1. 861–76), leading the fight against the
Earthborn (1. 989–97), and winning the rowing competition (1.
1161–71); the mishap which ends the last of those incidents is causally
linked to his disappearance, since his absence to find a new oar leaves
Hylas unsupervised and vulnerable, and leads to the confusion in
which he is inadvertently left behind. In the fourth book the course of
events is dictated for the most part by the seizure of the fleece and the
heroes' flight: they are compelled by the Colchian pursuit to take a
new route, but are then cut off; to escape from the trap they murder
Apsyrtus, and this crime leads to a further diversion. Only the Libyan
diversion is not given causal roots in the preceding action; yet even
here, the course of events has been interwoven with the rest of the
poem, for the heroes in the extremity of thirst are saved by a spring
opened by Heracles, abandoned in the first book (4. 1432–84).
Whether or not one finds these devices artistically satisfactory, it
seems clear that Apollonius has been striving to produce the kind of
unified structure which Aristotle describes as a single action of many
parts.[27]

The poem, then, is a single continuous narrative in many thousands of lines; and it is about heroes. Some recent interpreters have
maintained that the heroes' (or Jason's) stature is mitigated or

---

[27] More detailed discussions can be found in Vian's introductions to each book in his
Budé edition (Paris 1976–81).

reduced to the level of ordinary mortals.[28] I doubt whether this view is tenable, however; certainly, Apollonius seems explicitly to take a different view (1. 547–52, 4. 1381–92).[29] Nevertheless, in style and tone, and in the pervasive aetiological interest and mythological erudition, the influence of Callimachus is evident; one would hesitate to apply to this poem Callimachus' unflattering description of heroic epic as thunder or the braying of an ass. One might suppose that this effect was intended—that is, that the poem is an attempt to recover the old, traditionally prestigious epic form, without surrendering Callimachean criteria of style and artistic excellence (an unsuccessful attempt, some would argue). The rest of Apollonius' poetic output consisted largely of foundation-myths told in poems apparently not exceeding a single book; he generally composed on the scale of the *Hecale*, therefore, and his habitual theme was Callimachean (see *Aetia* fr. 43. 58–83); so one might imagine a poet making an experimental venture beyond the Callimachean epyllion. But it would be misleading to suggest that there is any actual evidence for this.[30]

In another case, however, such a development can be traced. Vergil's career began with neoteric miniatures in the *Eclogues*; the *Georgics*, though a more ambitious work, was still (as we have seen) neoteric or Callimachean in its models ('Ἡσιόδου τό τ' ἄεισμα καὶ ὁ τρόπος, as Callimachus said admiringly of Aratus) and aesthetic presuppositions; but Vergil ended up writing the *Aeneid*, a continuous narrative in many thousands of lines concerned with heroes—the 'reges et proelia' which he had deprecated in his earliest phase: contrast *Ecl.* 6. 3–5 (noting the Callimachean allusion) with *Aen.* 7. 41–2. To conclude this section, we shall look briefly at the response of two subsequent Roman poets of genius to the challenge of epic structure after its Vergilian rehabilitation.

In the brief proem to his *Metamorphoses*, Ovid describes the work as a 'perpetuum carmen' (1. 4) running from the creation of the world

---

[28] E.g. Lawall 1966; more persuasively Zanker 1987, 195–209.

[29] 4. 1773, ἀριστῆες μακάρων γένος; cf. 1. 970, 2. 1091, ἀνδρῶν ἡρώων θεῖον στόλον, 1. 548, ἡμιθέων ἀνδρῶν. Apollonius' most frequent descriptions of the Argonauts are as ἥρωες and ἀριστῆες.

[30] Brink finds in Neoptolemus of Parium (one of Horace's sources in *AP*) a theoretical position comparable to the practical line here ascribed to Apollonius ('an Alexandrian in his learned verse and in his scholarship; an Alexandrian, too, in the stylistic refinement which he demands of poems small and large; but an Aristotelian upholder of the long poem, and a believer in the unity of a large literary composition'); his conclusions are plausible, although inevitably they rest on conjectures in varying degrees precarious (1963, 43–74).

to his own day. That term looks very much like a translation of
Callimachus' 'continuous song' (ἄεισμα διηνεκές), in which case Ovid
would here be disclaiming Callimachus' disclaimer of long poems
with continuous plots; he would, in short, be aligning the work with
the traditional epic. This inference is strengthened by the analogy to
'perpetuum carmen' in Varro: he defines ποίησις (as distinct from
ποίημα) as 'perpetuum argumentum e rhythmis', citing the *Iliad* and
Ennius' *Annals* as examples (*Men.* 398). Similarly Lucilius (338–47
Marx) defines ποίησις as a complete (long) poem, such as the *Iliad*
and *Annals*, each of which is a single thesis; and the scholia to
Dionysius Thrax define ποίησις as 'in the strict sense, a complete
subject-matter (ὑπόθεσις) expressed in verse, possessing beginning,
middle, and end' (449. 24–6 Hilgard).[31] Certainly, the *Metamorphoses*
stands in contrast to the *Fasti*, on which Ovid was working at much
the same time. The latter is unequivocally a 'collective' poem in the
Callimachean tradition, the diverse stories being distributed according to the Roman calendar, that is 'in random order so far as their
content is concerned',[32] without any attempt to link them in a single
chronological or causal sequence. The movement of *Metamorphoses* is
quite different; at every stage carefully contrived circumstantial
connections give the reader the impression of a single, continuously
unfolding thread of narrative. But that impression is illusory since,
more often than not, there is no underlying causal sequence linking
the narratives thus artfully juxtaposed. Even in terms of a purely
chronological sequence, although the promised development from
the world's origin to the present is broadly observed, in detail it is
blurred and neglected; Ovid has devised instead a capricious structure of surprising insertions and associations.[33] Thus the deviation
from Callimachean principles is (as many commentators have
observed) more apparent than real; behind the pose of epic continuity one finds a collective poem in Callimachean style—and one on

---

[31] For these and similar references, see Dahlmann 1953, 118–27, and Brink 1963,
61–7; and cf. n. 2 above. Horace uses the phrase 'carmen perpetuum' of a poem on
Attica at *Odes* 1. 7. 6; some have suspected an allusion to Euphorion's *Mopsopia* (cf.
Nisbet and Hubbard ad loc.), but that poem, also called *Atakta* and containing
συμμιγεῖς ἱστορίας, was surely a Callimachean collection; if that is the reference—
which is quite uncertain—the sense of the term in this passage would be obscure.

[32] Steiner 1958, 223.

[33] Cf. Coleman 1971. Note also Little 1970 and 1972 for discussion of some
attempted thematic integrations of the poem.

a theme popular among the writers of such poetry.[34] With characteristic paradoxicality, Ovid offers this Callimachean poem in an epic
guise; but he does not really embrace the epic form.

It is quite otherwise with Statius (whose debt to Vergil, constantly
in evidence, is explicitly acknowledged at *Th.* 12. 816–7). The care he
takes over the structure and unity of his plot can be seen in the
opening lines of his *Thebaid*. He sets aside the 'longa retro series' (1. 7)
of events stretching back to the 'gentis . . . primordia dirae' (1. 4), in
favour of a strictly limited theme (1. 16, 'limes mihi carminis . . .').
That theme is the conflict of the sons of Oedipus; Statius passes
allusively over its remotest causal antecedents (cf. 1. 224–43 for the
causal relevance of this remote material), and its nearer antecedents
he handles concisely—indeed, they are rendered with admirable
economy as the preamble to Oedipus' curse, the proximate occasion
of the plot proper (1. 46–87; its motive force is seen at 1. 123ff.). Thus
Statius has chosen, not simply a 'single action', but that kind of
unified action of which Aristotle approved most highly; to reject the
whole story of Thebes or the Labdacid house is precisely to reject a
unified plot of many parts. That the plot extends to the burial of the
dead does not compromise this unity (any more than, in Aristotle's
view, it does in the *Iliad*); since at no prior point could one say that
there is no further event which necessarily or probably follows, there
is no prior point at which the plot would be complete or (therefore)
unified, in Aristotelian terms.[35] And, as Aristotle commends the
expansion of a poem narrating such a plot by means of digressive
epeisodia, so Statius—without compromising the Aristotelian unity of
his plot—devises narrative excursuses, such as the stories of Coroebus
(1. 557–668) and Hypsipyle (5. 29–498), and 'delays', such as the
drought which precedes and the funeral games which follow Hypsipyle's narration.[36]

---

[34] The suggestion that 'deducite' (1. 4; cf. 'deduxi', *Tr.* 2. 559–60) implies
Callimachean commitment (e.g. Kenney 1976, Gilbert 1976, 111–2) is doubtful;
'deductum' carries this sense elsewhere, but do other parts of the verb? Cf. Kovacs
1987, 461–2 (although I do not find his interpretation in general persuasive).

[35] I must emphasize that I am not suggesting that Statius set out to observe
Aristotelian precepts as such; rather, Statius was working within a continuous poetic
tradition, an earlier stage of which Aristotle had correctly analysed.

[36] For thematic integrations of the Coroebus and Hypsipyle narratives, see Vessey
1973, 101–7, 170–87; since I do not think that the digressiveness of these stories is an
aesthetic demerit or detracts from the poem's unity, I do not find it necessary to read

The opening of the *Achilleid* is not nearly so promising from an
Aristotelian point of view; Statius undertakes to tell the whole story,
'ire per omnem ... heroa' (1. 4–5), in a way that recalls Aristotle's
strictures on single-person plots (51a16–29).[37] Further inspection
suggests, however, that this may be unfair to the poet; Statius does
not include in his plot 'everything that happened' to the hero
(51a25): his youth and education are introduced digressively, as is the
wounding on Parnassus in the *Odyssey* (51a25–6; 2. 94–167). The
poem begins with Thetis' attempt to obstruct her son's involvement in
the Trojan war (1. 25ff.) and has in view as its *telos* the hero's death in
that war; the 'whole story', therefore, is a sequence of events with a
clear beginning and end, and the intervening events could in
principle have been treated as a causally linked (if multipartite)
series—since the epic did not progress far into its second book we can
only conjecture about the way it would have been developed, but
there is no reason at all why those conjectures should be loaded
against the poet. Certainly, it would not be plausible to claim that
Achilles' involvement in the Trojan war is strictly comparable to the
careers of Theseus and Heracles (Aristotle's examples of defective
plots), which it would be difficult to treat other than as a series of
discrete heroic deeds. Confidently, therefore, in the case of the
Thebaid, conjecturally and a little more hesitantly in that of the
Achilleid, I conclude that Statius' response to the problem of epic
structure may be seen as skilfully orthodox.

them as 'symbolically related to' or 'illustrating by parallel, antithesis and symbol' the
main or dominant themes of the whole (102, 170); and I do not in fact find Vessey's
parallels convincing evidence that the stories were designed to be read in that way.
(That Hypsipyle's narrative is designed to recall Aeneas' retrospective narrative in *Aen.*
2–3—compare *Th.* 5. 29–30 with *Aen.* 2. 1—is, of course, ambiguous: one might infer
that Statius wishes us to assume that his 'digression' is covertly, as Vergil's is overtly,
related to the outer narrative; but one might also conclude that Statius regarded it as
aesthetically indifferent whether or not an *epeisodion* had such relations.) Of course,
even if one admits digressions in principle, one might still find the scale and disposition
of those in the *Thebaid* inappropriate.

[37] So Dilke 1954, 8.

6
Dionysius and Historiography

ARISTOTLE referred to historiography to illustrate by contrast his theory of unity for narrative poetry; in this chapter I shall look more directly at ancient criticism of historical writing, taking Dionysius of Halicarnassus as my chief, though not my sole, guide. Our main concern is, of course, with the branch of rhetoric which deals with the selection, disposition, and development of a text's subject-matter (the πραγματικὸς τόπος, in Dionysius' terminology); before we turn to that, however, I shall try to provide a background for the discussion by looking briefly at some pertinent aspects of Dionysius' treatment of the branch of rhetoric which deals with questions of style and verbal expression (the λεκτικὸς τόπος).

In his major treatise on style Dionysius declares that good writing depends above all on four factors: melodic pattern; rhythm; variation(μεταβολή); and the appropriateness that attends the use of these three (τὸ παρακολουθοῦν τοῖς τρισὶ τούτοις πρέπον). Melody and rhythm give pleasure; but, in written compositions just as in music proper (from which, Dionysius says, rhetoric differs only in degree, not in kind), unvaried melody and rhythm produce only a sense of satiety (κόρος), while inappropriate melody and rhythm, or variation that is not in accordance with kairos (εὔκαιρος), jar and destroy the pleasurable effect (*Comp.* 11, ii 37. 9–12, 38. 13–40. 16 Usener-Radermacher). In the following chapter he takes up the question of variation, and recommends the juxtaposition of like with unlike—contrasting sounds, words of different length, words of different grammatical kind or form, different figures of speech; this helps to break up the uniformity (ὁμοιότης) of one's text and avoids satiety (12, 43. 17–45. 5). He insists that variety and diversifying embellishment (μεταβάλλειν, ποικίλλειν) are essential, but also that these effects are not to be sought mechanically; obsessive variation is a potentially irritating trick of style, which one must avoid by observing kairos—though kairos itself is not susceptible to systematic treatment in theoretical terms, being a matter of judgement (δόξα) rather than of

72   Dionysius and Historiography

science (ἐπιστήμη, 45.6–21).[1] As a general principle, uniformity is to be relieved (διαναπαύειν τὴν ταυτότητά φημι δεῖν) by introducing variation subject to kairos (μεταβολὰς εὐκαίρους εἰσφέροντα); for in everything variation is pleasant (46. 13–15, cf. Ar. Rhet. 1371a25–8). Dionysius returns to variation in chapter 19. Uniformity, he says, is to be relieved, since even the beautiful and pleasant induce satiety if unvaried; embellished by variation, they remain always fresh (ποικιλλόμενα δὲ ταῖς μεταβολαῖς ἀεὶ καινὰ μένει, 84.5–12). This theme is developed throughout the chapter, which ends with a contrast between the writers who have most successfully employed variation (Herodotus, Plato, Demosthenes), and Isocrates with his followers, who, whatever the virtues of their style, offend against the principle of variation by a monotonous use of period, of figure, of euphony, and of many other similar devices that are fatiguing to the ear (ἄλλα πολλὰ τοιαῦτα κόπτοντα τὴν ἀκρόασιν, 86. 21–87. 21). Earlier in the chapter Dionysius observed that poets are committed to some degree of uniformity by the repeated metrical schema of line and stanza (84. 12–86. 7); he returns to this point in chapter 26, stressing the potential difficulty faced by iambic and hexameter poets, whose stichic metres are uniform (ὁμοειδῆ) and do not permit metrical variation (οὐκ ἔξεστι πολλοῖς διαλαμβάνειν μέτροις ἢ ῥύθμοις τὰς ποιήσεις, ἀλλὰ ἀνάγκη μένειν ἐπὶ τοῦ αὐτοῦ σχήματος, 136. 13–17). He points out, using illustrations from Homer and Euripides, that this metrical uniformity can be offset syntactically by varied phrase-length and enjambment (136. 19–137. 1):

When they break up lines by dividing them irregularly into clauses (τοῖς κώλοις διαλαμβάνοντες ἄλλοτε ἄλλως), they confound and efface the severity (ἀκρίβεια) of the metre; and when they diversify (ποικίλας ποιῶσιν) the length and shape of the periods, they make us forgetful of the metre.

This discussion is an admirable piece of applied criticism, though one must feel somewhat uneasy at the persistent implication that metrical form is best when completely effaced; Dionysius could profitably have recalled here his earlier observation that similarity, as well as dissimilarity, can give pleasure (12, 45. 8–10), and considered how the charm of poetry is enhanced by the interplay of recurrent metrical pattern and syntactical variation.

The theory of style expounded in this treatise is applied in

[1] Cf. Isocr. 15. 183–4, cited in ch. 3 above; it is here that Dionysius comments on Gorgias' treatment of kairos.

Dionysius' critical essays on the orators. In *Demosthenes* the theory is concisely restated: when either melody or rhythm threatens to exceed due measure, variation steps in to regulate it; and when they have been restored to their proper place, appropriateness supervenes to supply the charm they deserve (*Dem.* 48, i 233. 13–17); the analogy with music is once again used to illustrate the necessity both of *poikilia* and of its restraint by *kairos* (233. 18–234. 6). Demosthenes is seen as the outstanding oratorical exemplar of these qualities: for his *poikilia* see 234. 9–12, 239. 16–23.[2] Isocrates is used to illustrate Demosthenes' virtues by contrast.[3] There is much, Dionysius agrees, to admire in Isocrates' style, but it has a number of faults, including a lack of variety. Because he uses the same manner consistently he frequently writes in a style inappropriate to the matter in hand—an offence against the fourth of Dionysius' stylistic requirements (*Dem.* 18, 166. 26–167. 10); but for the same reason he offends against the principle of variation, so that his style becomes tedious and unpleasant (*Dem.* 20, 171. 8–172. 3). The same criticisms are made in the essay which Dionysius devoted to Isocrates himself. His style is more ornate than that of Lysias, and so in one sense varied (ποικίλην, *Isocr.* 2, i 57. 3–7); but his enslavement to a uniform smoothness prevents him from adjusting the intensity of his style to the needs of the occasion, and limits the range of effects that he can achieve. Thus his lack of stylistic moderation leads him to violate the principles both of propriety and of variation (*Isocr.* 13–14). Isaeus offers a more successful, because more varied, contrast to Lysias' simplicity, and one which points the way to Demosthenes (*Isaeus* 3, i 95. 7–12; 12, 108. 1).

It is clear, then, that variety is a cardinal element in Dionysius' theory of stylistic excellence; the analogous treatment of variation in his approach to questions of subject-matter is one of the points which I wish to stress in what follows. I shall concentrate on his discussion of historiography, because it is in this connection that he attends most carefully to questions of subject and structure; but before we leave his essays on the orators, a brief survey of their contribution will be in order.

In his discussion of the treatment of subject-matter (the πραγ-

---

[2] Cf. *Thuc.* 53, where Demosthenes is considered an imitator of Thucydides' style who succeeds in avoiding his eccentric faults; μεταβολή and ποικιλία are among the traits imitated (413. 4–6). (Note the cross-references to *Comp.* in *Dem.* 49, 236. 10–14, and 50, 239. 14–16.)

[3] Cf. *Pomp.* 1. 6–8, ii 223. 2–234. 6, for a discussion of this critical technique.

μ ατικὸς τόπος) in oratory, Dionysius uses a fourfold, and sometimes a fivefold, scheme of headings: invention, selection, division (sometimes), arrangement, and development. Lysias, for example, is judged excellent in invention and selection; he can think out just the right points to make in any situation. But his economy, the way in which he deploys the points he has selected and develops them, is not recommended as a model, since his technique is too straightforward and too uniform (ὁμοειδής) to be effective (*Lys.* 15). Isocrates, despite his stylistic faults, comes into his own here (*Isocr.* 4, i 60. 9–21); he is Lysias' equal in invention and selection, but in arrangement, division, and development he is far superior. In particular—the point of most interest to us here—he is praised for breaking up the uniformity (τὸ διαλαμβάνεσθαι τὴν ὁμοείδειαν) of his speeches by maintaining variety in their treatment of the subject-matter (ἰδίαις μεταβολαῖς) and by introducing 'episodes' that digress from that subject-matter (ξένοις ἐπεισοδίοις). In his treatise on style, too, when praising Herodotus, Plato, and Demosthenes for their *poikilia*, Dionysius strays momentarily from his main theme to mention their use of *epeisodia* among the techniques by which they achieve that quality (*Comp.* 19, ii 87. 3–7).[4]

But Dionysius' fullest discussions of the questions of subject-matter are, as has been said, devoted to historiography. In his early treatise *On Imitation* he compared Herodotus and Thucydides, adding supplementary remarks on Xenophon, Philistus, and Theopompus; this work exists only in fragmentary epitomized form, but Dionysius partially reproduced the relevant sections in his *Letter to Pompeius*.[5] He subsequently developed his remarks on Thucydides at greater length in a separate essay. In this survey I shall adhere as far as possible to the headings under which Dionysius organized his earlier discussion (those of the later essay do not coincide exactly), introducing parallel material from other sources where appropriate.

(a) *Choice of subject:* The historian's first and most fundamental task, Dionysius observes in the *Letter to Pompeius* (3. 2–7, ii 232. 18–234. 15), is to choose an appropriate subject—one that is fine (καλή) and that will give pleasure to his readers. Herodotus, writing about a

---

[4] Cf. also *Isaeus* 3, and 14–15; the discussion of narrative there bears comparison with those cited from Ar. *Rhet.* and the *Rhet. ad Alex.* in ch. 2 above.

[5] Sacks 1983 argues that *Pomp.* does not reproduce but substantially reworks *Imit.*. I shall attempt elsewhere to establish that this view is mistaken, and that *Pomp.* in fact quotes an unrevised draft of *Imit.*; but that is immaterial to the present discussion.

great pan-Hellenic achievement, has clearly succeeded in this;[6] Thucydides has failed. The war about which he wrote was, despite his arguments to the contrary, on a smaller scale than his predecessor's, and since its consequences were wholly bad for Greece it should have been allowed to pass into oblivion; rehearsed as it is by Thucydides, it cannot fail to alienate the reader. That Thucydides attempts to justify his choice of subject by belittling those of previous historians shows that the error was the product of bad judgement, and not something forced on him by the necessity of handling virgin material.

In the essay on Thucydides Dionysius takes a more sympathetic view (*Thuc.* 5–8, i 330. 7–335. 13). Most of Thucydides' predecessors, he writes, devoted themselves to local history, composing separate monographs on each nation or *polis*. Since their aim was to record local tradition they inevitably included mythological accounts of the remote past and other colourful but foolish anecdotes. This model Thucydides rejected as too easy, and because it afforded too little useful instruction to his readers. The more ambitious project of Herodotus, a vast survey drawing together into a single work diverse events scattered over a wide geographical area, was also rejected, on the grounds that a 'synoptic' treatment (one of manageable length) of so large a subject could not have achieved the required degree of detail. Hence Thucydides' decision to treat in depth the course of a

---

[6] Dionysius remarks, punningly, that the proem of Herodotus' history is both the beginning and end of the work (*Pomp.* 3. 3, 233. 7–8): that is, Herodotus begins his work by stating its (in a teleological sense) 'end'—its subject-matter. Some modern critics have alleged that 'nowhere . . . does Herodotus explicitly state his theme' (Drews 1973, 70–1; cf. Immerwahr 1966, 17), but Dionysius was right; the first five lines of the history do contain such a statement. There Herodotus takes as his theme human affairs in general (τὰ γενόμενα ἐξ ἀνθρώπων), and more particularly the great or remarkable achievements (ἔργα μεγάλα τε καὶ θωμαστά) of Greeks and barbarians—a polar expression for the whole human race. The concluding transitional clause (τά τε ἄλλα καὶ δι' ἣν αἰτίαν ἐπολέμησαν ἀλλήλοις) indicates that Greek-barbarian conflict will be an important part of this theme, which in turn implies that the great Greek-barbarian conflict will be prominent. But Herodotus does not limit himself to the Persian Wars, or to anything else; he gives himself the widest possible scope for recording whatever seems to him worthy of record. This means that Herodotus' history is not in any substantial sense thematically integrated, a conclusion with which Dionysius was quite happy, but which modern interpreters have been reluctant to accept. For trenchant criticism of one attempt to integrate the work thematically (Cobet 1971), see Drews 1975; note in particular his remarks on the shift of interest from particular to general which this involves, and on the technique of the 'common denominator', by which apparently unrelated passages can be distorted into thematic harmony.

single war, a subject 'neither consisting solely of one section (μήτε μονόκωλον παντάπασι)', as were the simple subjects of the local historians, 'nor divided into many unconnected headings (μήτ' εἰς πολλὰ μεμερισμένην καὶ ἀσυνάρτητα κεφάλαια)', as was Herodotus' extremely complex theme; hence also the exclusion of myth.

We shall return to the question of myth in (c); but we should consider here whether this later discussion implies adverse criticism of Herodotus' choice of subject, reversing Dionysius' earlier approval. I think not. In the earlier discussion Dionysius did recognize that Herodotus' subject embraced many themes with little mutual resemblance (πολλὰς καὶ οὐδὲν ἐοικυίας ὑποθέσεις), and this, as we shall see in (d), only increased his admiration for the coherent way in which Herodotus had nevertheless drawn his material together. In the *Letter to Pompeius*, therefore, he was aware of the potential weaknesses of Herodotus' choice of subject; and nothing is said in *Thucydides* to cast doubt on the earlier judgement that Herodotus had managed to overcome the difficulties—for here Dionysius is not trying to assess Herodotus' handling of the subject-matter chosen (his οἰκονομία) at all.

As for the other historians, Dionysius praises Xenophon for choosing subjects that are 'fine, impressive, and suited to a philosophically-minded man' (*Pomp.* 4. 1, 241. 5–7). He mentions the *Cyropaedia*, presenting a model of good kingship, the *Anabasis*, an 'encomium of the Greek army', and the *Hellenica*, a continuation of Thucydides incorporating the overthrow of the tyrants and the liberation of Athens: these are all (it is implied) both edifying and attractive to a moral and patriotic readership. The Sicilian histories of Philistus are too narrow in scope to be of wide interest or very instructive (*Pomp.* 5. 1, 242. 16–21). The subjects which Theopompus chose for his histories, the rest of the Peloponnesian War and the career of Philip, are good (*Pomp.* 6. 2, 244. 16–19); no explanation of their excellence is offered.[7]

At the beginning of his own historical work, Dionysius emphasizes again the importance of selecting an elevated and instructive subject (*Ant.* 1. 1. 2–3), and explains the reasons for his own choice of Roman

---

[7] In particular, it is not explained why the Peloponnesian War is a better subject for Theopompus than for Thucydides. But the answer is implied in the description of Xenophon's *Hellenica*; because the story is continued beyond the end of the war to the liberation of Athens, the unpleasantness of the subject has been mitigated by a happy ending; cf. *Pomp.* 3. 10 (236. 1–5) and (b) below.

history at length (1. 2–6, cf. 5. 75. 1). The justification of one's choice of subject was in fact a regular *topos* of the historian's introductory material. Thucydides himself attempted it (1. 1–23)—an attempt severely criticized by Dionysius for exaggeration, rhetorical ineptitude, disproportion, and superfluous detail (*Thuc.* 19, 353. 6–354. 18).[8] Polybius justifies his choice of subject by emphasizing the importance of the Roman empire by comparison with its predecessors; and he lays particular stress on the universal nature of his history, it being useless to treat piecemeal a period in which the history of the whole world had become organically interrelated (1. 1–4, discussed further in (b) below). Diodorus also argues for the value of universal history (1. 1–3).[9]

(b) *Beginning and ending:* In the *Letter to Pompeius* (3. 8–10, 234. 16–236. 5) Dionysius argues that Thucydides has also erred in deciding where his history should begin and end. Herodotus has reasonably begun with the earliest origins of the conflict between Greeks and barbarians—significantly, for reasons we shall see shortly, the blame is placed on the barbarians (cf. Hdt. 1. 5. 3); and he has carried his narrative down to the defeat and punishment of the latter. Thucydides' starting-point is repellent, since it marks the beginning of the decline of Greece; and (by contrast with Herodotus) it was unpatriotic, since it implies that his own city was chiefly to blame for the war. He should have begun after the Persian Wars, when Athens' glory was at its height; that would have been intrinsically more attractive, and would have enabled him to place the blame for the outbreak of hostilities on Sparta's fear and envy of Athenian greatness. As for the end, instead of the abrupt and arbitrary terminus that we now have, the story should have been carried down—not, perhaps, to the end of the war (for the defeat of Athens would have been a disagreeable point at which to leave us), but to the subsequent liberation, 'an astonishing event and one exceptionally pleasing to his audience'.[10]

Dionysius' criticism of Thucydides' ending is of course absurd: the work is patently unfinished, as Dionysius himself was aware (*Thuc.* 16, though he had repeated the criticism in chapter 12). His comments on the beginning need more careful consideration. First, we must establish whether Dionysius' discussion is concerned with the

---

[8] More kindly treated by Aelius Aristides 27. 70.
[9] Further references in Scheller 1911, 38–41.
[10] Cf. n. 7 above.

level of the text (like Plato's) or the subject-matter (like Aristotle's). In the *Letter to Pompeius* Dionysius seems to have in view under this heading the temporal limits of the subject-matter. This is implied by the point at which the heading is introduced, after the choice of subject (a) but before inclusion and omission (c), and thus quite separate from the 'economic' heading of division and arrangement (d); and in *Imit.* 6. 3. 2 (ii 208. 17–19) we read that Philistus imitated Thucydides in leaving his subject (ὑπόθεσις), not his text, incomplete. In the parallel discussion in *Thuc.* 10–11 (i 338. 4–341. 23), however, the heading has been postponed to follow division as an aspect of arrangement (τάξις); that is, it has been attached explicitly to 'economy', the organization of the subject-matter in its textual realization. This might appear to be a distinction without very much difference, since Dionysius says that the natural order of exposition follows the temporal order of events; but he adds, as a distinct point, that the opening of Thucydides' narrative would have been 'superior' (κρείττων) if he had adopted that arrangement, which implies that in other circumstances departing from the natural order might have been technically advantageous.[11] So the definitions of beginning and end in *Thuc.* 10 (338. 6–9) must be taken to refer to the narrative propriety of a particular ordering of segments of text, rather than to the causal or temporal limits of an underlying subject-matter; compare *Lys.* 17, where, in a discussion of Lysias' skill in opening speeches (although his openings vary, Dionysius says, each is the most effective for that speech), he contrasts what someone might happen to say first with the appropriate (προσήκουσα) opening, that is, that which ought not be to anywhere other than at the beginning (cf. Pl. *Phdr.* 264b3–8).[12]

   In the *Letter to Pompeius*, therefore, Dionysius is criticizing the limits which Thucydides has set for his subject-matter. But this criticism is open to an obvious objection; it can be argued that Thucydides has done just what Dionysius recommends. Although his narrative begins (formally) with the Corcyra incident (1. 24), Thucydides subsequently extends his subject-matter backwards, returning to the withdrawal of the Persians from Europe, and tracing the rise of Athenian power from that point (1. 89–117); and he does make it

---

[11] This is the common notion of natural and artificial order: cf. *Rhet. Her.* 3. 9, Cic. *de Or.* 2. 307–9, Quint. 7. 10. 10–15; further n. 14 and ch. 8 n. 36 below.

[12] It must be added that the tidy contrast between the earlier discussion and that in *Thuc.* is blurred by the praise of Xenophon's beginning and end in *Pomp.* 4. 2 (241. 14–18), which is subsumed under economy, though preceding τάξις.

clear that the 'overt causes' with which he begins were basically pretexts, the Spartans' real motive being fear of Athenian power (1. 23. 5–6, 1. 88). (It remains true that Thucydides has not made as much patriotic capital as Dionysius requires out of Athenian glory and Spartan malice, but that is not a consequence either of the choice or of the arrangement of the subject.) It was presumably in recognition of this flaw in his argument that Dionsysius reformulated the criticism as a point about the economy of the text in *Thucydides*. Here he emphasizes the perversity of tucking away the 'truest cause' of the war—the most natural point of departure—into a formal digression; this inversion, and the disproportion of length between the accounts of the 'true' and 'overt' causes of the war, place undue emphasis on the latter.[13] This objection to Thucydides' arrangement is at least intelligible.

One possible line of reply is that Thucydides' narrative is concerned with the course, not the cause, of the war; a more extensive and emphatic account of the 'truest' cause would therefore be irrelevant to his subject in the way that a parenthetic clarification of the immediate background to the war is not. On this view, the Corcyrean and Epidamnian crises are related at length not (or not only) because they provided pretexts for the abrogation of the treaty, but because they, unlike the events of the Pentacontaetia, were continuous with operations in the north-western and north-eastern theatres in the early years of the war itself. The point that the prior events were 'outside the subject-matter' (ἔξω τῆς ὑποθέσεως) for a historian of the Peloponnesian War is made in an anonymous papyrus commentary on Thucydides in the course of a fairly detailed reply to Dionysius' criticisms (POxy. 853, col. i. 20–33, iii. 18–30); the commentator adds, rather lamely, that it is also more appropriate to begin with the causes openly discussed, and then to elaborate if the historian thinks that other, less obvious, factors were operative (iii. 30–iv. 9).[14] To be sure, this defence gives Dionysius the opportunity

---

[13] Since the 'overt causes' are Peloponnesian complaints, they tend to place Athens in a less favourable light than the 'truest cause' would warrant; thus the undue emphasis could be regarded as an aspect of Thucydides' alleged anti-Athenian bias—though Dionysius does not make that point here. (For further discussion of Thucydides on the causes of the war, see Heath 1986a.)

[14] The editors suggest that ἀνὰ μέσον and Ὁμηρικῶς in iv. 4–6 refer to 'Homerica dispositio', 'placing the weakest part of one's rhetorical forces in the middle' (cf. Quint. 5. 12. 14, with *Il*. 4. 297–300), in Dionysius' arguments; it is more likely, surely, to refer to Thucydides' beginning 'more Homerico in mediis' (see Quint. 7. 10. 11; Hor. *AP* 148–9; Σ bT *Il*. 1. 1; cf. n. 11 above, and Chapter 8 n. 36).

to reopen his original objection: the beginning of Thucydides' subject, redefined in this way, is unpleasing; but readers who do not share Dionysius' rhetorical approach to the evaluation of historiography are unlikely to find this objection compelling.[15]

Dionysius' concern with the appropriate delimitation of the writer's subject-matter is probably to be seen as a commonplace of Hellenistic historiographical theory.[16] Polybius explains that he has chosen the Olympiad 220/16 as his beginning because it was from that date that events began to be interrelated throughout the known world, history thus becoming an organic whole (σωματοειδῆ, 1. 3. 4–6). Like Thucydides' study of the Pentacontaetia, however, Polybius' first two books go back beyond the beginning of his subject to provide explanatory background; here, too, he is careful to establish an appropriate starting-point, and points out that the pursuit of ever more remote causes would rob his subject of a clearly defined beginning altogether (1. 5. 1–5, cf. 1. 12. 5–9); the necessity of such a beginning for the whole project is established theoretically in 5. 30. 8–32. 5 (he puns here, like Dionysius in *Pomp*. 3. 3, on the two senses of τέλος, 'end'). In 3. 1. 4–5 he explains that his subject has, as well as a beginning, a clearly defined end—the completion of the growth of Roman power, fifty-three years from his starting-point (3. 1. 9); however, when he subsequently revised his plan he had to explain how an extension beyond that apparently natural point of rest to another end would make the work more useful, and was therefore more appropriate (3. 4. 1–5. 6).

Polybius' use in 1. 3. 4 of the organic analogy, especially in a context of beginnings and endings, must raise the question of an Aristotelian connnection. Aristotle's point in *Poet.* 1459b17–30 is, as I suggested in Chapter 4, not that unity is a concept inapplicable to historiography, but that unity in a work of history is not to be defined in terms of the causal interrelation of the events constituting its subject-matter; histories do not typically display causal integration of that kind. Polybius does not impose on history in general the requirement of causal integration that Aristotle imposes on narrative poetry; on the contrary, he regards such integration as the peculiar and remarkable quality (τὸ ... ἴδιον καὶ τὸ θαυμαστόν) of his own work (1. 4. 1). Polybius' point is that he is dealing with a period in

---

[15] Cf., perhaps, the discussion of Homer's choice of opening word reported in the scholia to *Il.* 1. 1 (and cf. ch. 8 n. 26 below).

[16] Scheller 1911, 41–3.

which events all over the world were, for the first time ever, inextricably intertwined; consequently, to study or write about the history of that period in a piecemeal fashion could not yield any adequate understanding of the whole pattern: it would be like dissecting a living body (ἔμψυχον σῶμα) to get an impression of the whole animal (ζῷον, 1. 4. 5–11). This, clearly, is an observation, not on the correct way to write history, but on the correct way to write the history of the period beginning in 220/16.[17] Similarly, although both Polybius and Dionysius insist that the historian's subject-matter must have an appropriate beginning and end, they do not insist on the crucial element in Aristotle's criteria for epic and drama—that those limits must be defined in causal terms. Dionysius makes a patently rhetorical assessment of the appropriateness of Thucydides' beginning, in terms of the historian's *ethos* and the delectation of his readers. Polybius, though scrupulous to explain the causal background to the events of his chosen period, begins the period itself at a point of qualitative change in the nature of world-history: yet this change is the effect of continuing historical processes, not itself a cause of subsequent events; and his revised end, at least, is justified by its usefulness. There is no reason, therefore, to suppose that Hellenistic historiographical theory transferred Aristotelian canons to a genre which Aristotle himself specifically excluded from their application.[18]

(c) *Inclusion and omission*: Thirdly (*Pomp.* 3. 11–12, 236. 6–237. 5), Thucydides has shown inferior judgement to Herodotus over the inclusion and omission of material. Herodotus knew that a lengthy narrative will affect its readers with a painful sense of satiety (κόρος) if it concentrates unremittingly on a single series of events; to avoid this the reader must be 'rested' at intervals—he needs ἀναπαύσεις. Aware of this, Herodotus has tried to make his work varied (ποικίλην), in this respect imitating Homer. Thucydides, too, realized

---

[17] Scheller's treatment of this topic is therefore flawed, as is (e.g.) Walbank 1972, 66–9 (cf. also his commentary ad locc.): 'It is Polybius' claim, and indeed his achievement, that he succeeded in writing universal history in the footsteps of Ephorus, but at the same time produced a work with a subject and a pattern, which made it "as it were an organic whole"' (67). But since Polybius presents this as the appropriate historiographical response to a unique historical development, there can be no implication that Ephorus and other universal historians of earlier periods in which this pattern did not exist were failing to write in a historiographically appropriate way; the criticism is rather of authors of monographs on artificially abstracted aspects of Polybius' period.

[18] Other references to unity and the organic analogy in Hellenistic historiography will be discussed in (c) and (d) below.

that change (μεταβολή) makes history pleasantly varied, and has
made one or two token efforts in that direction (Dionysius mentions
the digressions at 2. 97 and 6. 2–5);[19] but for the most part he is
tedious: he goes breathlessly through a single war, battle after battle,
without relief. Xenophon, following Herodotus, has varied (πεποίκ-
ιλκε) his work (4. 2, 241. 19); Philistus, following Thucydides, is
uniform (ὁμοειδής) because of his refusal to admit material 'from
outside' (ἔξωθεν, 5. 2, 243. 1–3). Theopompus is praised for the
diversity (τὸ πολύμορφον) of his subject-matter, which is instructive as
well as entertaining (6. 3–5, 245. 9–21); similarly, he is praised for
poikilia in the events he describes (*Imit.* 6. 3. 3, 209. 16–17). But his
digressions (παρεμβολαί: *Pomp.* 6. 11, 247. 22–248. 5; παρεκβάσεις:
Imit. 6. 3. 3, 210. 6–10) are frigid, childish and contrary to *kairos*. In
terms of the distinction noted above from *Isocr.* 4, Theopompus
succeeds in breaking up the uniformity of his text by internal
variation (ἰδίαις μεταβολαῖς), but shows poor judgement in his use of
episodes (ξένα ἐπεισόδια).

Dionysius does not address himself to this point in *Thuc.*7–8, but his
remarks on myth might be thought to imply a change of heart.
Although he understands (he says) why the earlier local historians
had to embellish (ποικίλλειν) their works with mythological *epeisodia*,
he evidently approves of Thucydides' disengagement from the practice. Strictly speaking, however, his objection is not to *poikilia*, nor
even to *epeisodia* as a means of achieving it, but to the inclusion of
myth in history; for the point is made in the context of a discussion of
truth in history. So the point which he makes here is consistent with
the position which he took in the *Letter to Pompeius*, criticizing
Theopompus for the inappropriate content of his digressions while
simultaneously criticizing Philistus for not digressing at all.[20] It is
worth noting that Dionysius attributes the inappropriate use of myth
to the local historians, not to Herodotus; had it been Herodotus who
was subjected to criticism here, a conflict with his earlier position
would have been beyond question.

It is arguable, nevertheless, that Dionysius has taken up an austerer

[19] Cf. Westlake 1969, 1–38. I note in passing the following terms for 'excursus' in the
fifth-century historians: προσθήκη, Hdt. 4. 30. 1; παρενθήκη, Hdt. 3. 171. 1; ἐκβολή,
Thuc. 1. 97. 2.
[20] Cf. Theon *Prog.* 4 (II 80. 27–81. 4 Sp.): digressions (παρεκβάσεις) should not be
excluded entirely, as in Philistus, since they rest (ἀναπαύειν) the reader; but they should
not be so long as to make the reader lose the thread of the narrative, as in Theopompus,
whose digressions are too frequent, too long, and too remote from the main theme.

attitude to historiographical decorum in this essay, in which he attempts to think through the rationale of Thucydides' choice of subject, than he does in the more purely rhetorical criticism of the *Letter*; there the vantage-point for the comparison is external. Certainly, Thucydides' example did encourage a restrictive view of such matters. Dionysius himself cites Philistus as a follower of Thucydides who refused to digress. Marcellinus, in his *Life of Thucydides* (48–9), does not spare Herodotus, as does Dionysius, but is severely critical both of his liking for myth and of his digressiveness in general; superfluous declination from one's subject for mere gratification is not, in Marcellinus' view, part of the office of the historian. But this was a minority opinion. Plutarch (*Mor.* 855cd) does criticize Herodotus' digressions (παρεκβάσεις), but only because the historian seems perversely intent in them on malicious criticism (see (e) below): digressions, Plutarch says, in history are devoted primarily to myth, to stories from the more remote past (ἀρχαιολογίαι), and to praise; Plutarch is quite content, therefore, to have digressions as such, and even to have mythological digressions. Lucian agrees: he condemns the excessive use of myth and eulogy, but does not question their right to be present in due measure (*Hist. Conser.* 10).[21] The same line could be taken on speeches. Diodorus (20. 1. 1–2. 2) objects to over-lengthy or over-frequent speeches, on the grounds that they disturb the continuity of the narrative; however well-written the speeches may be in themselves, it is improper—an offence against *kairos*—to treat history as an appendage to rhetoric. The nature of history, he says, is simple (ἁπλοῦς) and self-consistent; like an animate organism (ἔμψυχον σῶμα) it loses its charm if damaged, but if it achieves its correct composition (σύνθεσις) then that very self-consistency makes the work clear and pleasant for the reader.[22] Out of context, such remarks might mislead us: in fact Diodorus goes on to insist that speeches should not be excluded from history altogether;[23] history

---

[21] Strabo remarks (1. 2. 35) that most historians deliberately weave myths into their work in order to entertain and gratify the reader's taste for marvels; usually, he says, they do so without admitting it: Theopompus is at least perfectly frank. (Certainly, historiographical decorum seems to have discouraged such admissions: see Dion. Hal. *Ant.* 7. 70. 1, Livy 9. 17. 1.) See further Wardman 1960.

[22] A further use of the organic analogy, but applied here to (appropriately varied) homogeneity rather than to structure. The phrase ἔμψυχον σῶμα seems to have been a cliché: cf. Plb. 12. 12. 3 (truth is to history as sight is to an ἔμψυχον σῶμα similarly, with ζῷον in 1. 14. 6), and 1. 4. 7 (see (b) above).

[23] The view taken by Cratippus: see Dion. Hal. *Thuc.* 16. On speeches, see Scheller 1911, 50–55; cf. Wiseman 1979, 28–9.

needs *poikilia*, which speeches can provide. For Diodorus, therefore, as for Dionysius, diversity is a necessary part of the appropriate constitution of a historical text; but, as always, the devices employed to secure this diversity must be used in moderation.[24]

Diversity is necessary, and may be achieved by digressing from one's subject-matter (whether for mythological material or not), or by interspersing the narrative with speeches; it may also be pursued in the choice of subject itself—as Theopompus was praised for the *poikilia* of his subject-matter. Dionysius refers slightingly in the introduction to his own history to those who treat only one aspect of history in their work: that is uniform (μονοειδές) and objectionable to the reader; he has mingled every kind of history (*Ant.* 1. 8. 3). Polybius apologizes for the uniformity (τὸ μονοειδές) which renders his work unattractive to most readers, and which results from his concentration on a single branch of history (9. 1. 2–6).[25] However, Polybius does, as we shall see in (d), have a rather clever way of laying claim to a certain *poikilia* of his own.

(d) *Division and arrangement:* Dionysius' fourth heading is division and arrangement (*Pomp.* 3. 13–14, 237. 6–238. 11), that is, the task of isolating the segments of one's subject-matter and assigning each to its appropriate place in the text. Here, too, Thucydides is inferior. Herodotus constructs his history on the basis of the continuities inherent in the events themselves (ταῖς περιοχαῖς τῶν πραγμάτων); the result is orderly and lucid. Thucydides tries to impose a rigid chronological framework; thus consequent chains of events are broken up and treated piecemeal, and the resulting discontinuities render his work obscure and difficult to follow. Philistus imitated the disorder (ἀταξία) and confusion of Thucydides' economy (*Imit.* 6. 3. 2, 208. 19–209. 1); his work is even harder to follow (*Pomp.* 5. 2, 242. 21–243. 1). Xenophon and Theopompus both divided and arranged their work well (*Pomp.* 4. 2, 241. 18–19; 6. 2, 244. 19–20). Dionysius' summation of the contrast between Herodotus and Thucydides

[24] This applies, of course, to other expository prose genres also. Pollux comments (1. 30) that 'didascalic' literature is austere and προσκορές, and he has therefore, in order to rest (ἵνα ... διαναπαύσω) his reader, included pleasant stories for ψυχαγωγία. Cicero writes (*ad Att.* 2. 6. 1) that geographical writing is ὁμοειδές, and offers surprisingly little opportunity for 'flowery writing' (ἀνθηρογραφεῖσθαι: for this term, cf. Eustathius 991. 8).

[25] Cf. Tac. *Ann.* 4. 33: his subject lacks the things which retain and refresh the reader; their uniformity creates satiety (cf. 6. 7, 16. 16; Woodman, 1988, 180–6). Cicero recommends a particular subject for treatment on the grounds of its variety (*Fam.* 5. 12. 4–6).

under this heading is of particular interest. He observes (*Pomp.* 3. 14, 238. 8–11) that, though Thucydides has selected a simple subject, his mode of presentation fragments its potentially unified body (συμ-βέβηκε τῷ μὲν μίαν ὑπόθεσιν λαβόντι πολλὰ ποιῆσαι μέρη τὸ ἓν σῶμα); Herodotus works with multiple subjects bearing little resemblance to each other, but has nevertheless produced out of them a harmoniously unified body (τῷ δὲ πολλὰς καὶ οὐδὲν ἐοικυίας ὑποθέσεις προελομένῳ σύμφωνον ἓν σῶμα πεποιηκέναι).[26] Here we see, as we concluded in (b), that a 'single subject'—one unified, for example, according to Aristotle's criteria of narrative unity—is not required, although the risks inherent in a multiple subject-matter are recognised; the organic analogy is applied, as by Diodorus (20. 1. 5, see (c) above), at the level of the text, and denotes appropriate order at that level: the text is 'a harmoniously unified body' if the subject, however complex, has been realized in a lucid and rhetorically effective manner, subject to the constraints of historiographical decorum.

In *Thuc.* 9 (335. 20–338. 3) Dionysius repeats his criticism of Thucydides' division and arrangement. His predecessors had constructed their histories on the basis either of regional divisions (Herodotus, for example, or Hellanicus), or of chronological divisions that were easy to follow: the reigns of kings, priests' terms of office, Olympiads, or—at the very least—annual magistracies. These periods were sufficiently long to allow the pursuit of a continuous chain of events to its end; Thucydides' adoption of a seasonal division means that such chains are broken far more frequently, so that the whole narrative becomes harder to follow.

The commentary on Thucydides introduced above (p. 79) summarizes these points (col. i. 7–20), and replies that the system of dating by archons or by Olympiads was not yet in use (ii. 6–8), and that because Thucydides' subject was not (as Dionysius supposed) simple, had he pursued individual chains of events to their ends intolerable confusion would have resulted (ii. 9–27).[27] The commentator adds that narrative disruption would have resulted even with the use of archon-years, a system of which Dionysius approves (ii. 27–iii. 1), and that Thucydides does follow continuous sequences

---

[26] Somewhat different is the comment (*Imit.* 6. 1, 203. 15–18) on Zeuxis' composite portrait of Helen: 'Whatever feature of each model was worth painting has been combined into a single portrait, and out of a collection of many parts art has composed a single complete image (ἕν τι ... τέλειον εἶδος).'

[27] There is a reference to Herodotus' system in this section, apparently applying the term ποικίλον to him, but the passage is too badly damaged to allow restoration.

through when the chronological framework permits (iii. 2–10). He
apparently goes on, though the papyrus is badly damaged, to point
out that Dionysius does not criticize Herodotus for digressing (ἔξωθεν
παραβαίνειν) or for changes of subject which interrupt narrative
continuity (iii. 10–17).

This was, in fact, a controversial issue.[28] Theon provides evidence
that Dionysius' criticisms of Thucydides' arrangement had wide
currency (*Prog.* 4, ii 80. 13–24 Spengel). Diodorus insists on the
importance of organization (οἰκονομία) for the historian (Timaeus,
he says, though an excellent historian in other respects, was at fault
here),[29] and recommends as a model Ephorus' practice of organizing
his work on a regional basis (κατὰ γένος: 5. 1. 1–2. 1); elsewhere he
argues that individual books within a history should, where possible,
follow self-contained actions from beginning to end (πράξεις
αὐτοτελεῖς ἀπ᾽ ἀρχῆς μέχρι τοῦ τέλους): discontinuity in the narrative
of such sequences he finds distracting (16. 1. 1–2). Polybius, by
contrast, generally adopts a chronological arrangement, keeping
events of a single year together. In 4. 28. 3–6 and 5. 30. 8–31. 7 he is
careful to explain that for the first few years of his period, when
events in different parts of the world had not yet become fully
interwoven, he would adopt a purely regional arrangement to make
the narrative easier to follow; subsequently, however, he would adopt
an annual chronology, though keeping to regional divisions within
each year. In 14. 12 he explains why, in one instance, he has departed
from this practice: the picture of Ptolemy Philopator has to be built
up from individually insignificant incidents, and would be obscured
if these were recorded each in its own year; so he has drawn them
together 'in bodily form' (σωματοειδῶς).[30] (His flexibility in the face
of the special demands of particular parts of his subject is evident also

[28] Scheller 1911, 43–6.
[29] Timaeus (though this is not a point Diodorus makes explicitly here) used a
chronological system; for his chronological care, see Plb. 12. 11. 1.
[30] Bizarrely rendered 'a life-like image' by the Loeb translator (W.R.Paton); in fact
it is identical to the σωματοειδῶς/κατὰ μέρος distinction observed in fourth century
sources in ch. 2 above. Lucian uses the introduction = head, main text = body analogy
(*Hist. Conscr.* 23, 55; in the latter passage he insists, like Isocrates, on smooth transitions
from point to point); he also remarks that the material collected by historians is a body
without beauty until order (τάξις) and verbal expression are imposed on it (48).
Josephus likewise speaks of economy and τάξις as furnishing τὸ σῶμα . . . τῆς ἱστορίας
(*BJ* 1. 15). It would be a mistake to read these casual uses of the organic analogy as
implying much about unity (as e.g. Walbank 1972, 67 insists on translating Cicero's
phrase 'modicum quoddam corpus' as 'a *unified* work of medium proportions' [my
emphasis]).

in 32. 11. 2–7.) He is aware of objections to the chronological system: some, he says (38. 5–6), will find fault with the interruptions of my narrative; readers like continuous narrative because it retains their interest and is easier to follow. His reply is ingenious: it is natural to prefer change (μεταβολή) to dwelling uninterruptedly on a single chain of events; all the senses require change and *poikilia* to avoid satiety, and the intellect above all. This is why older historians rested (προσαναπεπαῦσθαι) their readers with mythological and other digressions; Polybius' chronological structure is simply a systematisation of that earlier practice, and is superior in that the 'digressions' are themselves in due course followed through to their conclusions. Switching ground within a subject, one might say, means that the subject supplies its own digressions. Thus the rhetorical requirement of *poikilia* has been exploited cleverly to deflect rhetorical objections to the chronological organization of Polybius' work—though he in fact adopted that organization, we may suspect, on more strictly historiographical grounds.[31]

We may add as a brief pendant to this heading the criticisms which Dionysius makes in *Thuc.* 13–20 of Thucydides' working out (ἐξεργασία) of his material; the apportioning of care and textual space to the segments of his subject is unbalanced, following no consistent plan and often failing to correspond to the intrinsic importance (or insigificance) of the events recorded. This point, too, can be illustrated from other sources:[32] Diodorus frequently refers to the necessity of preserving 'proportion' (συμμετρία, 1. 8. 10, 1. 9. 4, 1. 41. 10 etc.); Polybius likewise criticizes other historians for giving disproportionate attention to unimportant topics (7. 7. 6–7, 14. 1a. 5, 15. 35. 1–7, 29. 12. 46). Compare Lucian *Hist. Conscr.* 27–8.

(e) *Attitude:* The fifth and final heading under which Dionysius compares Herodotus and Thucydides is that of the historian's attitude to his subject-matter (*Pomp.* 3. 15, 238. 12–22). Herodotus is fair, generous, and sympathetic; Thucydides is censorious and vindictive towards his own city because of his exile (cf. 3. 9, 234. 22–235. 16). Xenophon's *ethos* is outstanding, combining all the virtues (4. 2, 241. 19–21); Philistus' attitude is ingratiating and subservient (5. 2, 243. 3–4; cf. *Imit.* 6. 3. 2, 208. 15–17); Theopompus is praised for his

---

[31] For a summary of Polybius' structural devices, see Walbank 1972, 46–8, 99–117.
[32] Scheller 1911, 46–8.

scrupulously careful research (6. 2–4, 244. 20–245. 15), his philosophical and moral commentary (6. 6, 246. 3–6), and for his acute
moral judgement—Dionysius defends him here against a charge of
malice (6. 7–8, 246. 6–247. 4). This heading is not explicitly raised in
Thucydides, but a favourable view is taken there of Thucydides' care
in research, his devotion to truth, and in particular of his avoidance
of malice (*Thuc.* 6–8); his alleged lack of patriotism is mentioned at
Thuc. 41 (397. 3–10).

Dionysius' judgement of Herodotus is strikingly reversed in Plutarch's essay on his malice. Plutarch argues that Herodotus consistently exaggerates faults, suppresses virtues, prefers discreditable
variants and motives, and in general distorts his account to the
detriment of Greeks and, in particular, Thebans (Plutarch was
himself Boeotian). Praise and blame are typically seen as part of the
historian's moral function (D. S. 11. 46. 1, 15. 1. 1; Plb. 2. 61. 6
etc.);[33] and the historian must therefore strive to be fair to all and
well-disposed to virtue (D. H., *Ant.* 1. 6. 5). Dionysius' generous
estimate of Theopompus in this respect was not shared by Polybius,
who criticizes him as malicious (8. 10. 11–11. 2; cf. Lucian, *Hist.* 59);
indeed, he compares him unfavourably with Timaeus, whose censorious attitudes won him the punning nickname ἐπιτίμαιος, 'fault-
finder' (D. S. 5. 1. 3). But Polybius had in turn to defend himself
against the charge that his criticisms of Greek errors were malicious
and unpatriotic (38. 4). He argues that, although the historian should
be swayed in everyday life by patriotic and other partisan attach-
ments, in his historical writing he should be wholly impartial,
concerned only with truth (1. 14; a little mitigated at 16. 14. 6, 16. 17.
8).

I have obviously not attempted in this section to produce a
comprehensive study of Greek historiographical theory;[34] but I hope
to have done enough to indicate the kinds of consideration involved,
and to provide a context for some conclusions concerning unity and
diversity in historical writing. We may now sum up the conclusions
we have reached. Different views were held on what was appropriate
in history: contrast, for example, Dionysius and Marcellinus on
Herodotus. These differences arose from different conceptions of the
function of historiography—from the variable distribution of em-

---

[33] See Scheller 1911, 48–50, and—on *ethos* in general—34–7.
[34] For a provocative recent study of some further aspects, see Woodman 1988.

phasis, so to speak, between *prodesse* and *delectare*. To the extent that *delectare* was seen as an essential part of the historian's task (that is, as we might say, to the extent that aesthetic considerations were allowed to determine criteria of appropriate order in history), diversity (*poikilia*) was seen as an indispensable virtue; without it, an extended narrative could not retain the reader's interest and good will. *Poikilia* could be achieved by selecting a subject that was itself varied, by interweaving straightforward narrative with contrasting material (such as speeches), or by digressing from the main narrative. (If the historian is sufficiently liberal to admit them, excursions into mythology or the marvellous make ideal digressions, since they contrast most strikingly with sober historical narrative; but they must be kept within limit, and history's commitment to truth requires a certain reserve in their use.) At the level of the subject-matter as such, no minimum criterion of unity (analogous to that applied by Aristotle to narrative poetry) is proposed; the appropriateness of the choice and delimitation of one's subject is determined instead by a complex of factors, including the particular nature of the period chosen and its special historiographical demands, and the general demands of history's rhetorical and didactic functions. The decisive considerations of unity work at the level of the text and its economy. A complex subject makes orderly presentation difficult: a simple subject makes variety harder to attain; but if a historical text falls into neither error—if it is lucid and interestingly varied, able to retain and sustain the reader's interest without infringing such historiographical norms as truth and objectivity—then that text is, in the relevant sense, unified. For Dionysius and Diodorus a history is 'organically' unified—it constitutes a 'single and harmonious body'—not by virtue of thematic, or even causal, integration, but if all its elements, including substantially digressive elements, are brought together in the appropriate order so defined.

7

Later Rhetoric

ALTHOUGH in our discussion of Dionysius we looked only briefly at his remarks on the treatment of subject-matter in oratory proper, we did observe that his whole critical approach, even to historiography, was that of a rhetorician; in this chapter I shall look at some other sources of rhetorical theory in order to set Dionysius' view of historical writing in a broader context. I shall begin with Cicero, a slightly earlier contemporary of Dionysius; that Cicero was Roman is not, I think, of great consequence, for he learnt his rhetoric from Greek tutors, and it is possible to show from verbal parallels in later Greek rhetoric how directly he has embodied some of his teachers' formulae. As one might expect, this tendency is particularly marked in his early essay *On Invention*.[1] For example, the definition of narrative in 1. 27 ('narratio est rerum gestarum aut ut gestarum expositio') is exactly that found in the Greek progymnasmata: ἔκθεσις πραγμάτων γεγονότων ἢ ὡς γεγονότων ([Hermogenes] 4. 6–7 Rabe; Aphthonius 2. 14–15 Rabe; Theon ii 78. 15–16 Spengel; Nicolaus 11. 15 Felten); and Cicero's division of narrative into three genera is seen, not only in the roughly contemporary Latin rhetoric *ad Herennium* (1. 12), but also in the later Greek *Anonymus Seguerianus* (i 435. 12–19 Sp. = 363. 22–364. 3 Hammer). We shall return to the Seguerianus and other Greek sources in due course; for the moment I shall concentrate, first on Cicero's, and then on Quintilian's, exposition of the theory.

Cicero's threefold division of narrative (*Inv.* 1. 27) has two poles. On the one hand are narratives of the events actually at issue in a forensic speech; on the other hand are narratives 'remote from' forensic oratory: narratives of this latter kind might be mythological, or fictitious but verisimilar, or historical; the orator may compose them for pleasure, thereby deriving useful practice in composition. Between these two poles are narratives which, though not narratives of the contested events themselves, may be included digressively ('in

[1] See Cicero's own depreciatory remarks, *De Or.* 1. 5.

quo digressio aliqua extra causam . . . interponitur'). Such digressions might serve a number of tactical functions in a forensic speech: the speaker may praise himself or attack his opponent, strengthen his argument or his refutation of the opposing arguments, magnify the gravity of the alleged offence, and so forth; one may even include digressions to entertain ('delectationis causa'), as long as the entertainment is not 'alien' to the case—something for which no criteria are offered: presumably, if it has a plausible point of departure and helps one to win.

In this list of possible tactical reasons for digression I have conflated with 1. 27 a later passage (1. 97) in which Cicero attacks the view of Hermagoras (fr. 22 Matthes) that such digressions are a 'part' of the oration, in the sense of having a regularly localized seat; Hermagoras placed them between the proof/refutation and the peroration. Cicero rejects this theory on the grounds that one should not digress from the case at issue except for a *locus communis*—that is, for material which, by virtue of its generality, could be applied to any case of a given kind, as distinct from material dealing with the particulars of the individual case in hand;[2] material of this kind can be introduced at any point in the speech. In this passage, therefore, Cicero reflects a relatively conservative view of legitimate departure from the specifics of a case, and insists against Hermagoras that such departure as is legitimate cannot be localized restrictively; indeed, this view seems to be somewhat more conservative than that underlying the division of narrative in 1. 27.

Hermagoras' theory concerning the proper place of the digression is mentioned, without attribution, in Antonius' unenthusiastic survey of Greek rhetorical theory in *De Or.* 2. 80. The same speaker offers his own, more flexible, view at a later point (2. 311–12): passages emotive rather than argumentative in force are perhaps most apt in proem and peroration, but are also often of use as digressions, if the case at issue affords the opportunity and is of sufficient weight to warrant that degree of amplification and ornament; these may come after the narrative, or after the proof/refutation (Hermagoras' view), or indeed anywhere else. Amplification (*augere*) and ornamentation (*ornare*) are the two terms which Antonius uses in both passages to sum up the function of such digressions; Crassus adds entertainment

---

[2] Cf. *Inv.* 2. 47–8; in 2. 49 the *locus communis* is assigned, as one of its functions, the refreshment of the audience—a function ascribed to digression by the critics considered in ch. 6 above.

(*delectare*) at 3. 100. So in the course of a survey of older orators in
Brutus, Servius Galba is praised as the first Roman orator to introduce
digressions, 'for ornamentation, to give pleasure, to move, to amplify,
to excite pity, to employ *loci communes*' (*Brutus* 82); and Hortensius is
admired for (among other things) his unequalled ability to digress
'delectandi gratia' (322).[3]

Quintilian is another theorist who uses the threefold division of
narrative. The kind unconnected with forensic oratory is introduced
in 2. 4. 2 and, as in Cicero, is subdivided in turn into myth, verisimilar
fiction, and history. Those kinds of narrative used in forensic
speaking are excepted from discussion there, but Quintilian returns
to them in 4. 2. 11–10; they are divided into narratives of the case
itself, and narratives of events with a bearing on the case. This latter
class is large and diverse; it includes, obviously, narratives closely
relevant to the main argument (for example, those designed to show
that the accused is or is not the kind of person who would commit the
crime), but it also embraces the other tactical ends envisaged by
Cicero, and the last category in Quintilian's survey of the class is the
mythological narrative 'decoris gratia' (4. 2. 19, citing as an illustration Cicero's digression on Proserpina in *Verr.* 4. 106ff.).[4]

In 4. 3 Quintilian discusses digression more specifically. He rebukes
speakers who, more concerned with display than with their clients'
interests, indulge to excess their taste for appealing excursions. When
this taste is combined with a doctrine which localizes digression
(Quintilian cites the first of the three theories mentioned by Antonius
in *De Or.* 2. 311, that which places the digression between narrative
and proof), it undermines the economy of the speech; for material
that affords scope for digressive elaboration will tend to gravitate to
the part of the speech reserved for the digression, and it will therefore
not be available at the point where it would most appropriately be
placed. Moreover, introduced without regard to what the context
requires or permits the digression itself disrupts the continuity of the
speech, like a wedge inserted by force.[5] On the other hand, if inserted

---

[3] On *delectare* as one of the tasks of the orator, cf. *Orat.* 69: 'Sed quot officia oratoris,
tot sunt genera dicendi: subtile in probando, modicum in delectando, vehemens in
flectando.'
[4] On Cicero's digressions see Canter 1931, Davies 1968.
[5] In 4. 3. 4 Quintilian requires that digressions should 'cohere' (unlike a wedge), but
in 4. 3. 15–16 distinguishes between digressions that do and do not 'cohere', permitting
both. The sense is obviously different: in the former instance Quintilian is demanding
the appearance of continuity at the level of the text that the skilful working in of a

with due regard to context, digressions can be an effective ornament to the speech. In the latter part of this chapter Quintilian is at pains to stress the flexibility of the digression (the Greek term παρέκβασις is introduced in 4. 3. 12): it should not be restricted to one part of the speech, nor to any one class of material; it can be defined as the treatment of any material that goes beyond the specifics of the case treated in the five regular parts of a speech, at whatever point it may be introduced and for whatever purpose. Quintilian's only stipulation is that it should make some contribution to the presentation of the case: 'alicuius rei, sed ad utilitatem causae pertinentis, extra ordinem excurrens tractatio' (4. 3. 14). This includes material similar to or closely related to the case; such digressions, because they 'cohere' (see n. 5 above), do not seem digressive. But there are also many kinds of quite unrelated material which can be inserted as digressions in a less purely technical sense; these may justify their presence simply by refreshing or pleasing the judge (Quintilian again mentions Cicero on Proserpina as an example of mythological digression used in this way).

In Quintilian, therefore, as in Cicero, we have a broad category of digression (whatever goes beyond the five regular components of the exposition of a specific case). This includes much that is thematically integral to the case itself, and thus not digressive in a substantial sense; but it also includes as a limiting instance (and therefore as an legitimate technique, if used in moderation) material unrelated to the case—and even mythological material—introduced for ornamentation and to give pleasure. Though not thematically integral, such ornamentally digressive matter is justified functionally in so far as it pleases, refreshes, and allures the judges; and that is all the justification that Quintilian requires.

Let us now turn to the later Greek sources. We noted earlier that the threefold classification of narrative found in the *Rhetorica ad Herennium*, in Cicero, and in Quintilian appears also in the third-century Greek rhetoric known as the *Anonymus Seguerianus*. This author first divides narratives into two classes, those addressed to judges and those 'for their own sake' (καθ' ἑαυτάς); the latter category is divided, somewhat obscurely, into four subdivisions, rather than

digression secures; in the latter he is considering the relatedness of the underlying material, which is not a condition of 'coherence' in the former sense. Cf. 2. 4. 30–1 (a *locus communis* cannot 'cohere' unless it is supplied with some link to the context; it should be 'grafted in', not merely attached), and 7. 10. 16.

the three familiar from Cicero and Quintilian.[6] The threefold scheme is secured by a subdivision of narratives addressed to judges into those concerned with the disputed facts, and those which are inserted digressively (παρεμπίπτουσι), to provide proof or amplification, to attack the opponent, or for some other reason (i 435. 10–19 Sp. = 363. 20–364. 3 Hammer).[7] The term used 'by some' for this second division of narrative addressed to judges is 'subsidiary narration' (παραδιήγησις); but the writer subsequently makes a distinction between 'subsidiary narration' in a strict sense, which is concerned with something related to though not part of the matter at issue, and 'digression' (παρέκβασις), which is more substantially digressive: it is an excursus (ἐκδρομή) based on some similarity to the events at issue (καθ' ὁμοίωσιν ἢ μίμησιν τῶν γεγονότων, 436. 4–12 = 364. 21–365. 5). Unless 'similarity' is used here rather loosely, this limitation of digressive narrative to material related to or resembling the events at issue is in contrast with Quintilian's more liberal acceptance of matter that does not resemble or (in the sense of 3. 4. 15) 'cohere' with them. In fact Quintilian's broad definition of 'digression' (περέκβασις, quoted above) shows that he follows an alternative teaching, explicitly rejected by the Seguerianus, that equates 'subsidiary narration' and 'digression'. This equation is found in the scholia to Demosthenes, in a note which defines παρέκβασις as λόγος ἐξαγώνιος μέν, συναγωνιζόμενος δὲ πρὸς τὸν ἀγῶνα (Σ Dem. 21. 77, 575. 18–19 and 576. 23–4 Dindorf)—a formulation extremely close to that of Quintilian. On the other hand, a third view, even more restricted than that of the Seguerianus himself, is the one he ascribes in the same passage to Alexander, who rejected the concept of digression on the grounds that one should not speak 'outside the subject' (ἔξω τῆς ὑποθέσεως) at all; this is reminiscent of the view taken by Cicero in *Inv.* 1. 97.[8]

---

[6] As well as mythical and historical narratives there are βιωτικαί and περιπετικαί; for a guide to the intricacies of narrative classification see Barwick 1928. (I note that a threefold subdivision of non-forensic narrative can be found also in Σ bT *Il.* 14. 342–51.)

[7] The transmitted αἱ δὲ πρὸς ἰδέας διηγήσεις τῆς ὑποθέσεως λέγονται requires another category between these two, and is clearly corrupt; Barwick 1928, 264, suggests αἱ δὴ ἰδίως ... (cf. Theon ii 60. 4–5 Sp.: τὸ ἰδίως ἐν ταῖς ὑποθέσεσι καλούμενον διήγημα).

[8] An unusually narrow definition of παρέκβασις is found in *PS* 52. 14–18, 270. 28–271. 3, 271. 15–19, where it is defined as an account of the defendant's previous life; the term is applied, although not in so restrictive a way, to the equivalent part of the *locus communis* exercise in Aphthonius *Prog.* 7 (17. 11–12 Rabe); Theon (ii 108. 16–22 Sp.), pseudo-Hermogenes (12. 8–9 Rabe), and Nicolaus (43. 22–44. 17 Felten) refer to this part without using that term.

These austerer views of digression are not typical of the Greek rhetorical tradition, and even the Seguerianus can reflect more liberal attitudes. He begins a survey of the excellences of narrative by listing three necessary qualities: conciseness, clarity, and plausibility. Digression receives an unfriendly mention in connection with the first of these: to achieve concision, one should not use digression or *epeisodia*, and in general should keep to the matter in hand. Towards the end of his survey, however, he adds a rather disorderly supplemental list of qualities which make a narrative imposing or attractive; among them 'enjoyability' (ἡδονή). To achieve this quality, *poikilia* is recommended;[9] and the author mentions with approval the timely (εὔκαιρος) insertion of narratives based on ancient history and myth (ἀρχαιολογία)—that is, although he does not use the term here, he commends digression. He cites a widely admired passage of Hyperides to illustrate this technique (439. 15–18 = 369. 19–23; cf. [Longinus] 34. 2, and *PS* 214. 15–19). Similarly Hermogenes remarks on Lycurgus' use of frequent digressions (myth, history, and poetry) as contributing to his eloquence (402. 24–403. 2 Rabe). Although the Seguerianus does not discuss digression in connection with clarity, Theon, in a similar survey (ii 80. 27–81. 4 Sp., a passage already cited in connection with historiography in Chapter 6), does: lengthy digressions inserted into a narrative make it unclear; this does not mean that they are to be excluded altogether, as in Philistus, for they are necessary to rest (ἀναπαύειν) the audience; but they should not make the reader lose the thread of the narrative, as happens in Theopompus, who will bring together two or three stories digressively (κατὰ παρέκβασιν) without even touching on his main theme.

The more restrictive attitudes to digression mentioned above are, therefore, by no means typical of Greek rhetorical theory, and they are moreover generically weighted. The rhetoricians surveyed in this section are concerned primarily with forensic oratory, and their outlook is dictated by the strictly functional nature of that genre.

---

[9] *Poikilia* is a general requirement of the authors mentioned in this section; note also Himerius 68, an attractive little speech in which Himerius uses a series of analogies, itself very diverse, to encourage his pupils in the pursuit of *poikilia* in their composition (see also Kennedy 1983, 143–7 for an appreciative account of Himerius 48, a *prosphonetikos logos* of considerable *poikilia*). The following references are concerned with *poikilia* in style and treatment, rather than in large structure: Cic. *Inv.* 1. 76, *Part. Or.* 47, *De Or.* 2. 177, 3. 100, *Orat.* 109, 219; Quint. 8. 3. 52; Tac. *Dial.* 22. 5; Pliny *Ep.* 6. 33. 8 (more generally, cf. 1. 2. 4, 2. 5. 5–8, 4. 14. 4, 5. 17. 2); Theon ii 74. 27–75. 9, 91. 6–10 Sp.; Phoebammon iii 43. 8–14 Sp.; Hermogenes 222. 1–6, 320. 3–7 Rabe; *PS* 291. 6–11, 389. 16–21.

Quintilian insists that ornamentation, though admissible as helping
to promote victory by influencing the disposition of the judges, is
admissible only to the extent that it does so (e.g. 2. 4. 32); ornamentation or display for its own sake is out of place in forensic oratory. But
if ornamental digression is admissible at all in this functionally
austere genre, *a fortiori* it will be more freely admissible in genres for
which ornamentation and pleasure (that is, purely aesthetic effects)
are in some measure ends, and not simply means to an end.

This is, in effect, to return to the distinction observed in Chapter 3
between forensic and epideictic propriety; and the distinction is a
recurrent theme in the rhetoricians. Quintilian, after condemning the
abuses which render declamation useless as an exercise for the
forensic speaker, grants (2. 10. 10–12) that declamation is in some
degree a matter of display (*ostentatio*) and should therefore make
concessions to the audience's entertainment (*voluptas*); epideictic
oratory in general, he says, though not unconcerned with truth, aims
to give pleasure (*delectatio*), and so admits more, and more overt,
artistry than does the forensic speech. Declamation, therefore, is
amphibious: it is an 'image' of forensic speaking, and so should
adhere to its norms, but it is also partly epideictic, and may therefore
allow·itself greater liberties. Quintilian regards the modern practice
of declaiming solely with a view to pleasure (*voluptas*) as a corruption
(5. 12. 17); still worse is the infiltration of declamatory display into
genuine forensic speaking: there was a time, he says, when oratory
aimed at *utilitas* rather than *ostentatio*, but now *voluptas* has taken over,
even when the life or fortune of a client is at stake (4. 2. 122, cf. 4. 3.
1–3).[10] Forensic *utilitas*, therefore, is set against epideictic *ostentatio* and
entertainment. Poetry is placed at the epideictic extreme of this
scale—it, too, is composed for *ostentatio* and aims solely at *voluptas* (10.
1. 28); history is a kind of poetry in prose (10. 1. 31), and so is a safe
model for the (forensic) orator only in his digressions—that is, in
those parts of his own work which tend, for tactical reasons, more to
the epideictic end of the scale.

Cicero takes the same view. In *Orator* 37–42 he excludes from
consideration epideictic—the kind of oratory that Isocrates and other
sophists composed; it is remote from forensic struggles and aims at
delectatio, enjoying therefore the licence to employ artistic devices
more often and more openly than the forensic speech; it is written not

---

[10] For a more favourable view of 'modern' oratory, praising its pointed, ornate, and
entertaining manner, see Tac. *Dial.* 20. 2–7.

'ad iudiciorum certamen', but 'ad voluptatem aurium'; it is 'pompae quam pugnae aptius' (cf. *De Or.* 2. 341). Again in *Orator* 65: the 'sophistic' manner aims less to move and persuade than to please and delight; here Cicero mentions digression and the inweaving of stories (*fabulae*) among the devices used more frequently in this genre. History, he says, is closest to epideictic (66, cf. 39).[11]

In this passage Cicero contrasts forensic oratory successively with the philosophical style (*Orat.* 62–4), with epideictic oratory (65), with history (66), and with poetry (66–8). Hermogenes likewise classifies as 'panegyric' (the term is here equivalent to 'epideictic') philosophical dialogue, history, and poetry.[12] Poetry is all 'panegyric'—indeed, it is the 'most panegyrical' of all kinds of writing (389. 7–9); Homer, naturally, is the best poet (389–95). Plato is the best composer of panegyric in prose (386. 16–27; cf. 384–9 and, for other writers of dialogues, 404–7). History, too, is prose panegyric (404. 10–16); Herodotus is the 'most panegyrical' of historians (408. 9–10)— indeed, in his representation of character and emotion he is like a poet (408. 19–20)—and he is judged, in a revealing phrase, 'more panegyrical and more pleasant (ἡδίων)' than Thucydides and other historians (409. 12). The essay on mistakes in declamation falsely attributed to Dionysius condemns the lavish use of graphic descriptions (ἐκφράσεις) as irrelevant to forensic speaking, a kind of futile display (ἐπίδειξις) that has infiltrated from history and poetry (ii 372. 4–373. 2).[13]

We have seen, then, that with exceptions and qualifications the Greek rhetoricians accepted and indeed commended digression as a means of diversification; but what did they say about unity, and in particular about 'organic' unity? Before we consider their comments, it might be helpful to review briefly the various uses of the organic analogy that we have already encountered. First of all, we should note that those uses do not all bear on the question of unity; for

---

[11] Cf. also *Part. Or.* 12: epideictic ('quibus in orationibus delectatio finis est': cf. 10–11) seeks variety in its ordering of material, which affords *exornatio* and hence pleasure.

[12] In fact, Hermogenes considers epideictic oratory as too closely related to the forensic and symbouleutic kinds to be fully 'panegyrical' (388. 15–389. 1, 407. 23–408. 6).

[13] The author stresses the functionality of forensic oratory (πρὸς τὴν χρείαν, 372. 14); for a contrast between forensic and historiographical narrative see also Theon 83. 23–84. 5. On poetry and history, cf. Wiseman 1979, 143–53, Woodman, 1988, 98–101 (41–2, 95–101 for history and epideictic); on the epideictic forms in general, Burgess 1902, 89–261.

example, when Polybius says that truth is to a historical text what sight is to a 'living body' (12. 12. 3, cf. Chapter 6 n. 17), this clearly has nothing to tell us about the structure or integration of the historical text. At the boundary of uses significant in this connection are those in which the 'body' is merely an aggregate; this would include the use of 'in bodily form' (σωματοειδῶς) to designate all the parts of a text, or of some component of a text (such as the narrative component of a forensic speech), placed together, as opposed to their dispersal piecemeal (κατὰ μέρος: see Chapter 2, Chapter 6 n. 30). The analogy becomes more centrally significant as it acquires the implications of completeness (so that the parts aggregated are all and only the parts that ought to be present), of orderliness (those parts being disposed appropriately in relation to each other), and functionality (the appropriateness of this selection and disposition of parts being determined by the end or function of the text). In this central use, the parts may still be parts of a text or of some component of a text; Plato, as we saw, applied the analogy at the level of the text itself (Chapter 2), while Aristotle was concerned with the structure of the subject-matter as one abstracted component of the text (Chapter 4). The criteria of appropriateness applied to the subject-matter might include requirements related to unity (as in Aristotle's theory of plot in narrative poetry), but need not (as in rhetorical theories of historiography); but in neither case is the text required to deal exclusively with its subject-matter—substantive digression is permitted. Where the requirement of unity is applied at the level of the text, what is required is a lucid, interesting, connected surface into which everything has been worked skilfully, and in which everything satisfies. In effect, the unified or organic text in Greek criticism is a metaphor for the well-constructed and well-written text, judged by whatever criteria of excellence are held applicable to a text of that kind.

The rhetoricians surveyed in the previous section do not diverge from this pattern. First, a use of the organic analogy with no bearing on structure or integration. Aper, in Tacitus' *Dialogue*, comparing the more colourful and ornamental style of modern oratory favourably with the sparer manner of older speakers, observes that a speech, like the human body, is more attractive if clothed in healthy flesh (21. 8); Quintilian neatly reverses the point: the attractiveness of a healthy body derives from the same source as its strength, and is rendered ugly by effeminate cosmetics and affected dress (8. Pref. 18–20).

Second, the 'boundary' usage mentioned above appears in the Seguerianus (i 444. 8–17 Sp. = 374. 24–375. 7 H.): should the narrative in a forensic speech be made one 'body' or divided into several parts? The view of Alexander is commended: when the charges bear on a single point we should 'make them like a body by uniting them (σωματικὰς ποιεῖν ἀναγκαῖον ἑνοποιοῦντας)'; when they are diverse, or when the length of the narrative demands it, they should be split up.[14] It is scarcely more significant when the author *ad Herennium* says of a figure too diffuse to be illustrated by quotation that it is not separable, like a limb, but like blood 'perfusus . . . per totum corpus orationis' (4. 58, cf. Cic. *Orat.* 126, 'toto corpore orationis fusa'). A more central usage is found in pseudo-Longinus, where the role of composition (ἐπισύνθεσις) in rendering an aggregate 'as it were like a body' (10. 1) is recognized. This is perhaps less clear in 10. 1–3, where the term ἐπισύνθεσις is used in parallel with a term like πύκνωσις, which implies no more than aggregation, than in 40. 1; there the contrast between elements scattered (σκεδασθέντα) and organically unified (σωματοποιούμενα) is explicitly related to the 'harmony' of a period's structure and to the 'complete structure (σύστημα)' that results from the composition of a body's limbs. Pseudo-Dionysius identifies neglect of the 'necessary sequence (ἀκολουθία)' as a common fault in declamation, and cites Plato's requirement in the *Phaedrus* that one's arguments should not be deployed 'at random' and that a speech should 'be like a body, from head to foot, its parts (μέρη) and limbs (μέλη) appropriate to each other and to the whole structure (σύστημα) of the body' (ii 364. 12–18). In the transition between his discussions of *inventio* and *dispositio* Quintilian points out that one's inventions will remain an unordered heap unless given order and connection, and he uses the organic analogy to make the point; in the preface to Book 7 he points out that a statue, or a human or animal body, needs not only its full complement of limbs, but those limbs in their right places—otherwise it is a monstrosity (7. Pref. 2).[15] His attack on modern oratory includes a scathing reference to those whose speeches resemble the notebooks in which schoolboys

---

[14] The problems which this decision can present in practice are discussed in the *protheoria* to the 49th declamation in Libanius (vii 648–50 Foerster; the reference to ἦθος and τὸ πρέπον on p. 651 bears comparison with the passages of Hermogenes and pseudo-Dionysius cited n. 20 below). For convenient illustrations of the two techniques, see the examples of *anaskeue* and *kataskeue* in Aphthonius' *Progymnasmata*.

[15] Cf. 7. 10. 16: parts of parts, as well as parts, need to be ordered—and connected: 'qui non modo ut sint ordine conlocati laborandum est, sed ut inter se vincti atque ita

jot down the most striking parts of each others' declamations—that is,
unordered assemblages of purple passages; such speakers concentrate
their effort, not on the case, but on individual *loci*, and produce
fragments ('abrupta quaedam') without regard to the *corpus* as a
whole (2. 11. 5–7).[16]

Hermogenes has a number of pertinent references. We mentioned
earlier his admiration for Lycurgus' digressions, including quotations
from the poets; commenting elsewhere on the pleasing effect of poetic
quotations in a prose text he observes that if they are to have this
effect the quotations must not merely be inserted, like the laws cited
in a forensic speech, but must be woven into the context in such a way
that they appear to form 'one body' with the prose (337. 23–338. 18);
one may recall here the 'wedges' to which Quintilian objected
(4.3.4).[17] Elsewhere he defines 'genuine eloquence (δεινότης)' as using
all the elements that go to make up the 'body' of a speech in
accordance with *kairos* (368. 22– 369. 9). Hermogenes makes more
elaborate use of the organic analogy when introducing the stylistic
idea 'beauty' (κάλλος). He begins by distinguishing beauty in the
limited, stylistic sense that he proposes to analyse from beauty 'in the
strict sense (κυρίως)', and he uses the organic analogy to expound the
two factors in terms of which this latter, more general notion of
beauty is defined (296. 15–298. 10). First, all the elements of a text
that constitute its stylistic idea (or ideas)[18]—thoughts, figures, diction,
rhythm, and so forth—must fit together appropriately and harmoniously (τὸ ἐκ πάντων τῶν ποιούντων τὰς ἰδέας αὐτοῦ πάσας ...
εὐάρμοστον καὶ σύμμετρον); this is compared to the composition of a

cohaerentes ne commissura perluceat; corpus sit, non membra'; see n. 5 above. The
point is cunningly illustrated by the smooth transition which 7. 10. 17 effects to the
discussion of style in Book 8.

[16] Modern poets, too, neglect economy: 1. 8. 9. Elsewhere Quintilian observes that
Ovid's use in *Metamorphoses* of strained and paradoxical transitions, such as ought not
to be tolerated in oratory, is justified there by the need 'res diversissimas in speciem
unius corporis colligere' (4. 1. 77): that is, like Herodotus in Dionsyius' assessment
(*Pomp.* 3. 14, ii 238. 8–11), Ovid has taken πολλὰς καὶ οὐδὲν ἐοικυίας ὑποθέσεις and
made σύμφωνον ἓν σῶμα.

[17] Quintilian, too, values the effect of poetic quotations, 'cum poeticis voluptatibus
aures a forensi asperitate respirant' (1. 8. 11).

[18] Hermogenes envisages a single idea, or a selective combination of ideas, or a
comprehensive combination; the last is exceedingly rare (on the difficulty of mixing the
ideas, see 279. 14–280. 12): Demosthenes made his style ποικίλον by combining all the
ideas, but still contrived by virtue of their interpenetration to make his text stylistically
unified (τὸν λόγον ἓν εἶναι πασῶν αὐτῷ δι' ἀλλήλων ἠκούσων τῶν ἰδέων, 221. 17–23, cf.
217. 21–218. 3); similarly Homer (τὸ ποικίλον καὶ ἐξ ἀπάντων ἓν ὅτι κάλλιστον ὁ μάλιστα
ἐργασάμενος, 390. 24–391. 1).

body, the ideas and their constituents being analogous to the body's 'limbs and parts'; Hermogenes goes on to explain that this was what Plato meant by his use of the analogy in *Phaedrus*.[19] Secondly, there must be 'a single quality of character pervading the whole text and appropriate to its (stylistic) idea (μετά τινος ἐμφαινούσης δι' ὅλου τοῦ λόγου ποιότητος ἤθους μιᾶς πρεπούσης τῇ ἰδέᾳ)'; this is analogous to the good complexion of a healthy body (καθάπερ ἐν σώματι χρῶμα). This notion of character or *ethos* recurs in a similar attempt to distinguish the stylistic idea of that name from a broader sense of the term (320. 16–321. 18). The idea, like any other idea, can be used throughout a speech or in a particular section, and may be combined with any one or more of the other ideas; the *ethos* that is necessary to beauty and analogous to complexion necessarily pervades the whole text (τὸ δι' ὅλου τοῦ λόγου ἀναγκαίως ἔχον ἐμφαίνεσθαι), and consists in making the text apt to the persona of the speaker—or, in a dialogue or narrative text, speakers (εἴ τις τοῖς ὑποκειμένοις προσώποις οἰκείους καὶ πρέποντας τοὺς λόγους περιάπτοι τις).[20] For Hermogenes, therefore, the organic analogy requires an appropriate disposition of the constituent elements of the text, together with an appropriate and successfully realized characterization of the speaker or speakers: συμμετρία μελῶν καὶ μερῶν μετ' εὐχροίας (296. 25–297. 1); this aptly summarizes the rhetorical consensus.[21]

---

[19] In 297. 14–21 Hermogenes says that Plato's objection to Lysias' speech in *Phdr.* is that the thoughts (ἔννοιαι) are not used εὐαρμόστως, but at once clarifies the point: Plato does not object to the thoughts in themselves—they fail of εὐαρμοστία because of their poor τάξις.

[20] Since a dialogue or drama may have many characters, it is unclear why Hermogenes stresses the singularity of this kind of *ethos*. Contrast pseudo-Dionysius; he distinguishes two kinds of *ethos* (ii 375. 9–19): common (κοινόν) or philosophical, by which he means 'the overall moral tendency of the work' (Russell 1978, 120); and particular (ἴδιον) or rhetorical, that is, appropriate characterisation—Hermogenes' 'complexion'. But pseudo-Dionysius recognizes the multiplicity of character in this sense, and sets it against the unity of the philosophical *ethos* which is the proper foundation of rhetorical characterization (as the emotive and appetitive components of the soul need to be governed by reason, so δεῖ κἂν τῷ λόγῳ ἓν μὲν ἦθος ἐκεῖνο τὸ μέγιστον τὸ ἐκ φιλοσοφίας ὥσπερ λογισμὸν ὑποκεῖσθαι τῷ λόγῳ, τὰ δὲ ἄλλα ἐπάγειν, 360. 8–17). Russell comments: 'It seems to say that the unity of a speech or poem depends not only on the fact that the parts should cohere to effect a single purpose, but also on the nature of that purpose, to wit that it should reflect the reason-controlled life' (124); but pseudo-Dionysius says nothing of a 'single purpose'—only that the text (whatever its purpose or purposes) should tend to promote virtue and dissuade from vice; and he presents this as a condition, not of the unity of the text, but of its dignity or elevation (τὸ μεγαλοπρεπές).

[21] The idea that visual beauty consists in the συμμετρία of parts with each other and the whole, together with εὔχροια, is criticized by Plotinus, who describes it as almost universally held (1.6.1); cf. Cic. *Tusc.* 4.31, Chrysippus *SVF* iii 278, 472.

8

The Homeric Scholia

WHEN Dionysius wished to praise Herodotus' *poikilia*, his skill in avoiding tedium by resting his reader frequently and diversifying his text, he described him (as we saw in Chapter 6) as 'emulating Homer'.[1] Plutarch also testifies to Homer's supremacy in this respect, affirming (*Mor.* 504d) that he alone among the poets remains immune to men's ready susceptibility to satiety (κόρος); he is always fresh (καινός), always charming; by leading us always from one narrative to another he evades 'the satiety that lies in ambush for every text (τὸν ἐφεδρεύοντα παντὶ λόγῳ κόρον)'.[2] In short, as one of the ancient commentators on the *Iliad* remarked (Σ B 13. 219–329), Homer is 'a lover of variety (φιλοποίκιλος)'.[3]

This theme, clearly, will be worth pursuing deeper into the scholiastic thickets; but some effort should be made, first of all, to mitigate their unflattering reputation.[4] The critical tools which these commentators used were derived primarily from rhetoric, and the rhetorical analysis of poetry meets with some resistance today; moreover, the problem of anachronism is particularly acute when one is examining Hellenistic exegesis of pre-classical texts. Nevertheless, I believe that if we consider the treatment of similes in the

---

[1] Cf. [Longinus] 13. 2, where Herodotus is described as Ὁμηρικώτατος—the reason is not indicated; in Dion. Hal. *Dem.* 41 (ii 220 Usener-Radermacher), the point of the comparison is stylistic; in Nicolaus *Prog.* 12. 14–19 Felten (= iii 455. 25–9 Sp.) Herodotus and Homer are linked as exemplars of the 'mixed' style of narrative. Cf. Woodman 1988, 1–5.

[2] At *Mor.* 25cd Plutarch asserts that poetry is particularly attached to τὸ ποικίλον καὶ πολύτροπον, since it is change (μεταβολαί) that creates the effects of pathos and surprise on which poetry's emotional impact (ἔκπληξις) and charm (χάρις) depend.

[3] In the fifth century, Democritus had expressed a sense of ordered diversity in Homer: ἐπέων κόσμον ἐτεκτήνατο παντοίων (DK 68 B 21); for further references see Verdenius 1983, 16 n. 5.

[4] See Griffin 1976, Richardson 1980, for a sympathetic view of the literary criticism of the scholia; Richardson gives a useful summary of their approach, and a more detailed survey can be found in Griesinger 1907. There is an excellent critical review of the secondary literature in Schmidt 1976, 39–65; see also Wilson 1983. I collect some references to other poetic scholia in Appendix B.

Homeric scholia we shall find that rhetorical theory was able to furnish Hellenistic critics with a flexible interpretative model, and one rather well adapted to their object of study. The question of the Homeric simile is, in addition, of direct relevance to our larger project, since the similes have often been seen as digressive, the description in the 'vehicle' of the comparison having a tendency to autonomous (or, in our term, centrifugal) development.

First, how did the rhetoricians approach similes in theory? The crucial point to observe is their recognition of two kinds of correspondence between illustrand and illustration: global and partial correspondences are both allowed for. The (probably third-century) treatise on tropes ascribed to Trypho (iii 200–1 Spengel) divides comparison (ὁμοίωσις) into three classes: visual comparison (εἰκών: defined as λόγος ἐναργῶς ἐξομοιοῦν πειρώμενος); paradigm, or historical exemplum (παράδειγμα); and the generalized exemplum (παραβολή), lacking the historical specificity of the paradigm (ἐξ ἀορίστων καὶ ἐνδεχομένων γενέσθαι). Under the first class, the author distinguishes between those images which compare wholes to wholes (ὅλα πρὸς ὅλα), and those in which the comparison is in various ways incomplete: part to part (μέρη πρὸς μέρη), or shape, or colour, or size. Polybius of Sardis, who classifies comparisons in a rather different way (iii 106–9 Sp.)[5] similarly distinguishes an image (εἰκών) that corresponds globally (ὁλοσχερῶς) from one which corresponds partially (ἀπὸ μέρους). As we found in Chapter 7, doctrines which appear in the relatively late Greek rhetorical treatises that have come down to us can often also be traced in earlier Latin rhetorics, suggesting that lost Greek texts of the second and first centuries BC would have contained the same ideas. In this case, it is the *Rhetoric to Herennius* that provides the parallel (4. 61): 'It is not necessary for one thing to correspond to another in its entirety ['res tota totae rei': cf. ὅλα πρὸς ὅλα], but the point in respect of which the comparison is made must correspond.'[6]

[5] Various classifications of comparison are found in the rhetoricians: Minucianus (i 498–9 Spengel = 362–3 Hammer) agrees with 'Trypho', while Polybius and Apsines (i 372–3 = 279–80) give different accounts. In practice, it makes little difference; the Homeric scholia apply the terms ὁμοίωσις, εἰκών and παραβολή indiscriminately. It is worth noting that 'Trypho' and Polybius illustrate their discussions of comparison from Homer; Apsines and Minucianus, who do not distinguish global and partial correspondence, cite the orators.

[6] Clausing appeals to *Rhet. Her.* 2. 46 to show that ancient rhetoric was committed to global correspondence ('simile vitiosum est quod ex aliqua parte dissimile est'); but this

This scheme of global and partial correspondence is applied in the scholia.[7] We must first distinguish between the function of a simile in its context and the function of details in a simile. As to the former, the scholia recognize a general function of 'resting' the reader (διαναπαύουσι τὸν πόνον αἱ παραβολαί, BT 15. 362–4: the image here is in particularly striking contrast to the battle-narrative) and embellishing the text (the simile is one of the many ἡδύσματα with which Homer 'seasons' his poetry: Eustathius 176. 20–22); they recognize that clusters of similes are used at moments of crisis or special significance to point to the importance of the events (BT 14. 394–9, 15. 624–5);[8] and, naturally, the illustrative function—making the action clearer and more vivid—is never in doubt. However, precisely because illustration can always be invoked, the function of the simile within its context only becomes problematic when the function of details within the simile is obscure; when the detail seems to drift away from the illustrand, this *prima facie* centrifugal movement makes illustration insufficient as an explanation of the simile as a whole.

The scholia frequently note global correspondence. When they do so explicitly, their terminology is similar to that of the rhetoricians: ὅλον πρὸς ὅλον (BT 18. 318–22), ὅλον ὅλῳ (ABT 8. 306–8, T 20. 495–7), ὅλη [sc. εἰκών] πρὸς ὅλον (BT 17. 747–51); πάντα πᾶσι (BT 17. 61–9, 20. 490–2, cf. 16. 406–9, 18. 161–2) or πρὸς τὸ πᾶν (BT 16. 633–4).[9] But global correspondence is also implicit in the many notes which

is a mistake. The author is there discussing the use of comparison as a mode of forensic argumentation ('exornatio' is being used in a special sense of part of the *argumentatio*: cf. 2. 28), where naturally precision of analogy is important (so also Cic. *Inv.* 1. 82); in the discussion of comparison as a figure the author denies the necessity of complete correspondence (4. 61). Quintilian makes the same distinction between *similitudo* in proof and as *ornatus* (5. 11. 5–6, 8. 3. 72).

[7] McCall 1969, 252 n. 25, expresses doubts about the dating of the relevant notes: 'The terminology employed and the types of comment made are so analogous to those in the late treatises that it seems most natural to associate them principally with late antiquity.' But, as we have seen, there is a Latin parallel reflecting earlier Greek texts ancestral to the late treatises; and there is nothing inconsistent with an earlier origin in those scholia. As McCall notes, the evidence of Vergil's acquaintance with the scholia on similes (cf. Schlunk 1974, esp. 36–48) supports this view.

[8] This latter, the point at which the Trojans at last break through to the ships, is a particularly striking example: in 15. 592–638 there are five similes, progressively longer (1, 2, 5, 6, and 8 lines) and more complex, while the intervals between them become shorter. (For the sense of the scholion, πρὸς ἔμφασιν τῶν πραγμάτων, see 'Trypho' iii 199. 15–16: ἔμφασις is an expression δι' ὑπονοίας αὐξάνουσα τὸ δηλούμενον.)

[9] See also on *Od.* 6. 102: κατὰ πάντα ἀπαράλλακτος. (Friedrich 1975, 60, distinguishes πάντα/πᾶσι from ὅλον/ὅλῳ as point-for-point and structural global correspondence; but this distinction cannot be sustained from the scholia.)

simply work out the correspondences in detail: for example, BT 4. 130–1, 4. 275–8, 11. 113–19, 15. 381–4.[10] The last two references, in particular, reflect the enthusiasm which the scholia feel for a vivid comparison that can be applied in detail; but it should not be inferred from this that the commentators responsible for these notes would not have allowed and admired incompletely corresponding similes also. The situation in the scholia has generally been misunderstood by modern scholars as a conflict between rival modes of interpretation;[11] in fact, as the rhetorical evidence makes clear, what we have is not two conflicting principles, but a single and admirably flexible principle applied in different ways to different cases.

For the scholia do also acknowledge quite freely partial correspondence. For example, BT 11. 475 remarks that the comparison is partial (μερική): Odysseus' wound and the multiplicity of attackers correspond, and Ajax' subsequent intervention corresponds to the arrival of the lion; but the cowardice implied by comparison with a deer must be excluded (ABT 11. 475), and the additional detail that the lion eats the deer is a development of the image with no application to the subject (οὐ πρὸς τὸ προκείμενον, T 11. 481, cf. Eust. 856. 39–49). Compare A 10. 5 (not πρὸς ἅπαντα), T 12. 41–8 (πρὸς ἓν μόνον, cf. BT 17. 523, 17. 666); BT 16. 770–1 refers to τὸ συνεκτικόν, a term comparable to our *tertium comparationis* and *Vergleichspunkt*; and A 8. 560, noting the shift from a qualitative to a quantitative term of comparison (ὡς 8. 555, τόσσα 8. 560), suggests that the point of the comparison (τὸ παραβολικόν) is given by the introductory term, while the concluding term 'suggests incidentally (παρεμφαίνει)' a further point.

When dealing with partial correspondence the scholia are willing to discern various functions in the non-corresponding development. Most frequently, it is seen as intensifying the vehicle of the simile— not, that is, reinforcing its similarity to the subject, but enhancing its

[10] Usually the exegesis is restricted to what is made explicit in the simile, but there are exceptions. The brief simile at *Il.* 3. 222, words 'like winter snowflakes', is explained with reference, not only to the density of the snowfall, but also to its whiteness (the clarity of the speech) and coldness (the shiver, φρίκη, of emotional response in the hearer); winter snow, because snowfall in spring is harmful to crops. Compare ABT 2. 87 (although this is not represented as a global correspondence: see n. 17 below).

[11] Clausing 1913, 70: 'Beide Betrachtungsweisen haben sich gegenseitig bekämpft'; accepted by Schmidt 1976, 53 and Friedrich 1975, 60, with nn. 140–1 and 146 (Friedrich's presentation makes very clear the projection of modern controversial positions onto the ancient commentaries).

impressiveness and importance.[12] For example, ABT 17. 520–2: Homer has 'amplified' both elements of the vehicle—a *sharp* axe wielded by a *vigorous* man—to make the stroke more effective. Compare BT 23. 222–3 (the whole simile αὐξητικῶς ἔχει), 11. 305–8, 16. 385, 17. 676–7, and numerous other passages. Other functions are suggested sporadically. BT 16. 753 sees the addition of 'and his own courage destroys him' to the description of the lion as a foreshadowing of Patroclus' death.[13] The introduction of Zeus' anger into the storm-simile at *Il.* 16. 384–93 is explained as a device of amplification (πρὸς αὔξησιν, BT 16. 385), but also as didactic in intent (παιδευτικὰ ... ταῦτα, BT 16. 387, cf. 16. 385) and as an expression of piety (πρὸς τοῦτο ἡ πᾶσα παραβολή, τὰ δ' ἄλλα εὐσεβείας χάριν παρέθηκεν, BT 16. 393). Eustathius, commenting on the same passage (1065. 28–35) mentions—in addition to relaxation (διανάπαυσις), clarity, and *poikilia*—the display of Homer's wide learning as a function of similes, and his note on *Il.* 4. 452–5 (497. 29–33) alleges that Homer often includes 'superfluous' detail (περιττά) in his similes for this reason (πολυμαθίας χάριν); this, of course, reflects the view of Homer as a universal expert common in antiquity. Finally, the scholia are quite willing to accept that some similes are developed in a purely decorative manner; BT 4. 482: '"he fell like a poplar": the comparison extends so far, and the rest he adds luxuriating in abundance and pursuing pleasure (ἐκ περιουσίας ἐναβρυνόμενος ... καὶ διώκων ἡδονήν)';[14] BT 7. 208: 'the poet is ambitiously lavish (προσφιλοτιμεῖται) with the rest'; T 12. 41–8: 'he applies the image to one thing only ... and the rest has no bearing on the subject of the comparison ... but is introduced as poetic ornament (κόσμος)';[15] BT 21. 257–62: 'he narrated the rest incidentally (παραδιηγήσατο) for the sake of ornamentation (κόσμου ἕνεκα)'.

For many modern critics that 'for the sake of ornamentation' would probably take on derogatory implications—'mere' ornament 'for its own sake', as we are prone to write; it is important to emphasize again, therefore, that the phrase would not have struck an ancient critic in that light. As we have seen in previous chapters,

[12] Cf. Clausing 1913, 72–6.
[13] An important principle in the scholia: cf. Richardson 1980, 269 and n. 9.
[14] BT 4. 484 sees a further point of contact—a difference, not of principle, but in the application of a shared principle to a particular case; so BT 22. 193 offers a partial and, tentatively (and unpersuasively), a more global explanation of that simile.
[15] The text is corrupt (see van der Valk 1963, i 511), but this does not affect the point.

ornamentation was an important principle of literary composition, above all in a 'panegyrical' or epideictic form—and poetry is the 'most panegyrical' of all kinds of writing (Hermogenes 389. 7–9 Rabe, cf. Chapter 7 above); no poet, therefore, could be blamed for taking such opportunities to ornament his text, just because the ornamentation is digressive. Here, too, we find that centripetal composition is not required by ancient criticism. Thus while Richardson is right to say that 'unlike many (but not all) modern scholars . . . the Scholia tend to regard the detailed elaboration of the similes as adding significantly to the effect of the scene with which they are compared, and they often admire their close correspondence or ἀκρίβεια',[16] a misleading impression will be given unless we add the converse: that they do not always insist on close correspondence, and are (in turn, unlike many modern scholars) aesthetically appreciative also of similes that do not correspond globally. This flexible approach seems to me correct, for some—but not all—similes in Homer are centrifugally composed to some significant degree.[17]

Let us now return to the testimonia with which we began the chapter. Dionysius considered that Herodotus, knowing that any extensive narrative needs 'rests' (ἀναπαύσεις) to ensure that its audience remains well-disposed, and that to dwell on the same material at length will produce a painful sense of satiety (κόρος), wished to emulate Homer by making his text varied (ποικίλην). Plutarch, too, commented on the perpetual freshness (καινότης) of Homer's text, and its consequent avoidance of satiety. The two preceding chapters have shown that these themes—*poikilia* and its opposite, uniformity (τὸ ὁμοειδές), which is tedious (προσκορές, that is, which leads to κόρος), together with the consequent need for 'rests'—were staples of the rhetorical critics' aesthetic. The view that Homer was especially concerned with, and especially skilled in the use of, these techniques is reflected extensively in the scholia.[18]

---

[16] Richardson 1980, 279.

[17] *Il.* 2. 87–93 compares the Greeks congregating in one place to bees scattering from their hive: Eustathius uses this occasion to expound the notion of partial correspondence at length (177. 12–47); cf. Friedrich 1975, 62 (his discussion of Homeric similes, 59–75, is admirable). Moulton 1977, 39 n. 44 comments on this passage: 'It is to be noted that some details in the simile do not exactly correspond with those in the narrative . . . For all that, the passage is an effective image, and can hardly be used as evidence for similes' completely independent existence from narrative.' But has anyone ever maintained their *completely* independent existence?

[18] For *poikilia* in the scholia see Richardson 1980, 266–7, Griesinger 1907, 62–7.

Some comments on the poet's use of similes will provide a convenient introduction to the scholiasts' perception of Homer's love of *poikilia*. BT 15. 362–4: similes provide rest (διαναπαύουσι τὸν πόνον).[19] BT 5. 523: there is *poikilia* in the juxtaposition of similes taken from blustery winds (5. 499–502) and windless calm (5. 522–6). BT 15. 630–6: the poet has taken many similes from the attacks of lions, but here (by introducing the figure of the inexperienced herdsman) he is still able to produce one that is fresh (καινόν).

The devising of 'fresh' variants is an important element of Homeric *poikilia* in the scholiasts' view—particularly so, since of its nature a poem of this kind will contain a number of recurrent motifs or repetitive incidents. There will, for example, be many blows, many wounds, many deaths; but Homer constantly varies (ποικίλλει ABT 16. 339; cf. T 11. 378, 20. 397) his descriptions of them, and by doing so he rests the reader (ἐπαναπαύει BT 4. 539)—indeed, to avoid tedium (τὸ προσκορές) he sometimes omits the description altogether (T 20. 460). That innovativeness (καινοτροπία) is one of the best features of Homer's poetry (Eust. 952. 60–2, in a defence of *Il.* 13. 657 against athetesis). The confrontation between two warriors is sometimes developed into a scene of supplication to avoid monotony (πρὸς ἐξαλλαγὴν ταυτότητος BT 6. 37–65; παραλλάσσων τὸ ὁμοειδές BT 20. 463–9) and vary the narrative (ποικίλλων τὴν διήγησιν BT 21. 34); the last in this series itself departs from the model of its predecessors, being complicated and rendered more pathetic by the history of Lycaon's previous dealings with Achilles.[20] In the *Odyssey* there is a series of recognitions, and the commentators admire the way in which these have been varied.[21]

These examples are concerned with contrasts between comparable segments of the poems; *poikilia* is also observed in the presentation of individual segments, from minute details of phrasing upwards. Eustathius, in a stylistic analysis of *Il.* 2. 100–8, remarks (181. 23–36) that the conjunctions have been alternated for the sake of *poikilia*, to avoid monotony (Homer uses αὐτάρ in 103, 105, 107, but δέ in 104, 106). On a slightly larger scale, he sees the chiasmic presentation in *Il.* 7. 206–18 (Ajax-Greek reaction: Trojan reaction-Hector) as, in part, a device of *poikilia*, avoiding ὁμοιοσχημοσύνη (677. 56–64; it also

---

[19] Cf. BT 17. 426 for this use of πόνος.
[20] The scholion regards this story as an example of *peripeteia*, a device invented by Homer, 'varied, dramatic, and emotive' (ποικίλον ὂν καὶ θεατρικὸν καὶ κινητικόν).
[21] Richardson 1983.

serves to secure a connected, συνεχές, exposition). Chiasmus in the service of variety (τὸ ποικίλον) is also detected by T 12. 129–130a: two victims are named, following the order 'patronym-epithet-name: name-epithet-patronym'.[22] BT 9. 125–7 remarks on how the inclusion of those lines mitigates uniformity (τὸ ὁμοειδές) in Agamemnon's list of gifts. On a still larger scale, the structure of whole scenes is governed by the principle of *poikilia*. Consider the *teikhoskopia* (*Il.* 3. 161–244): first, Priam asks the identity of one conspicuous Greek leader, Helen identifies him as Agamemnon, and Priam praises him; second, Priam points to another man, Helen identifies him as Odysseus, but this time it is Antenor who interjects praise, adding unprompted a description of Menelaus; third, Priam points to another man, and Helen identifies him as Ajax—but very briefly, passing unprompted to Idomeneus, and ending with a reference to her brothers, who (by contrast with the others mentioned) are not to be seen. Eustathius remarks on the Homeric *poikilia* of this; by presenting the heroes in various ways (πολυτρόπως, πολυειδῶς), the poet has avoided uniformity (τὸ μονοειδές) (409. 9–25).[23] In 4. 223–421 the contingents inspected by Agamemnon are all found in a different state of readiness, the king addresses each in a different way, and receives a different response from each; thus the poet displays his characteristic *poikilia* (Eust. 466. 31–467. 12). T 10. 158: the Greek leaders are not all awakened uniformly (μονοειδῶς: Eustathius again remarks on Homer's 'customary *poikilia*' and the avoidance of τὸ ὁμοειδές: 794. 32–3). In this way, just as repetitive incidents scattered through the poem are varied, so in single incidents any potentially repetitive sequence or pattern of motifs is broken up.

If we move to a still larger scale of structure, the striving after *poikilia* is seen also in the sequence of segments; incidents are juxtaposed so as to maximize contrast. Eustathius on Hector's return to the city in *Iliad* 6 (650. 5–12): the poetry's grim countenance becomes more genial, washing off the blood of the fallen.[24] T 11. 599: Patroclus' visit to Nestor's tent avoids uniformity (τὸ ὁμοειδές), providing a rest (ἀνάπαυσις) from the fighting.[25] T 13. 168: Meriones

[22] This assumes that 12. 130a (= 2. 746) is read; see West 1967, 99–101.

[23] By contrast Kirk finds the brevity with which Ajax is treated 'surprising', and proposes (rather unconvincingly) a psychologizing interpretation (1976, 82–4, 142–3, cf. also his commentary ad loc.).

[24] Van der Valk refers us ad loc. to Eust. 95. 12–21, 159. 10–13.

[25] The role of this visit in the larger economy of the poem is, of course, also recognized; see Richardson 1980, 268–9.

is sent out of the battle to fetch a spear so as to rest (ἀναπαῦσαι) the audience from the fighting; Idomeneus is manipulated to the same end: on hearing of Poseidon's anger (13. 206), the audience expects the fighting to continue with added fury, but the poet, being a lover of variety (φιλοποίκιλος), introduces other things—the god's meeting with Idomeneus, the arming of that hero, and his meeting with Meriones while the latter is fetching his spear (BT 13. 219–329). BT 14. 1: again we switch from the battle to the Greek camp, where the wounded leaders consult and decide to resume fighting; the poet 'diverts us from the uniformity (τὸ ὁμοειδές)'.[26] Again at BT 18. 1: 'the poet introduces variety (ποικίλλει) by transferring us to the camp'. A special case of this is the move to Olympus; BT 4. 1: the poet moves us from 'the tumult below' to heaven, adding dignity (σεμνύνων) and variety (ποικίλλων); BT 8. 209: he introduces a divine dialogue to rest us (ἀναπαύων) from the narrative of Greek reverses. Compare BT 16. 431–61 (the divine dialogue preceding Sarpedon's death), 16. 666 (the divine recovery of Sarpedon's body), 17. 426–8 (Zeus' pity for the horses of Achilles after Patroclus' death).[27] This use of divine interludes was sufficiently well-established for Zenodorus to employ it as one of his arguments for the athetesis of 18. 356–68: Homer is in general eager to vary (ποικίλλειν) his poem, and so customarily moves from the human to the divine, and from the divine back to the human, level; but here he has put a dialogue between Zeus and Hera immediately before Thetis' visit to Hephaestus, anomalously juxtaposing similar (ὅμοια) rather than contrasting incidents (BT 18. 356).

One particular means of contrast and variation is the interleaving of separate strands of narrative—a technique developed on a much larger scale in the *Odyssey*.[28] In *Iliad* 1, Thetis' meeting with her son and her interview with Zeus are separated by the embassy which

---

[26] Specifically, he does not wish to dwell on the Greek reverses: the scholia assume that the poet and his audience are philhellene; since κόρος will occur more readily when the material is unpleasing, Greek defeats are particularly difficult for the poet to make acceptable (cf. Dion. Hal. on Herodotus and Thucydides). For discussion of this point of view, see Richardson 1980, 273–4, and the references given there.

[27] Homer includes two divine interludes in his (by comparison with the other days' fighting, brief) account of the Greek defeat on the second day: 8. 198–212, 350–484. Both are interludes in a strict sense: they are causally inconsequent in the action, the philhellene gods in each case drawing back from confrontation with Zeus. (T 8. 246 comments also on an omen: ὑπὲρ ἀναπαύσεως τοῦ ἀκροατοῦ.)

[28] For this technique see Fenik 1974, 61–104 ('interruption sequence').

brings to an end Chryses' involvement in the poem (1. 430–487, picking up from 1. 308–11); BT 1. 430 observes that by intermitting the two continuous series Homer rests (διαναπαύει) his audience, removing satiety (κόρος) from the one sequence of events while satisfying our interest in the other. Similarly in *Iliad* 11, the poet varies (ποικίλλει) the interval between Thetis' meeting with Achilles and her approach to Hephaestus by inserting the continuation of the battle over Patroclus' body (BT 18. 148). The scholia see this technique applied especially, as here, to filling the 'blank section' (τὸ διάκενον) left while a character is in transit from one place to another: cf. BT 11. 619–43, 15. 405. When the poet does not use a continuing strand of narrative for this purpose, other, more digressive, resources are available: similes (BT 3. 2), or the description of a local landmark (BT 22. 147–56: while Achilles is pursuing Hector, the poet himself entertains (ψυχαγωγεῖ) the audience with a description of the two springs), or a self-contained incident. The most striking instance of this is in *Iliad* 6, where the 'empty space' of Hector's return to the city is filled by the encounter between Glaucus and Diomedes—which, since it passes peacefully with an exchange of stories, genealogies, and gifts, is itself in contrast to the preceding battle-narrative, so that the poet is resting (διαναπαύει) his audience (BT 6. 119, 6. 237).

Eustathius uses the term 'to episodize' (ἐπεισοδιάζειν) in connection with this incident, and describes Hector's encounter with Andromache as an *epeisodion* (628. 39, 650. 6); what does this term imply for the scholiasts? AD 2. 212 (= Porphyry *QH* 30. 8–15 Schrader) offers (as is usual in the scholia) two kinds of explanation of Thersites' presence at Troy with the army—for it is obvious that he cannot have been brought along for his prowess as a fighter; one is naturalistic (he was too subversive to be left behind), the other technical: he is introduced by way of an *epeisodion* to bring about a shift of mood in the Greek army from the despondency shown in their reaction to Agamemnon's test to a good-humour receptive to Odysseus' exhortation. The scholion compares the use of Hephaestus towards the end of Book 1, and we might refer also to the introductory note to *Iliad* 11 (BT 11. 0), which points out that the nocturnal Greek success of *Iliad* 10 (described as an *epeisodion*, BT 10. 38–9) makes more plausible the Greek advance at the beginning of the third day's fighting by restoring the beaten army's morale. The note on Thersites adds a general comment on the functions of *epeisodia*: they are used for plausibility (πιθανότης: as e.g. the beginning of *Iliad* 11 would not be plausible without the Doloneia); or, as here, for some other practical purpose (χρεία); or, finally, for ornamentation or elevation (κόσμου καὶ ὑψώσεως χάριν). No definition of the term is offered; but an implication of (in some sense) superfluity must be present, or there would be no need to explain the use of *epeisodia*. We might infer, therefore, that an *epeisodion* is an incident that does not form an indispensable part of the narrative's causal structure, but which is included in the narrative for any of a range of possible reasons—from the strictly practical (e.g. enhancing the plausibility of the narrative) to the 'merely' ornamental.

This view is upheld by other major examples. Discussing the Catalogue, Eustathius observes that narrative continuity (ἀκολουθία) would require the description of Agamemnon with which the muster and the beginning of the Greek advance reaches a climax (2. 477–83) to be followed by the Trojan reaction (2. 786ff.); what intervenes— the listing of the Greek leaders—is an *epeisodion* (259. 25–7). Similarly of the duel between Paris and Menelaus: we expect battle to be joined, but Homer keeps this in reserve, introducing the duel (παρ- εισοδιάσας: note how this compound reinforces the digressive impli- cation); *epeisodia* involving duels, he adds, are a relish or condiment (ἄρτυμα)[29] to Homer's poetry (386. 34–387. 8). It will be observed that this duel, like that of Hector and Ajax in *Iliad* 7, is causally without consequence in the development of the plot. We have already commented on the *poikilia* of the internal structure of the *teikhoskopia*; it, too, is an *epeisodion* in this sense (Eust. 391. 32)— indeed, it is one used to fill in the 'blank section' while messengers are sent to fetch Priam to ratify the truce before the duel: an *epeisodion*, therefore, within an *epeisodion*.[30] BT 14. 153, on the deception of Zeus: the reader anticipates an imminent threat to the ships, but the poet has freshened (ἐκαινοποίησε) his narrative by introducing another *epeisodion*, one which involves a switch of attention to the divine level, an erotic narrative and a moral lesson—that is, it is both in contrast with its context and internally diverse (so, too, in more detail, Eust. 973. 37–55); cf. T 13. 1–7: Zeus' inactivity is used to extend and diversify the narrative (μῆκος ἅμα καὶ ποικιλίαν περιποιεῖ). A papyrus scholion to 21. 240 (POxy. 221 = Erbse XII, xii 19–24) describes Achilles' fight with the river as an *epeisodion* used to interrupt (διαλαβεῖν) the fighting and make a transition to the theomachy—an

---

[29] ἡδύσμασι παραρτύων also of similes, 176. 20–4.

[30] The alternations of scene in this book are striking.

interpretation which the commentator attributes to Protagoras (80 A 30 DK);[31] BT 21. 18: having gone through every other kind of battle, Homer can still devise something fresh (καινόν)—Achilles' battle with the river; this avoids uniformity (μονοείδεια), but the introduction of the river and of the conflict between the gods also solves the problem of how to supply material for a fourth day's fighting, especially when Achilles is facing manifestly unworthy opponents.[32]

Other examples of the use of the term *epeisodion* which might be mentioned are BT 6. 37–65: Adrastus' supplication of Menelaus (mentioned above); T 13. 521: Ares' (abortive) attempt to avenge his son (15. 113–42); A 18. 36: underwater lamentations ('further ἐπεισόδια καινά'); BT 23. 63: Achilles' dream, a pathetic *epeisodion* (cf. BT 23. 65: 'after Achilles' laments, the poet has devised something fresh (καινότερον)'; Eustathius refers to the *poikilia* of the incident, 1287. 51ff.). A possible counter-example to our interpretation of the term is to be noted at BT 15. 219, which refers to Apollo's use of the aegis (15. 229–30, 318–27) as an *epeisodion*, although the same note describes it as one of the causes of the Greek defeat; the implication may be that since the defeat is causally overdetermined this incident is strictly superfluous, and has been included primarily for its exotic character (precisely κόσμου καὶ ὑψώσεως χάριν).

Sometimes (as in Eustathius' account of Glaucus and Diomedes, cited above) the term *epeisodion* is applied, not to an incident introduced into the main narrative, but to a secondary narrative, whether told by the poet in a formal digression or placed in the mouth of a character; 'digression' (παρέκβασις) is also frequently applied in these cases.[33] BT 14. 114, on Diomedes' rehearsal of his family history: 'it is characteristic of Homer to rest (διαναπαύειν) his audience with digressions' (Eust. 970. 61: the poet rests the reader by the παρένθεσις of a historical *epeisodion*). Phoenix's use of the Meleager

---

[31] Cf. app. A.

[32] 'Adding μῆκος', as T 13. 1–7 (cited above) says of the Deception of Zeus. Note also that, while the Doloneia may be (as the scholia say) πιθανότητος χάριν, in that it renders the Greek successes plausible, those successes themselves do not forward the plot at all, and could be seen as adding μῆκος. The question of length is, as we saw in ch. 4, one which concerned Aristotle also (see especially the discussion there of *epeisodion* in *Poet.* 59a35–7, and of Aristotle's comments on 'watery' narrative in 62b7).

[33] BT 16. 166 says of the rescue of Sarpedon's body: 'he rests (ἀναπαύει) the flagging audience with a brief παρέκβασις'; thus the term can be applied to a secondary incident of the main narrative—an *epeisodion* in the former sense. So Friedrich's distinction between the two terms (1975, 15–16, cf. 55) involves an element of regimentation; but this does not affect his substantive point.

story in *Iliad* 9 is cited by the rhetoricians to illustrate the term παρέκβασις (Trypho iii 203. 20–3, Gregory of Corinth iii 224. 5–12); the paradigmatic and persuasive character of the story is, of course, understood (BT 9. 527 observes that the device introduces an element of *poikilia* into the attempts to sway Achilles), but Eustathius points out also that Phoenix interpolates additional material that is strictly superfluous (ἔτερα παρεισάγει κατά τινα περιττότητα), introducing *epeisodia* into *epeisodia*, and he stresses the internal *poikilia* of Phoenix's narrative (760. 64–771. 9).

In fact, many of the *epeisodia* (in the sense, secondary incidents in the main narrative) cited above are interpreted by the scholia as, at least in part, occasions for the insertion of such secondary narratives as a means of securing *poikilia*. The Catalogue, for example, is an *epeisodion*, introduced partly for practical reasons, to identify the heroes to the audience (an element of χρεία, in the scheme summarized earlier), but also ornamentally (an element of κόσμος); indeed, a list of names may be felt dull and lacking in emotional force (κίνησις), but that is averted by stylistic virtuosity and by the introduction of stories, descriptions of places, genealogies, and so forth, which provide *poikilia* and remove uniformity.[34] The *teikhoskopia* is an *epeisodion* 'opportune for furnishing stories' (Eust. 391. 30–33). Priam's speech at 3. 182–90 is one of the stories; he 'weaves an old story into the text in the manner of the Greek rhetor Nestor, as the poet resourcefully makes a skilfully-managed display of his *poikilia* and breadth of learning' (Eust. 402. 3–6, cf. 409. 20–1). Nestor's readiness to deliver rambling secondary narratives is familiar, of course, from both the *Iliad* and the *Odyssey*;[35] it is a point to which we shall return shortly. See also Eust. 100. 29–43: the poet did not want to dwell exclusively on the matter of Troy (τὰ Τρωϊκά), but to season (παρ-αρτύειν, implying digressive ornamentation) his poem with older stories; and he uses Nestor, an old man and so driven to reminisce by present incapacity, as a plausible opportunity for the insertion of these stories (παρένθεσις; also παρεμπλέκει, παρεισοδιάζει).

Other occasions are also used for the insertion of secondary narratives. Eust. 450. 8–9: the description of Pandarus' bow (4. 105–

---

[34] This summary is based chiefly on B 2. 494–877, Eust. 260. 42–6, 263. 9–16, 272. 5–9, 369. 36–8, Dion. Hal. *Comp.* ii 67–8 U-R.

[35] In the *Cypria* (according to Proclus: 103. 20–3 in vol. 5 of the OCT Homer) Menelaus consults Nestor about the planned expedition against Troy, 'and Nestor tells him in a παρέκβασις how Epopeus was killed after raping the daughter of Lycus, the story of Oedipus, Heracles' madness, and the story of Theseus and Ariadne'.

11), which is included for rest (ἀνάπαυσις), includes a hunting *epeisodion* (cf. 829. 47–51, on Agamemnon's shield). Eust. 484. 19–20: in the scene in which Agamemnon criticizes Diomedes for slackness 'here, too, the poet skilfully introduces as an episode (παρεισοδιάζει) a lengthy Greek story about the famous Theban war' (4. 376–399); the story is told at greater length than is necessary, for the sake of *poikilia* (486. 35–8). Tlepolemus' taunting of Sarpedon (5. 630–55) is developed in the same way; Eustathius 590. 12–13: the poet 'weaves in' a story 'not unrelated' to that of Troy (οὐκ ἀλλοδαπήν; it is, in fact, that of the sack of Troy by Heracles), 'rousing the audience from uniform (μονοειδές) flatness'. The obituaries of those killed in the fighting are another opportunity for this technique; BT 20. 383–5: it is Homer's custom to diversify (ποικίλλειν) his text in this way, and now, after so much fighting and so many deaths, it is especially opportune to use ornaments drawn from outside the plot (καλλωπίσμασι χρήσασθαι ἔξωθεν), both because of the threat of tedium (τὸ προσκορές), and also to show that Achilles' first victim after his return to action was not insignificant. These two factors—*poikilia*, and amplification (αὔξησις) of the victims, and thereby of the victors—are frequently mentioned in notes on such obituaries: BT 5. 70 (with Eust. 522. 38–523. 1), 11. 104–5 (with Eust. 834. 10–12), 20. 213. Gods are also useful; for example, Eustathius identifies the mythological digressions in the deception of Zeus (14. 249–61, 315–28) as one element in its *poikilia*, and Zenodorus, in a discussion of 18. 356–68 already cited, mentions this as one of the functions of divine interludes: but this is a scholion to which we shall have to return after discussing a further point.

The secondary narratives that we have been considering are sometimes described as 'completing' the poem's subject (for example, BT 9. 328; compare T 11. 625); the very broad view of the subject of the *Iliad* which this description presupposes, though initially surprising, is found throughout the scholia. B 2. 494–877: the poet omits no part of his subject-matter (ὑπόθεσις); he narrates each event (the strife of the goddesses, the abduction of Helen, Achilles' death) at an appropriate point, but following an inverted order (ἐξ ἀναστροφῆς), since the straightforward narrative order (ἡ κατὰ τάξιν διήγησις) is a 'modern and historiographical' style (νεωτερικὸν καὶ συγγραφικόν), unsuited to poetry. Eust. 7. 27–42: Homer begins with Achilles' wrath, passing over earlier events, but he does not omit them altogether; he inserts them—and events subsequent to the wrath—

elsewhere; this technique, which he uses also in the *Odyssey*, had many ancient imitators, especially Euripides, who 'beginning from the middle of his dramatic subjects then introduced previous events and also inserted subsequent events skilfully into his text (managing the latter by conjecture from probability or by prophecy), so that the audience should not be left uninformed of any part of the story in hand (προκειμένη ἱστορία) or, in a word, of the subject-matter (ὑπόθεσις)'. To start 'in medias res' (Hor. *AP* 146–9) and complete the subject-matter retrospectively is 'economic' (AD 1. 1, cf. Eust. 7. 6–21), a 'poetic merit' (BT 1. 1).[36]

There is here a contrast between the concept of 'hypothesis' or subject-matter in the scholia and Aristotle's concept of the *praxis* of a narrative text (cf. Chapter 4 above). Aristotle's *praxis* is a causally structured underlying sequence of events, into the narrative of which other events may be introduced digressively; the scholiasts' hypothesis is a 'field' of events (in the present case, the matter of Troy), from which a single sequence (the wrath of Achilles) may be extracted to provide the core of a text in which the whole field is narrated by inversion (ἐξ ἀναστροφῆς).[37] Thus where Aristotle contrasts poetry and history in terms of the structure of 'the underlying events' (τὰ ὑποκείμενα πράγματα: cf. Chapter 4 n. 37 above), the scholia contrast the way in which a—possibly common—hypothesis is realized in the text: narrative 'by inversion' is poetic, narrative 'in order' (κατὰ τάξιν) is historiographical (B 2. 494–877, cited above; cf. Macrobius *Sat.* 5. 2. 8–11, 5. 14. 11); naturally, it is likely that the events held over in an inverted narrative text will be treated in less detail and more selectively[38] than would be appropriate in a historiographical

---

[36] See further Brink 1971, 219–22. In a *paignion* which maintains, *inter alia*, that Helen was Paris' lawful wife and that the Greeks never took Troy, Dio Chrysostom argues that to begin at the very beginning would have been more artistic, and that the disruption of the natural order is a liar's trick, designed to obscure the issue (11. 24–33); this is, of course, tongue-in-cheek. Homer's practice is also noted in AT 1. 1, [Plut.] *de vita et poesi Homeri* 162, and Macrobius *Sat.* 5. 2. 8–11, 5. 14. 11. Narrative ἐξ ἀναστροφῆς is praised as more interesting and more entertaining in BT 11. 671–761 (Nestor to Patroclus). The scholiastic comments on inverted and historical narrative cast more light on the nature of the weakness of Apollonius' poem than does the Aristotelian question of unity: cf. ch. 5 above.

[37] But BD 4. 494 applies ὑπόθεσις to the core sequence (Homer's hypothesis is concerned with the tenth year of the war). And AT 1. 1 uses the term in a quite different sense: the wrath is the ὑπόθεσις of the events Homer records, i.e. their basis or presupposition.

[38] More selectively, despite hyperbolic claims for Homer's comprehensiveness; as we shall see in connection with *Odyssey*, the scholia concede that much Iliadic material was in fact 'left out' of the poem.

narrative.[39] It is worth noting, however, that Aristotle's preference for Homer's choice of a plot with a single part (*Poet.* 59a35) is similar in practice to the scholiastic preference for inverted narrative; the core-sequence of the scholiasts' hypothesis corresponds to the Aristotelian *praxis*, while the other parts which, according to Aristotle, Homer uses as episodes correspond to the parts of the hypothesis taken out of order in an inverted narrative.

A further consequence of the scholiasts' concept of hypothesis is that, while the rhetorical criticism of history recognized the subject and digression from the subject (see Chapter 6 above), the scholia on Homer have to reckon with two levels of digression: purely formal digressions, which remain within the hypothesis, and digressions that are strictly outside the hypothesis (ἔξωθεν: BT 20. 383–5; cf. Eust. 100. 29–43, cited above, and Σ *Od.* 5. 336, ἔξω τῆς ὑποθέσεως).[40] These two levels are recognized by Zenodorus in his discussion of 18. 356–68 (BT 18. 356). One of his arguments is that divine dialogues are introduced 'either to convey information about the events which make up the *Iliad*, or to expound an old story'; for the latter he cites the stories which Dione tells to comfort Aphrodite in 5. 382–415, and for the former Athene's (he says, mistakenly, Hera's) sharp remark to Zeus (5. 421–5), which informs us that Helen was deceived by Aphrodite when she eloped with Paris. The present interview, he argues, contributes nothing to 'the underlying events (τὰ ὑποκείμενα πράγματα)' and tells no story, and is therefore inauthentic.[41]

If we apply the scholiastic concept of hypothesis to the *Odyssey*, we shall conclude that the subject-matter of that poem is the homecoming of Odysseus from Troy in its entirety, and that it is treated by inversion—the core sequence begins with Odysseus already near the end of his long stay with Calypso, and his earlier adventures are

---

[39] In fact this view of historiography is not easy to sustain, as Herodotus' habitual order of exposition and (on one interpretation of the structure of Book 1: cf. ch. 6 above) Thucydides' make clear. Theon's discussion of narrative ἐξ ἀναστροφῆς (ii 86–7) refers indifferently to the *Odyssey* and the two historians. It could, however, be argued that Herodotus is, after all, 'Ὁμηρικώτατος, a poet among historians, and that the other interpretation of Thucydides (the Pentacontaeteia being ἔξω τῆς ὑποθέσεως) is correct.

[40] A passage like *Il.* 5. 630–55, in which the story is Trojan, but not from this war, falls, perhaps, between the two extremes: it is οὐκ ἀλλοδαπή (Eust. 590. 12–13, above).

[41] A complication: Zenodorus actually says that divine dialogues are not introduced ἐκτὸς τῆς ὑποθέσεως, but for one or other of the purposes given; but one of these purposes other commentators would describe as 'completing the hypothesis', the other precisely as 'outside the hypothesis'—and it is difficult to see what other sense the phrase could bear here; we must assume that he has used it rather loosely.

incorporated into the poem by means of the Phaeacian narrative (cf. Theon ii 86. 8–17). Other material, related but less integral (recollections of Troy, and the homecomings of other heroes), is also introduced; thus BT 24. 804: the *Odyssey*'s hypothesis, concerned solely with Odysseus and his family, was rather slight, so Homer kept back some of the material from the *Iliad* and placed it in the mouths of Nestor, Menelaus, and Demodocus in the later poem; Σ *Od.* 1. 284: since the *Odyssey* had insufficient *poikilia* in itself, the poet sent Telemachus to Sparta and Pylos, so that some Iliadic material could be recounted by Nestor and Menelaus in digressions (παρεκβάσεις; [Longinus] 9. 12 uses *epeisodia* to make the same point; cf. also Eust. 1459. 24ff.). In the latter part of the poem, the poet uses another means of interpolating digressive narratives, the exchange of biographies: Odysseus' false tales to Athene (13. 256–86) and Eumaeus (14. 192–359, 462–506), and Eumaeus' tale (15. 403–84), to which we may add Theoclymenus' story, told by the poet himself (15. 225–55), and the story of Odysseus' scar (19. 392–466; cf. Eust. 1869. 64–1870. 1: παρεισοδιάζει). One should also consider the structure of Odysseus' journey to the Underworld. As we have said, the whole Phaeacian narrative is an account by inversion of the earlier stages of the subject-matter; within that, however, the Nekuia is blatantly an *epeisodion*—for the ostensible reason for the journey (10. 538–40) could be, and is, fulfilled as well by Circe (12. 37ff.); Σ *Od.* 10. 491 offers, as is usual, both a naturalistic explanation (Circe suspected that Odysseus would distrust her) and a technical one: the poet wanted to include this *epeisodion* for the emotional effect (τὸ φρικῶδες καὶ ἐκπληκτικόν) of dealings with the dead. But there is a further level of digression; the *epeisodion* as a whole consists of two panels, divided by an interlude of dialogue with the Phaeacians (11. 330–84), and each panel is brought to a climax with material quite remote from the poem's subject-matter: a catalogue of women (11. 225–330), and a catalogue of illustrious dead (11. 566–635); Eustathius rightly admires the skill with which the poet inserts these stories, thereby avoiding monotony (τὸ μονοειδές, 1696. 35–8).[42]

I say 'rightly'; but is this cheerful admission that Homer is

---

[42] There has, of course, been much analytic discussion of this part of *Od.*: see e.g. Page 1955, 21–47, Kirk 1962, 236–40; but these scholars were not helped by their failure to understand the aesthetics of *poikilia*. I agree with Goold 1977, 19–22, in seeing progressive elaboration of a fixed text by the poet himself—although I cannot accept Goold's premiss 'fixed, that is to say written' (33).

digressive right? There is—as one might expect—a good deal of reluctance to concede this among many modern interpreters.[43] The most systematic attempt in recent years to develop a more centripetal approach is to be found in Norman Austin's article on the function of digressions in the *Iliad*.[44] Austin stresses (what no one would dispute) the paradigmatic nature of most digressions (209–305), but recognizes that this is not a sufficient answer: 'We may find the paradigmatic intention relevant but the manner of execution inopportune. It is just the amount of detail, the discursiveness, which has made the digression the subject of such controversy' (306). He argues, however, that the apparently unnecessary detail is never centrifugal elaboration, but is a (to us) unfamiliar rhetorical device in the service of the centripetal, paradigmatic intention: 'The length of the anecdote . . . is as relevant as its intent. The expansion of the anecdote is a form of *amplificatio*, or what later Greek rhetoricians called αὔξησις, a heightening of the subject, and so itself a form of persuasion.' This approach will certainly succeed in some cases; an obvious example is the digression (παρέκβασις, A 1. 234–40) on the sceptre in *Iliad* 1: by dwelling on the sceptre Achilles emphasizes and renders more solemn his oath.[45] But the theory is not uniformly successful. It will hardly account for the length of Glaucon's genealogizing in his encounter

[43] It is true that a significant number of recent scholars have accepted, indeed emphasized and over-emphasized, the digressiveness of Homer, inspired by the discovery of his orality; for a cautious assessment, see Hainsworth 1970. My own view, as by now will be apparent, is that Aristotle was right to think of the poems in Aristotelian terms, and that there is little profit in regarding as peculiarly pre-classical, paratactic (cf. Notopoulos 1949) or oral, techniques of composition practised throughout antiquity and recommended by the highly literate rhetorical theorists of the Hellenistic period.

[44] Austin 1966. Austin's interpretations do not always avoid the fanciful; I find his interpretation of the digression on Odysseus' scar as a psychological drama played out in the Nurse (310–11) quite unconvincing—as Austin himself says, 'the details go beyond Eurykleia's actual memory to mingle with what only Odysseus could have known'. De Jong 1985 renders this view no more plausible. Eurycleia is involved in the first part of the digression (19. 401)—naturally, for Odysseus is still an infant; but she is not mentioned when Odysseus returns (462–6). It may well be true, as de Jong argues, that Euryclea would probably have been present at the later scene; but the poet's failure to mention her presence hardly suggests that the passage has been contrived to 'explain' her knowledge of the story. Nor can I see why de Jong thinks that 463–4 would be 'superfluous' if the story were 'told from the perspective of the (omniscient) narrator' and that 'rejoiced' in 463 'also indicates a personal point of view'; the parents' reaction to their son's return is entirely natural, and is just the kind of detail that a skilful epic story-teller would use to complete his story.

[45] Griffin 1980, 11: 'Six lines describe the history of the sceptre before Achilles reveals what it is that he is about to swear by it—a powerful device of emphasis.'

with Diomedes (6. 150–211); Austin merely labels that an 'apologetic paradigm' (301) without attempting to account for its discursiveness. Nor is Austin's treatment of Nestor's story in *Iliad* 11 wholly satisfactory; but this passage will reward closer attention.

'In paradigmatic digressions', Austin writes, 'the length of the anecdote is in direct proportion to the necessity for persuasion at the moment. The more urgent the situation, the more expansive the speech and its illustrative paradigm. The two longest digressions, the story of Meleager in Book 9 and Nestor's story of the Pylians and Eleians in Book 11, mark the two most desperate stages in the deteriorating situation' (306). But Austin has exaggerated the urgency of the situation: the Trojans have not yet breached the wall, and there are four whole books before they reach the ships—books which allow a short-lived Greek rally, aided by Poseidon, and during which Patroclus dallies attending to Eurypylus. Nor is Nestor trying to sway the obdurate Achilles in person; he is speaking to Patroclus—he will conclude by asking Patroclus to intercede with Achilles, but little persuasive skill is necessary to gain that request. When Patroclus does make his appeal to Achilles, at the beginning of Book 16, with the crisis really upon us,[46] his speech is brief and to the point (16. 21–45); the same is true of Ajax's speech in *Iliad* 9 (9. 624–42), which is the speech which has most effect on Achilles.[47] Nestor himself, when he really has an exhortatory point to push home by means of a reminiscence, elsewhere speaks concisely rather than expansively (see 1. 259–74, 23. 629–43). Moreover, Victoria Pedrick has noted that Nestor's speech differs in several other respects from normal paradigms: the exhortation is implicit, the addressee is absent, it is substantially longer, and it is not adapted to the circumstances of the addressee.[48] It would be reasonable to infer from this (as Pedrick does not) that the story is not meant as a paradigm. This is suggested too by the way in which it is introduced (11. 666–9); it expresses Nestor's sense of grief at his incapacity in extreme old age to do anything to prevent the imminent disaster. Although at the end Nestor draws a contrast with Achilles (762–3) this does not receive much emphasis, and serves rather as a transition to the appeal to Patroclus. So

[46] The crisis is marked not by expansion but by frequent shifts of attention: BT 15. 390.

[47] Austin 1966, 306 n. 21: 'A comparison of Achilleus' reply to Odysseus with his reply to Phoinix will show at once which ambassador was the more ineffectual.' A comparison of Achilles' reply to Ajax with his reply to Phoenix is also relevant.

[48] Pedrick 1983, 57.

Austin's account of the rhetoric of this digression does not really match the evidence. Nor is this surprising. Elaboration can be used to amplify and emphasize, but there must be a limit to its effectiveness; unlimited elaboration is not unlimited amplification. It seems reasonable to conclude, therefore, with the ancient commentators, that the poet has exploited Nestor's characteristic garrulity for his own digressively ornamental ends.[49]

Austin begins his essay with the observation that, as a result of recent studies in orality, 'scholars are more cautious about imposing their own aesthetic bias on Homer and making anachronistic demands on him' (295). But he adds:

A danger of this new receptive attitude, however, is that while Homer may be vindicated as a historical personage, as an artist he may be merely excused. Some modern studies, particularly those on the paratactic style of Homer, have not so much settled the question of unity in the Homeric poems as evaded the issue by denying the value of the search for unity, or at least any unity which we would recognise as such, in an oral poet.

I am far from wanting to abandon the search for unity in Homer;[50] but it does seem rather as if Austin is here retracting with one hand the methodological concession he has just made with the other. If failing to have 'any unity which we could recognise as such' is something that would need 'excuse'—a fault, therefore—and if drawing the conclusion that Homer fails thus is a 'danger'—to be shunned, therefore—how are we to avoid 'imposing our own aesthetic bias' on the poems? For that, surely, is precisely to require that the poems be unified in a way that 'we would recognise'.

Combellack, in a review of Moulton's book on Homeric similes, is firmly opposed to anachronistic demands:[51]

This is another book on Homer of a type that has become quite common in this country during the last decade or two: a great deal of ingenuity will be employed in discovering beauties that had not previously been noticed. Many of these beauties will be of a sort that modern American critics believe are essential to a great poet.

---

[49] On Nestor's speech see Cantieni 1942, 18–23. It should be added that the scholia do also see it as a paradigm addressed to Patroclus: T 11. 670–764, A and BT 11. 717–8, BT 11. 721, T 11. 747, BT 11. 761.
[50] See n. 43 above for my reservations about the studies which Austin has in view (references 295–6 n. 1).
[51] Combellack 1978, 129, reviewing Moulton 1977.

Taplin, citing this passage in his own review of the same book, comments:[52]

The insinuation is to be doubly resisted. First there is no reason to suppose that the virtues looked for by modern critics are necessarily inappropriate to Homer; secondly, we have no secure external guide to the proper virtues of a primitive heroic bard.

This is, up to a point, true. But what is not 'necessarily inappropriate' may still not, in fact, be appropriate; and when a critic finds realized in a text the artistic preferences of a culture remote from that in and for which it was composed, the interpretations on which that discovery rests merit some reserve. To overcome this reserve it is not enough to point, as Taplin does, to the indubitable presence of those virtues in the text: 'The poem itself is the only sound evidence for the presence or absence of any particular set of "beauties".' That is hermeneutically naïve. We do not inspect 'the poem itself' without presupposition, and our presuppositions dispose us to find plausible or implausible interpretations of one or another kind; that for readers of Homer in other cultures other sorts of artistry have been there 'for all to see' (Taplin's phrase again) should make us hesitate in believing the evidence of our own eyes. Can we impose a control, therefore? Again, Taplin is right when he says that we have no secure external guides; but we do have some guides, admittedly insecure. We know something of how Greeks of various periods read and valued the Homeric (and other) poems. It must be stressed: the danger of anachronistic imposition arises here also, since the culture of Hellenistic scholarship, too, was remote from that in and for which the Homeric poems were composed. But there is—one must insist—'no reason to suppose' that the virtues looked for by ancient critics are 'necessarily inappropriate'; and their culture was, at any rate, less remote—the cultural continuity was greater, not least because of the extent to which the Homeric poems formed and dominated later Greek literary practice.[53]

The reading of Homer by later Greek critics has, therefore, to be taken seriously; even if it is not accepted, in whole or in part, it will

[52] Taplin 1980, 184. I should stress that I am concerned here with the methodological point, and not with the merits—which are genuine—of Moulton's book.

[53] The continuing availability of Homer as a shared point of reference was the single most important factor in promoting the continuity of the Greek literary tradition. This is not, of course, to deny that, since perceptions of Homer themselves changed, the reference-point was not simply stable.

serve to remind us how rash it would be to assume the validity of our own preferred modes of reading. I do believe, in fact, that a good case can be made out for the general approach which the scholia adopt, at least to the questions we have been studying here; their aesthetic bias does appear to give a better account of the evidence afforded by the texts. Nevertheless, the interpretation of Homer as such inevitably remains beyond the scope of the present study; our immediate concern here is with the Greek secondary literature as such. I hope to have done enough in this chapter to show that the scholiasts' approach agrees with the rest of the Greek critical tradition in its tolerance of centrifugal composition.[54]

[54] I add, for completeness, the one reference to unity which I have found in the scholia (Eust. 5. 33–6): 'the *Iliad* is a single body, continuous (συνεχές) throughout and well-constructed (εὐάρμοστον)'; this is not further explained, but is contrasted with the book-division imposed by the Peisistratean and later editors.

9

The Neoplatonist Turn

I HAVE been arguing that the Greek critical tradition takes a consistently centrifugal view of literary unity; in this chapter we shall consider the one important exception to this general pattern, the theory of unity developed by the later Neoplatonists.[1] Critics of this school were convinced that a literary work must have one single *skopos* (σκοπός), one target, goal, or intention. In order to accommodate the texts they studied to this assumption, they used exegetical methods strikingly similar in some respects to modern techniques of thematic integration; but within the Greek tradition the Neoplatonist approach was a definite innovation.

The fundamental premiss is most clearly formulated in the anonymous *Prolegomena to Platonic Philosophy*, a text probably of the sixth century AD. This treatise provides a list of ten principles to be observed when establishing the *skopos* of a dialogue, the first and most important of which is unity (21. 18–26):

One or many: we must maintain that a dialogue has a single *skopos*, not many. How could Plato's dialogues have many *skopoi*, when he praised the divine on account of its unity? Moreover, he says himself that a dialogue resembles a living organism, since every text does so; for any well-written text is analogous to a living organism; so if a dialogue is analogous to a living organism, and a living organism has a single *telos*, i.e. the good (for that is the reason for its existence), then a dialogue too should have a single *telos*, that is, one *skopos*. So one cannot accept the view that *Phaedo* has three *skopoi*—the immortality of the soul, dying well, and the life of the philosopher; this is mistaken, as we have said, since there should not be many *skopoi*, but only one.

This strict thematic integration of the text does not necessarily exclude diversity. Although Proclus does emphasize Plato's moral disapproval of literary *poikilia* in his commentary on *Republic* (e.g., i

---

[1] For a general discussion of Neoplatonist theories of literary unity see Coulter 1976, 77–94.

46. 14–19, 49. 21–30 Kroll; cf. Chapter 3 above), other Neoplatonists were willing to stress its virtues. Olympiodorus, for example, draws a somewhat unexpected conclusion from the organic analogy: a well-composed text should resemble, not any living organism, but the best; the best living organism is the cosmos as a whole; and as the cosmos contains within it a diversity of lesser organisms, so a dialogue should be full of contrasting characters (*In Alc.* 56. 14–18 Westerink, Creuzer's pagination).² The author of the *Prolegomena*, too, asks why Plato, disapproving as he did of variety (τὰ ποικίλα τῶν πραγμάτων), wrote dialogues containing diverse characters (ἐκ ποικίλων προσώπων). He points out that this variety is less open to objection in a philosophical dialogue, in which the bad characters are instructed and improved, than in drama, and then lists seven positive reasons for adopting the dialogue form: of these the first three explore the analogy between cosmos and text, concluding (with Olympiodorus) that the dialogue's resemblance to the cosmos makes it the most perfect fulfilment of the organic analogy, while the seventh observes that to have a variety of speakers is more interesting than continuous exposition by one person (14–15 Westerink). Nevertheless, whatever diversity there is in a text must, in the same author's view, be subordinated strictly to the text's unifying *skopos*.

The application of this principle can be illustrated well from Hermias' commentary on *Phaedrus*.³ Hermias discusses at length the dialogue's putatively single *skopos* (8. 15–9. 10, 10. 26–12. 25 Couvreur), mentioning various opinions: (i) it is about love, the topic with which the dialogue starts; (ii) it is about rhetoric: the speeches are included for the purpose of comparison and criticism, and it is to true

² Cf. Plotinus 3. 2. 11: Providence makes 'the things which are called bad'—i.e. inferior levels of being—to achieve *poikilia*, just as the painter does not only use beautiful colours (cf. Pl. *Rep.* 420cd) and the tragedian includes inferior characters as well as heroes in his play. Among Latin authors I note that Macrobius uses the cosmic analogy ('non aliam secutus ducem quam ipsam rerum omnium matrem naturam') when describing Vergil's range of diverse styles as 'concordia dissonorum' (*Sat.* 5. 1. 18). He describes in a similar way ('concordia ex dissonis', 1 *Praef.* 9) the structure of his own work; but this is designedly and professedly a mixture of diverse subjects (i.e. it has no single *skopos*), even though the imposition of order nevertheless makes it a unified body ('in ordinem instar membrorum cohaerentia', 1 *Praef.* 3; 'unde unum fiat', 1 *Praef.* 8). In his commentary on Cicero's *Somnium*, however, Macrobius does raise the question of the '*propositum*, which the Greeks call σκοπός' (1. 4. 1), and seeks to exculpate Plato and Cicero from the charge of having included 'superfluous' material in their work (1. 1. 3).
³ This commentary seems to have been based largely on the lectures of Syrianus: see Praechter 1912, 733–5; Bielmeier 1930, 29–39.

rhetoric and the nature of excellence in composition that the dialogue returns at the end; (iii) it is about the soul as motive principle (περὶ τῆς ψυχικῆς ἀρχῆς): this view (which takes as 245c9 as the key to the dialogue's *skopos*) combines the two preceding suggestions, since love is an internal movement of the soul, while speech is its movement outward; (iv) it is about the soul as such: hence the discussion of immortality, and the charioteer-analogy designed to establish the nature of the soul; (v) it is a theological dialogue concerning the good: hence its climax is the vision of transcendent reality in 247c; (vi) it is about original beauty (περὶ τοῦ πρώτου καλοῦ). Hermias objects that these all take part of the dialogue and illegitimately generalize from it a *skopos* that fails to account for the whole; the organic analogy requires not only a single *skopos*, but also one that accounts for every element of the text (9. 6–9, 11. 11–19).[4] This is the third principle propsed in the anonymous *Prolegomena*, that ἐκ τοῦ ὅλου καὶ μέρους (22. 1–6):

> *Total or partial*: we should not make the content of a small part of the dialogue its *skopos*, but the teaching of the whole. Thus we reject the view that the *skopos* of *Phaedrus* is rhetoric; for that is discussed there only briefly, while the dialogue as a whole deals with universal beauty (τοῦ διὰ παντὸς κάλλους), which should therefore be regarded as its *skopos*.

Hermias himself adopts Iamblichus' theory concerning the *skopos* of *Phaedrus*, that it is about beauty in all its forms (περὶ τοῦ παντοδαποῦ καλοῦ, 9. 9–10). The dialogue begins with phenomenal beauty—the physical beauty of the beloved of Lysias' speech (whom Hermias assumes to be Phaedrus himself);[5] thence it ascends to beauty in speech (Phaedrus' love of λόγοι is more elevated than Lysias' physical passion); to spiritual beauty—virtue and understanding—in Socrates' speech, and in his palinode to the beauty of the cosmic deities (τὸ τῶν ἐνκοσμίων θεῶν); finally to 'intelligible beauty and the very source of beauty and the god Eros and beauty itself'; there is then a

---

[4] In his note on *Phdr.* 264bc, the passage from which the organic analogy is derived, Hermias argues on metaphysical grounds that the principle of the single, all-embracing *skopos* is necessary (231. 6–10): 'Why must a text be unified? Wherever the light of beauty or excellence is shed, the source of that light is unity; nothing whatsoever is capable of excellence that does not participate in unity. Thus beauty itself is not beautiful unless all its elements are unified. So, for example, Lysias' speech, because it did not possess unity, possessed no beauty either.'

[5] Although Hermias does not make the point, this is an example of the thematic integration of the dialogue's circumstantial details recommended, as we shall see, by Iamblichus, Syrianus, and Proclus.

descent through spiritual beauty in the rest of the palinode to beauty in speech, so that the dialogue as a whole executes a circular movement (συνάπτει τελευτὴν ἀρχῇ: 11. 19–12. 5).

Hermias' account of the ascending and descending movement of *Phaedrus* is illuminating, but it might be thought to display, not the unity of the dialogue's *skopos*, so much as the skill with which Plato has drawn many *skopoi* into an artistically ordered whole. For while it is true that beauty occurs in the various sections of the dialogue, it hardly follows that beauty is what those sections are about—that is, that beauty is their common *skopos*. To write about the soul's vision of and yearning for transcendent beauty, for example, is not to write about beauty as such; in this context, surely, it is to write about love. But, as Hermias rightly says, love is not a *skopos* of the whole. In Chapter 2 I argued that the *Phaedrus* need not be read as a thematically integrated composition; and I think it is clear that Plato's statements of principle—including his use of the the organic analogy—do not, as the Neoplatonists supposed, imply their theory of unique *skopos*.

The novelty of the Neoplatonist approach can be seen very clearly if we compare Proclus' treatment of Plato's *Republic* with that of Dio Chrysostom. In his *Euboean Discourse* (7. 127–32) Dio argues that digressions (ἐκτροπαὶ τῶν λόγων) should not be criticized as departing from the subject-matter of the whole, even if they are very long, provided they are not about trivial or inappropriate topics, since the speaker in a philosophical discourse has not really departed from his overall subject-matter (ὑπόθεσις) if he is still treating of philosophically serious matters (περὶ τῶν ἀναγκαίων καὶ προσηκόντων φιλοσοφίᾳ). Dio suggests the image of a hunter who, while following one trail, comes across another; he will follow up the fresh trail, and then return to take up his original pursuit. There is an obvious echo here of the Socratic notion of following an argument where it leads, and Plato himself uses hunting imagery in this connection.[6] Although unannounced, it is the *Republic* which Dio has in mind: one should not find fault, he says, with someone who sets out to discuss the just individual and justice, but having introduced the city and constitution as an illustration goes on to discuss the constitution exhaustively. Dio adds: 'But if what is said has nothing to do with the question in hand (τὸ προκείμενον), and if it throws no light on the subject of

---

[6] *Rep.* 35d1–2, cf. (e.g.) 432b7–d3, *Laches* 194b5–9, *Lysis* 219c4–5.

enquiry on account of which the discussion was originally taken up—
in that case, if at all, criticism is not wholly unjustified' (7. 131). In
isolation this might be understood as demanding unity of *skopos*; in
context, however, the meaning is clear: if an intended illustration
does not function as such at all, then its presence is unjustified; but if
it does so function, then it is legitimate to develop it to an extent
disproportionate to that limited use, so long as that development has
some philosophically serious intent.

Dio's position seems to be this: if on the course of discussing one
topic another topic suggests itself, then it is perfectly legitimate to
pursue the new topic far beyond its bearing on the original theme, as
a subject of discussion in its own right. It must have some bearing on
the original theme, or its introduction would be arbitrary; but beyond
that point of connection (or departure) the criterion to be applied is
not relevance to the main theme or any abstract principle of artistic
proportion, but intrinsic philosophical interest. This, as we have seen
in previous chapters, is a wholly conventional position. Dio says
something similar, and throws a little more light on his idea of
philosophical importance, in 12. 38: the philosopher finds it hard to
check the course of his discussion, since the various points that occur
to him all seem useful and important for his audience (ξυμφέροντος
καὶ ἀναγκαίου τοῖς ἀκροωμένοις); after all, he continues, as someone or
other said, we are not subject to the water-clock. That 'someone' was
of course Plato himself; the image is taken from *Theaetetus* 172de, one
of the passages which we discussed in Chapter 2, and we saw reason
there to conclude that Dio's interpretation is essentially correct.

Proclus' commentary on Plato's *Republic* takes a very different view.
The first prefatory topic is the question of the dialogue's *skopos* (i 7. 5–
7 Kroll). Proclus mentions two opinions: some say that its theme
(πρόθεσις) is justice and the just man—for that is the first question
raised in it, and the discussion of the state is introduced in order to
provide an answer to it; others, including Aristotle and Theophrastus,
argue that the question of justice is raised only to prepare the way for
the discussion of the state, so that the dialogue's real theme is
constitutional (i 7–11). Proclus accepts and tries to reconcile the
arguments of both parties; the dialogue is about justice and it is about
the state. But that does not mean that it has two distinct *skopoi*; rather,
the 'two' topics are essentially one, justice being to the individual soul
what a good constitution is to the state—an analogy crucial to Plato's
own argument, as Proclus reminds us. So the dialogue does not move

between two different questions, but between two ways of formulating a single question (i 11–14). Proclus is insistent that the dialogue cannot be thought to have two *skopoi*; if it resembles, as it ought, a living organism (ζῷον) it must have one *skopos* only, just as the parts of an organism are disposed according to a single ordering principle (ὁμολογία: i 11. 8–12). Proclus has already referred to the organic analogy in a preliminary review of his prefatory topics. The seventh and last of these is 'to display the coherent thread of doctrine running through the whole work, and to demonstrate—as Plato puts it in *Phaedrus*—that the treatise as a whole has the structure (σύστασις) of a single organism, the parts and limbs of which are ordered in relation to each other' (i 6. 24–7. 1); this, he says, will clarify the individual headings and their interrelation, and will show how they all look towards a single *skopos* (i 7. 1–4).

The distinctiveness of the Neoplatonic approach is evident also in the treatment of the dramatic aspects of Plato's dialogues. Proclus begins his commentary on *Parmenides* by discussing the occasion and place of the dialogue's setting, the participants, the course of the discussion (618–30 Cousin); he then moves on to the question of the dialogue's unique *skopos*. Just as one ascends from sensible phenomena to the intelligible, he says, so one must ascend from the dialogue's circumstantial detail (τὰ ὑποκείμενα ... περιστατικά) to its single theme (πρόθεσις) or end (τέλος); time, place, participants—all must have a bearing on that one *skopos* (630. 21–36). In interpreting Plato, therefore, one must pay careful attention to the dramatic circumstances of each dialogue and the way they are set forth in the prologue; to suppose that Plato's prologues are, like those of Heracleides and Theophrastus, unrelated to what follows (ἀλλότρια ... τῶν ἑπομένων) is intolerable, since that would violate Plato's own principle of organic order (659. 12–23). The same point is made in the commentary on *Alcibiades* I: 'The prologues of Plato's dialogues are in accord with their overall *skopoi*; he did not devise them for the sake of dramatic entertainment (δραματικῆς ἕνεκα ψυχαγωγίας) ..., nor is their purpose purely historical, as some have supposed.' In opposition to the historicizing theory he points out how unlikely it is that everything said and done on a given occasion should tend, like the elements of a carefully ordered text, to a single end; rather, Plato selects from and supplements the record of what actually took place so that each text contains exclusively what will bear on the particular *skopos* he has in view in that text (18. 13–19. 10 Westerink; Creuzer's pagination). He credits this approach to 'my masters (καθηγεμό-νες)'—that is, in particular, Syrianus;[7] so, too, in discussing the Atlantis-myth in *Timaeus*, Proclus records that Iamblichus and 'my master' did not regard Plato's account as merely historical in intent (as did Crantor), nor as a philosophical myth without foundation in history: they accepted its historicity, while also reading it allegorically as a text of the widest philosophical significance, 'just as we are accustomed to relate what precedes the subject-matter (ὑποκείμενα) of the dialogues to the same *skopos* as the dialogues themselves' (i 77. 24–78. 11 Diehl).

This is clearly polemical. Although Proclus and his masters would have contested my claim that Plato did not anticipate their theory, they were well aware that their treatment of the prologues of Plato's dialogues was opposed to an orthodox opinion in rhetorical theory. Pseudo-Hermogenes observes that the dialogue interweaves passages expressive of character (ἠθικοὶ λόγοι) and passages of argument and enquiry (ζητητικοὶ λόγοι); he continues (*Meth.* 455. 1–5 Rabe):

When one combines conversation and enquiry, the insertion of passages expressive of character allows the mind to relax (ἀναπαύουσι τὴν ψυχήν); and when that has been done, the enquiry is reintroduced. Thus tension and relaxation alternate, as in a musical instrument.

As we have seen, the concepts employed here are wholly typical of Greek rhetorical theory. Among those who took this rhetorical view and adopted a correspondingly relaxed attitude to Plato's dramatic prologues was Longinus, a critic and minor philosopher contemporary with Plotinus; Porphyry studied under him, and Plotinus himself is reported to have held a low view of him as a philosopher. Proclus reports with disapproval his views on the Atlantis-myth (*In Tim.* i 83. 19–25):

Longinus found it difficult to see Plato's intention in including this narrative: he was not giving his audience a relaxing interlude (διαναπαύων), nor was there any need to mention it. He resolved the problem (as he thought) by saying that Plato inserted it before the discussion of physics so as to entertain (ψυχαγωγῶν) his readers and prepare them (προθεραπεύων) to face the rigours of that exposition.

That is to say, Longinus thought that the myth was devised purely

[7] For Proclus' debt to Syrianus see Sheppard 1980, 39–103 (see also n. 3 above).

to give pleasure (δι' ἡδονήν, 83. 27–8).[8] Later Proclus records that Longinus did not treat the whole prologue of Timaeus as 'super-fluous', but only the account of Atlantis and Egypt (i.e. 20c–27a); by contrast, Severus had omitted the entire prologue from his exposi-tion;[9] but Porphyry and Iamblichus both, though in different ways, gave an account of the prologue that coheres with the overall theme (πρόθεσις) of the dialogue (i 204. 16–27).

This mention of Severus brings us to a further point: that we can discern the development of the principle of unique *skopos* within the Neoplatonist tradition itself; the decisive innovations are attributable to Iamblichus.[10] This is not to deny that there was discussion of *skopoi* before the Neoplatonists. For example, an anonymous first- or second-century commentator on *Theaetetus* remarks in his introduc-tion:[11]

Some Platonists have considered that the dialogue is about the criterion of knowledge; it would, however, be preferable to say that it is about knowledge simple and uncompounded: to this end it necessarily investigates the criter-ion.

Porphyry, too, discusses the theme (πρόθεσις) of Aristotle's *Categor-ies* in his commentary—he asserts that it is concerned with words rather than with categories of being (57. 16–59. 33 Busse). He goes on to argue that Aristotle was not being neglectful of this *skopos* in the

---

[8] Cf. Longinus' concern with stylistic and artistic explanation of the details of Plato's text: Proclus records his comments on the exallage in the first sentence of *Tim.* (I 14. 7–20), and his claims that Plato used stylistic embellishments (καλλωπίσαντα τὸν λόγον) for entertainment (ψυχαγωγία, i 59. 10–31) and that he took pains over the grace and *poikilia* of his diction (i 86. 19–24). In the last case Proclus cites Plotinus' remark that Longinus was a φιλόλογος, not a φιλόσοφος (i 86. 24–5), and approves a suggestion of Iamblichus, who saw in Plato's lexical variation a reflection of the variety of reality; this, he says, is worthy of Plato, not that 'preoccupation with style (πολυπραγμοσύνη τῆς λέξεως)' (i 87. 6–15).

[9] So, too, Calcidius: 'Denique de principio libri, quo simplex narratio continebatur rerum ante gestarum et historiae veteris recensitio, nihil dixi, rationem tamen totius operis et scriptoris propositum et ordinationem libri declaranda esse duxi' (58. 26–59. 1 Waszink); he begins his commentary at 31c.

[10] On what follows, see Praechter 1910, Larsen 1972, 428–49 (449–62 give a historical survey of the influence of Iamblichus' hermeneutics, but it is flawed by a failure to distinguish concern with *skopos* as such from Iamblichus' insistence on strict unity of *skopos*), Pépin 1974.

[11] Ed. H. Diels and W. Schubart (Berliner Klassikertexte II, Berlin 1905), ii 11–23. One might also consider here the 'second titles' of Plato's dialogues, descriptive of their subject; these can be traced back to the Hellenistic period (Call. *Ep.* 23. 4, with Pfeiffer ad loc.), and probably to the fourth century: see Hoerber 1957, Tigerstedt 1977, 110 n.4.

introductory discussion of homonymy, synonymy, and paronymy
(59. 34-60. 19); but when he suggests that Aristotle included this
material in the introduction so as not to disrupt the text's continuity
by digressions (ἵνα μὴ . . . παρεκβάσεις ποιοῖ καί διακόπτοι τὸ συνεχές),
his underlying concern seems to be as much with clarity of exposition
as with unity of theme. More significantly, Porphyry's exegesis of the
'Cave of the Nymphs' in the *Odyssey* does not adhere to the centripetal
principle of unique *skopos*; Pépin speaks aptly of its 'pluralisme
calculé'.[12] Diverse allegorical significances are discerned in the
Homeric text, and no systematic attempt is made to subordinate them
to a single theme. Porphyry evidently took a more liberal view of
skopos.

The strict insistence on integration that we found in Proclus and
other later commentators, and the association of that requirement
with Plato's organic analogy, seems to have been due to Iamblichus.
Certainly he adopted a more systematic and self-conscious approach
than did his predecessors, as his criticisms of previous commentators
reveal. In particular, his application to exegesis of the concept of an
analogical relationship between different levels of reality made
available a far more powerful mode of integration; the presence, for
example, of ethical discussion in a physical or metaphysical dialogue
can be systematically reconciled with the presupposition of unique
skopos by transposing it into physics or metaphysics—as, for example,
Proclus reads the myth of Atlantis in *Timaeus* allegorically as a
reflection on the role of conflict in the cosmos. We have seen that
Proclus praises Porphyry and Iamblichus for giving an interpretation
of the prologue of *Timaeus* 'in accord with the overall theme
(πρόθεσις) of the dialogue'; he adds, however, that Porphyry did this
in a more partial manner (μερικώτερον), Iamblichus more 'epopti-
cally' (ἐποπτικώτερον, i 204. 24–27). Porphyry has already been
criticized for giving an ethico-political interpretation of the prologue
of a physical dialogue (i 19. 24-9):[13]

    [12] Pépin 1965, 246. On Neoplatonist exegesis of Homer in general, see Friedl 1936,
Lamberton 1986 (esp. 108–33 for Porphyry).
    [13] Cf. i 24. 12–24, 29. 31–30. 19, 116. 27–117. 28. The first two of these references
are to comments on *Tim.* 17a and 17bc respectively; since these passages are
summarizing *Rep.*, one might have thought an ethico-political interpretation acceptable; but that would offend against the principle of unique *skopos*—for a summary
included in *Tim.* must be referred to the *skopos* of *Tim.*—and the passages must
therefore be read εἰκονικῶς (30. 2–15, cf. 1. 17–24). Iamblichus himself is criticized for
interpreting the text μερικώτερον, contrary to his own precepts, in i 174. 28–175. 2.

Porphyry interprets almost everything that precedes the discussion of physics in terms of politics, applying it to virtue and . . . obligation, while Iamblichus interprets it in terms of physics; for everything should be in accord with the current *skopos*, and this dialogue is physical rather than ethical in nature.

It follows that the claim that both interpreters connect the prologue with the theme of the whole dialogue can be taken only loosely (Proclus means: by comparison with Severus and Longinus). But since he does make that claim, however loosely, the term 'partial' (μερικώτερον) applied to Porphyry's reading cannot be meant in the sense of the canon 'total or partial' (ἐκ τοῦ ὅλου καὶ μέρους) which we saw applied by Hermias; that is, it does not imply that Porphyry's interpretation accounted for only part of the text to be explained. Rather, Porphyry is being criticized for his failure to ascend analogically to the more elevated and esoteric (ἐποπτικώτερον) philosophical plane on which Iamblichus' reading moves. Thus the contrast refers to the second of the rules recorded in the anonymous *Prolegomena*, that ἐκ τοῦ καθόλου καὶ μερικοῦ (21. 29–35):

General or particular: we should choose the more general and comprehensive *skopos* in preference to the more particular one. So one cannot accept the view that the *skopos* of *Sophist* is the sophist; rather, one should accept the view that it is the non-existent. For a sophist is something non-existent, but non-existence as such is more general than a non-existent particular; and if it is more general, it is more comprehensive, so that the more general *skopos* embraces the partial one.

There is, however, an indirect relation to the third rule, 'total orpartial', for it is by means of his analogical ascent to the more general or 'epoptic' level that Iamblichus achieves his superior thematic integration of the dialogue. This evidence therefore supports our earlier conclusions about Porphyry's liberal approach to thematic unity, and confirms that the strictly centripetal theory was an innovation of Iamblichus.[14]

We have seen, in this chapter as in Chapter 7, that for traditional rhetoric neither unity nor the organic conception of the text excluded digression or entailed a unitary subject-matter—a single *skopos*, in Neoplatonist terms. To take one further illustration, an essay on

---

[14] Larsen 1972, 438–442, notes Proclus' reference to 'canons . . . for discovering the *skopoi* of Platonic dialogues' (*In Remp.* i 6. 1–4), and argues that they were initially formulated by Iamblichus; those of the *Prolegomena* would represent a later elaboration. For the Iamblichean shift of levels in Hermias on *Phdr.*, see 28. 13–14, 54. 19–28.

'figured speeches' falsely attributed to Dionysius of Halicarnassus analyses Plato's *Apology* as combining (i) a defence of Socrates, (ii) an attack on the Athenians who tried him, (iii) an encomium of Socrates, and (iv) instruction on the philosophical character; thus it is a 'tying together' (συμπλοκή) or 'mixture' (κρᾶσις) of four subjects (ὑποθέσεις, ii 305. 5–306. 10, cf. 347–8). It is clear that a Neoplatonist exegete could not have accepted an analysis of this kind.

But rhetoric itself in due course came under Neoplatonist influence.[15] In this new context the question of *skopos* is commonly raised, and unity of *skopos* is sometimes explicitly required; this is so, for example, in the anonymous (fifth- or sixth-century) prolegomena to Aphthonius' *Progymnasmata* (*PS* 73. 18–74. 8), copied by John Doxapatres (*PS* 134. 10–135. 2), who elsewhere denies the possibility of multiple *skopoi* (*PS* 306. 9–22). Nevertheless, the principle of thematic unity does not seem to have been attached to the organic analogy by these authors, even though the analogy flourished in diverse and often exotic forms.

Hermogenes was the authoritative rhetorical text for the later Neoplatonists; we have commentaries on *Peri Staseon* and *Peri Ideon* by Syrianus, Proclus' 'master'.[16] He comments only briefly on the elaborate use of the analogy in the introduction to 'beauty' (κάλλος);[17] but when Hermogenes subsequently alludes to that discussion in defining eloquence (δεινότης) as 'the correct use of all the previously mentioned forms (εἴδη) and their opposites, and of the other things of which the body of the text consists' (368. 23–369. 2 Rabe), Syrianus explains that 'forms' is used catachrestically for the stylistic 'ideas', and that the 'other things' are the στάσεις, or kinds of case, and the formal divisions of the text: 'for when all these are assembled in one place they construct a most beautiful body for the text, and—as Plato says—they make it resemble a complete organism' (i 84. 20–85. 2 Rabe). Thirdly, he cites Porphyry as the source of a novel application, in which the expression (ἑρμηνεία) of a text is analogous to its body, while the content (νοημάτων εὕρεσις) is analogous to its soul (i 93. 9–13, ii 14. 9–14).

---

[15] See, in general, Kustas 1973, 5–26; Hunger 1978, i 65–196; Kennedy 1983.

[16] See Kennedy 1983, 77–9, 109–12.

[17] He explains that, in the συμμετρία μελῶν καὶ μερῶν, the two terms represent respectively limbs (e.g. head, arm, leg) and their constituent parts (e.g. eyes, ears, fingers, toes), and that these are analogous to the ideas and their constituents (i 62. 21–63. 2). (The passages of Hermogenes are discussed in ch. 7 above.)

Porphyry's version of the analogy enjoyed a long career; it was used to explain the order of treatises in the Hermogenean corpus, being elaborated as that corpus expanded. An introduction to the *Peri Staseon* conjecturally attributed to the sixth-century rhetorician Marcellinus explains the order *Peri Staseon*, *Peri Ideon* thus (*PS* 291. 12–18; cf. 204. 25–205. 4, and—at wearisome length—Doxapatres, *PS* 308. 21–309. 17):

The ancients, too, worked on the assumption that a text consists, like a living organism, of a body and a soul; 'soul' was the term they applied to the arguments ... and 'body' to the phrasing and the external beauty which is produced by the [stylistic] ideas. As the soul is superior to the body, so that which resembles the soul takes precedence.

When *Peri Heureseos* was added to the corpus, one could apply 'body' to invention and redesignate expression as the external shape (μορφή) of the body (*PS* 345. 21–5).[18] A less satisfactory approach to the same question was to regard the text itself as a body, and stasis, invention, and idea as progressively smaller parts of that body (*PS* 345. 17–21)—or, a slight improvement, idea as the shape (μορφή) of the larger and smaller parts of the body (*PS* 257. 6–258. 1, taken over almost verbatim by Doxapatres, *PS* 367. 11–368. 1). Or: stasis is the whole body, invention its parts, idea its shape, and 'method' its behaviour (τρόποι): thus *PS* 348. 18–25.[19]

The analogy of the body and its parts was applied more plausibly to the formal partition of a speech, the sections of the speech being made to correspond to parts of the body. The comparison of proem with head is, of course, commonplace: we met it in the fourth century (see Chapter 2 above), and among later rhetoricians one might mention Nicolaus (40. 14–17 Felten) and the Seguerianus (i 431. 6–8 Spengel = 358. 1–3 Hammer); but John of Sardis (eighth- or ninth-century) has a modestly elaborated version (*PS* 358. 17–20), and John Siceliotes (eleventh-century) one of astonishing elaboration (*PS* 398. 3–23).

[18] In Marcellinus' scholia on *Peri Staseon*, the words of a text are described as the embodiment of the hypothesis, the idea as the μορφή of that body; the soul-content/body-expression analogy is added as the opinion of 'some' (*RG* iv 184. 30–185. 7 Walz). This is perhaps a difficulty in the attribution to Marcellinus of the passage quoted above.

[19] John Siceliotes analyses the constituents of the ideas according to a similar scheme: ἔννοια is soul, λέξις body, σχῆμα shape, μέθοδος the motion of the soul (*RG* vi 117. 32–118. 25, 139. 11–140. 2).

Finally, a more sophisticated use of the analogy is found in Phoebammon's debate with those opponents of Hermogenes who denied that the stylistic 'ideas' are knowable or imitable—a fundamental attack on the rhetorically crucial concept of stylistic imitation. Porphyry's version of the analogy—soul-content/body-expression—is restated (*PS* 376. 12–14), and becomes the basis for one of the arguments against Hermogenes: if the organic analogy is pressed, then styles are particulars, not universals, and thus innumerable and unknowable (*PS* 376. 18–21). Phoebammon turns the argument around: although it is not possible to give a full account of the individual quality of an animate body, one can have a partial understanding of its material composition; one can say that a human body comprises such-and-such parts, without being able to explain why it has precisely the complexion that it does (*PS* 382. 15–22).[20]

[20] See Brinkmann 1906, Kennedy 1983, 120–2.

10

Some Post-Classical
Developments

It is impossible to give a full account of the history of 'unity' in post-classical criticism in a single chapter; nor, indeed, would I be competent to provide an adequate account of the matter. But the subject is one of considerable interest, and potentially also of considerable use. We will find it hard to make ourselves aware of the characteristic assumptions of our own literary culture, if we are unable to trace their sources; and without self-awareness, there can be no self-criticism. Here I shall offer only a brief survey of some important trends in the criticism of narrative, lyric, and dramatic poetry.[1]

Many critics have complained that much medieval literature is marred by its uncontrolled digressiveness and thematic pluralism; Curtius' remark is representative:[2]

> The Middle Ages was far from demanding unity of subject and inner coherence of structure in a work of literature. Indeed, digression (*egressio*, *excessus*) was regarded as a special elegance ... Nor did anyone have any qualms about treating completely different subjects in a single work.

I hope that the aesthetic which is described here will seem a little less perverse in the light of the conclusions which we have reached in our investigations of ancient poetics; but it will be worth pursuing Curtius' two complaints a little further.

As to the charge of uncontrolled digression, it is noteworthy that in the flowering of poetic theory in the late twelfth and early thirteenth centuries strict control of digression was required.[3] Geoffrey of

---

[1] There is little of substance in Orsini 1975. For an interesting comparative perspective, note van Gelder 1982, a study of polythematic poetry and its treatment in classical Arabic criticism.

[2] Curtius 1953, 501–2; cf. e.g. the very unsympathetic recent presentation in Vickers 1988, 238–44.

[3] Klopsch 1980 provides an invaluable introduction to the field; note also Atkins 1943, 91–118, Murphy 1974, 135–94. D. C. Kelly has contributed two important papers relevant to our present inquiry (1966, 1969).

Vinsauf, the most influential of these theorists,[4] insists that the poet must plan his material and its disposition in the poem before putting pen to paper, and that he must keep the plan in view throughout the process of composition. He devotes much space to the techniques of *amplificatio*—not in the classical sense of intensification (although this sense is familiar to him: cf. *NP* 166off., on hyperbole), but in the more characteristically medieval sense of the expansion of one's text.[5] But Geoffrey is aware of the risks which these techniques incur. With Horace in mind (cf. *AP* 24–31) he insists that, just as one must beware of obscurity when treating a subject briefly, so one must avoid incoherence when pursuing diffuseness through amplification; the poet who wishes to 'amplify' his text in this sense must respect the 'universum corpus materiae', following its lineaments so that all the parts of one's text 'cohere' and the fault of 'incongrua partium positio' is avoided (*Doc.* 2. 3. 154). One of the techniques in question is digression ('digressio . . . ampliat et decorat materiam', *Doc.* 2. 2. 17). There are two kinds of digression (though the uses of digression are manifold): internal, when one moves from one part of the *materia* to another; and external, when one introduces comparison or simile (for this involves a reference to something that is not part of the 'corpus materiae': *Doc.* 2. 2. 21). But if one does introduce a digression, it must be 'competens et ad rem pertinens'; for example, a description that makes no contribution to the *materia* is faulty (*Doc.* 2. 3. 156). And one must be able to effect a return from it to one's *materia* (*Doc.* 2. 3. 135).

Similar views were expressed by John of Garland,[6] and by Gervaise of Melkeley, whose *Ars Poetica* adopts a scholastic approach in contrast with Geoffrey's rhetorical approach.[7] For Gervaise, it is legitimate to depart from one's material to something that is appropriate to it ('digressio est quando eximus ad aliquid materiae conveniens'); this might be a piece of poetic fiction, a comparison, a description—and description may be 'intrinsic' or 'extrinsic' (the latter being the description of something that is not strictly part of one's *materia*). But no digression is legitimate unless the author can

    [4] Text in Farel 1923.
    [5] This was discussed by classical rhetoricians under other headings: e.g. *ad Alex.* 1434b1–11. Cf. Cave 1979, 7–9, on medieval *amplificatio* and Renaissance *copia*; the whole chapter is relevant to our present theme.
    [6] Text in Lawler 1974; see pp. 72 (c. 4, 314–8), 84 (c. 5, 20ff.)—a rather confused discussion.
    [7] Text in Gräbener 1965; see pp. 65–7.

derive from it 'aliquod argumentum'; that is, it must make some contribution to the *res* in hand: 'descriptio vero nihil ad rem faciens nulla sit vel brevissima'. A similarly restrictive view was taken by Matthew of Vendôme, although his observation that older poets delighted in diversions and expansions to excess could be cited in support of the judgement of Curtius quoted above.[8]

Gervaise gives as an example of extrinsic description that does contribute to the *res* the Funeral Games in Statius' *Thebaid*; the description is warranted, because it enhances our impression of the authority and dignity of the Seven ('ut ex magnis actibus haberentur ... magis auctentici'). A number of similar explanations can be found in the commentary of Arnulf of Orleans on Lucan; for example: 2. 67: for *amplificatio* (in the classical sense); 4. 661: to display Curio's folly; 9. 734: to display Cato's *virtus*.[9] His notes illustrate Geoffrey's observation that the two modes of digression are used 'pluribus ex causis'; but it is also worth noting that, despite the restrictive attitude of contemporary theorists, the limiting case of digression 'causa delectationis' is still recognized in practice (9. 318).

The other point on which Curtius remarked was the lack thematic unity. The theorists we have mentioned do not formulate a requirement of unity of theme. They do require an appropriate choice and disposition of parts, but as with the classical texts we have considered, where thematic integration is not explicitly stated as a condition of appropriate composition, it would be rash to impose it. Gunn has impressively demonstrated that the structure of the thirteenth-century allegorical poem *La Roman de la Rose* conforms to the rhetoric and poetics of the period, refuting the unsympathetic view of Jean de Meung's continuation of Guillaume de Lorris' fragment taken by, among others, C. S. Lewis.[10] But Gunn's larger argument for the poem's 'unity', in the sense of a strict integration to a single basic theme, depends on implicit links and symbolism (for example, the rainbow as suggestive of Cupid's bow) of a kind which we have found reason in this study to treat with caution; Lewis, in a generally favourable review, was rightly sceptical in this respect.[11] That the

---

[8] *Ars Versificatoria* 4. 5 (Farel 1923, 181): 'Antiquis siquidem incumbebat materiam protelare quibusdam diversiculis et collateralibus sententiis, ut materiae penuria poetico figmento plenius exuberans in artificiosum luxuriaret incrementum. Hoc autem modernis non licet.'

[9] Text in Marti 1958; see pp. xxxix-xl of her introduction for discussion.

[10] Gunn 1952, Lewis 1936, 137–42.

[11] Lewis 1953; the example is from Gunn 1952, 266.

diverse topics on which the poet touches are reached by intelligible steps, each from the exposition of another, does not of course entail that they are all to be regarded as contributing to the exposition of some one theme in common.

We mentioned above Geoffrey of Vinsauf's concept of 'internal' digression, in which the poet moves between different parts of his *materia*; the distinction between natural and artificial order, which we have already encountered in classical contexts, was also important to medieval poetic theory.[12] It has been plausibly suggested that these two techniques explain the intricate structure of the medieval and early Renaissance romance, with their complex interweaving of separate strands of plot and inverted narrative order.[13] This point is of some interest for the history of concepts of unity, since this very structure was in due course to become a centre of unitarian controversy.

The rise and fall of Neoclassical norms in the criticism of epic is itself a fascinating illustration of the mutability of taste and, more specifically, of changing concepts of literary unity. In the opening pages of his book on Spenser, the eighteenth-century critic Thomas Warton remarks on the (to him) surprisingly slow advance of classicizing taste even after the Renaissance rediscovery both of the models (Homer) and of the precepts (Aristotle) of antiquity:[14]

But it was a long time before such a change was effected. We find Ariosto, many years after the revival of letters, rejecting truth for magic, and preferring the ridiculous and incoherent excursions of Boyardo, to the propriety of the Grecian and Roman models.

It is certainly true that the theorists of the Italian Cinquecento responded in diverse ways to Aristotle's requirement of unity of action in epic, and an Aristotelian—or would-be Aristotelian—consensus was only gradually established. Some critics rejected the requirement. Castelvetro, for example, held that a number of actions by one person, or indeed a number of actions by several people, are as legitimate in poetry as the single action of a single person demanded by Aristotle (note the common misunderstanding expressed in 'of a single person'); the single action is superior, in the sense that it

[12] See ch. 6 n. 11, ch. 8 n. 36 above. Scholia Vindobonensia in Hor.*AP*, 4–5 Zechmeister; Kelly 1969, 131–2, Quadlbauer 1982, Vickers 1988, 241; for the early Renaissance, see Herrick 1946, 16–20.
[13] Vinaver 1967, i. lxvii–lxviii, cf. iii. 1268–75.
[14] Warton 1762, i. 2 (first ed. 1754).

displays the ingenuity and skill of the poet more clearly—but that is only because multiple actions, being more varied, more interesting, and more enjoyable, are more readily handled with success.[15] Others, more subtly, side-stepped confrontation with Aristotle by recognizing the romance as a legitimate genre distinct from epic; while epic was subject to Aristotelian norms, romance was characterized by multiple actions. Giraldi Cintio took this line, citing Ovid's *Metamorphoses* as a model;[16] he describes the advantages of romance thus (23/264):

Diversity of actions carries with it variety, which is the spice of delight, and gives the author wide scope for introducing episodes, or pleasant digressions, and for bringing in events which in poems dealing with a single action cannot come about without some hint of blame.

He adds at once that these digressions must 'depend on one another and be well joined with a continuous thread and a continuous chain to the parts of the subject he has undertaken to treat'; but it soon becomes clear that he is thinking of formal rather than causal continuity, and in particular of the techniques of interruption, suspension, and resumption which Ariosto uses so skilfully in his interweaving of actions. Because this is form of narrative is technically more demanding, Giraldi regards romance as more praiseworthy than the continuity of epic, which is simply the sustained narrative of a single subject (39/267).

Giraldi did recognize that there are many 'episodes and digressions' in Homer and Vergil, 'which ... can bring about so much variety and delight that the poem will become very attractive and pleasing, without those breaks in the action that have been used by our writers' (42/268-9). Purists such as Tasso, a strenuous opponent of the romance and its multiplicity of plots, used this fact to disarm the argument from diversity; if variety is laudable 'it is laudable up to the point where it turns into confusion, and unity is itself quite capable of variety up to that point'—as the diversity of incident in Homer and Vergil proves.[17] The question at issue, therefore, was solely that of integration of plot; this leaves scope, as in Aristotle (see

[15] Castelvetro 1576, 179, tr. Gilbert 1940, 318-9. In general, see Weinberg 1961 (an account somewhat marred by the author's questionable understanding of Aristotelian theory), especially 433-6 (Giraldi), 509-10 (Castelvetro), 651-2 (Tasso), and (on Ariosto *vs* Tasso in general) 954-1073. For a more concise summary, see Spingarn 1908; note also Forcione 1970, 11-45.)
[16] Giraldi 1549, 19, tr. Gilbert 1940, 262-3.
[17] Book III of Tasso 1594 (tr. Tasso 1973, 65-86).

Chapter 4 above), for digression without prejudice to unity. Pontanus, for example, insists on unity of plot: 'Although there may be
many actions in an epic poem, nevertheless it is essential that they
constitute a single plot [*fabula*], just as many limbs constitute a single
body, and do not give birth to a Horatian monster'; but he continues:
'Over and above this, an epic poem should be dilated and amplified
with numerous episodes or digressions; their variety is extremely
charming, decorative, and pleasant.'[18] But Neoclassical criticism was
to become increasingly restrictive in this respect. Dryden reflects the
newly constrained concept of 'episode' in his account of the heroic
poem: 'The action of it is always one, entire, and great. The least and
most trivial episodes, or under-actions, which are interwoven in it, are
parts either necessary, or convenient to carry on the main design.'[19]

Tasso had been forced to recognize that in modern times romance
had enjoyed greater success than epic, although authority and reason
alike prove the superiority of the latter's unified action; Ariosto was
admired, Trissino forgotten. But Tasso's advocacy and his example
proved effective; during the dominance of Neoclassicism his *Gerusa-
lemme Liberata* was seen as, if somewhat imperfect in view of its
concessions to 'Gothic' taste, nevertheless part of the genuine epic
tradition of Homer and Vergil, in a way in which the structurally
flawed poems of Boiardo, Ariosto, and Spenser were not. This brings
us back to Warton. Most of his first chapter is devoted to castigating
Spenser's defective treatment of plot: 'It is an action consisting of
twelve actions, all great and unconnected between themselves, and
not composed of one uninterrupted and coherent chain of incidents,
tending to the accomplishment of one design.'[20] Warton is dismissive
of the various palliatives that had been proposed, and is willing to
concede only that the *Faerie Queene* is less at fault than *Orlando
Furioso*:[21]

---

[18] Pontanus 1597, 58 (first ed. 1594); note the post-classical sense of *amplificatio*. In
Book I of his *De Poetica* (1579) Viperanus devotes chapter 9 to the plot, chapter 10 to
episodes and digressions. A recent English translation renders the opening of the latter
('sed de ipsa tamen fabulae conformatione multa saepe vel ornandi, vel amplificandi
causa interseruntur . . . episodia') thus: 'Nevertheless in the structure itself of the story
many . . . episodes are often interposed for the sake of embellishment or amplification'
(1987, 29); but 'in the structure itself' is nonsensical here, and *conformatio* must be
meant in a sense more like 'fashioning, realization' (cf. the use of *confirmare* in Cic. *de Or.*
1.17).

[19] From the 'Dedication of the Aeneid' (1697); Dryden 1961, ii. 154.

[20] Warton 1762, i. 10–11.

[21] Warton 1762, i. 12. Cf. Kames's biting comment: 'If unity of action be a capital
beauty in a fable imitative of human affairs, a plurality of unconnected fables must be

There is indeed no general unity which prevails in the former, but, if one considers every book, or adventure as a separate poem, we shall meet with so many distinct, however imperfect, unities, by which an attentive reader is less bewildered, than in the maze of indigestion and incoherence, of which the latter totally consists, where we seek in vain for partial or universal integrity.

In the very last pages of the chapter, however, Warton produces a defence of the poem as 'the careless exuberance of a warm imagination and a strong sensibility' (i 15). He concludes (i 16):

If the Faerie Queene be destitute of that arrangement and oeconomy which epic severity requires, yet we scarcely regret the loss of these while their place is so amply supplied, by something which more powerfully attracts us: something, which engages the feelings of the heart, rather than the cold approbation of the head. If there be any poem, whose graces please, because they are situated beyond the reach of art, and where the force and faculties of creative imagination delight, because they are unassisted and unrestrained by those of deliberate judgement, it is this. In reading Spenser, if the critic is not satisfied, yet the reader is transported.

An intriguing situation has arisen. Warton the Neoclassical critic is horrified by Spenser's plot-construction; Warton the proto-Romantic reader is enchanted by his 'creative imagination'; neither has any conception of the distinct intellectual and aesthetic satisfaction to be derived from Spenser's, and still more from Ariosto's, cunning interlacing of disparate threads of action.

Warton's proto-Romantic move finds an interesting parallel in a near-contemporary study of Pindar. J. G. Schneider, taking up the controversy over Pindar's apparent digressiveness that had raged throughout the eighteenth century, argues that a correct understanding of the epinician programme greatly reduced the scale of the problem; but he concedes that there remain in Pindar myths 'to which one may reasonably object that they are alien and superfluous to the main theme (*Hauptinhalt*), that they are lacking in interest and

---

a capital deformity. For the sake of variety, we indulge an under-plot that is connected with the principal: but two unconnected events are extremely unpleasant, even when the same actors are engaged in both. Ariosto is quite licentious in this particular: he carries on at the same time a plurality of unconnected stories. His only excuse is, that his plan is perfectly well-adjusted to his subject; for everything in the *Orlando Furioso* is wild and extravagant' (Kames 1785, ii. 407–8, cf. i. 323–4; first ed. 1761). Kames refers here (cf. Warton, n. 14 above) to the magic and fantasy of romance: another controversial feature in Renaissance criticism where 'classical' decorum eventually triumphed.

proportion'.[22] The conventional explanation of this phenomenon was that Pindar was compelled to compensate for the barrenness of his subject—praising successful athletes—by introducing 'irrelevant' material. While for many critics this merely explained the fault, for some it removed it. Robert Lowth, for example, admired the poet's 'felix audacia' in digression: Pindar's limited and repetitive subject would have been tedious, had the poet not treated it with the greatest freedom; once one has understood the technical rationale of the poet's apparent waywardness, all objections are seen to be beside the point: 'Thus he has the excuse of necessity; it is not only pardon that he has won, but also—and deservedly—praise. What in other poets would be indefensible and intolerable can on this account be seen to warrant approval, and even praise.'[23] Schneider is aware of Lowth's treatment of this defence, but finds it unsatisfying; rather than appeal to technical necessity, he would prefer to abandon any attempt to defend Pindar's poetic practice and see in it 'a product of his heady and prodigal imagination' (83).

The earliest modern interpreters of Pindar, the commentators of the sixteenth and early seventeenth centuries, had noted his digressions and his plural themes with equanimity, and subjected them to rhetorical analysis. If Pindar's poems sometimes appeared wayward in their composition, they recognized the artifice with which the poet had contrived an illusion of spontaneity and inspiration, and looked beneath this surface to discern the underlying structure of each poem; if that structure proved digressive and thematically diverse they were not perturbed, for they had read the ancient rhetoricians with care. The criticism of lyric poetry indeed continued for some time to be an oasis of calm, by comparison with the criticism of epic and dramatic poetry, where demands for unity and integration were making themselves heard with increasing force. This anomalous treatment is explicable. In the absence of an Aristotelian or similarly authoritative formulation of the criteria of unity in lyric, classical norms for lyric must be derived directly from classical practice; as Dryden says: 'Thus Pindar, the author of those Odes, which are so admirably restored by Mr. Cowley in our language, ought for ever to be the standard of them; and we are bound, according to the practice of

---

[22] Schneider 1774, 73. I have discussed the history of Pindaric criticism, including eighteenth-century developments, in greater detail in Heath 1986b; the discussion is extended here.

[23] Lowth 1753, 257–8.

Horace and Mr. Cowley, to copy him.'[24] In such a case, the apparent waywardness of Pindar's practice itself becomes a norm, and one may, precisely on Neoclassical grounds, accord the lyric poet a *licentia digrediendi* that classicizing taste would normally have rejected. Masenius, writing in the mid-seventeenth century, reflects these conflicting inclinations; he cites from Horace's *Odes* examples of digression arising from the subject (1. 3, 1. 7) and of more remote digressions (2. 13, 3. 3), adding of the latter: 'Such *episodia* Horace defends rather by his authority and by his imitation of Pindar than by the excellence of a correctly ordered poem. Therefore, although I am unwilling to criticize, neither will I commend them; in imitation, one would do well to follow the former examples.'[25]

It is only with the advent of the eighteenth century, and even then only gradually, that this tolerant approach, reflected in Lowth's defence of the poet, was abandoned. The critics who first decisively rejected Pindar's authority as a lyric model were the 'modernists' of the *querelle des anciens et des modernes*, critics like Perrault and La Motte—for the *querelle* was precipitated not least by the discovery that classical authors were not in fact particularly 'classical'.[26] These critics were unable to regard digression and thematic plurality as components of an ordered underlying structure, and consequently could see no more in Pindar than his superficial waywardness; where predecessors had seen, in Boileau's phrase, 'un beau désordre', Perrault found a 'galimatias impénétrable'.[27] As the centripetal aesthetic gradually established itself in the study of Pindar, it manifested itself at first in the contention that Pindar's poetry was flawed by its failure to conform to such an aesthetic, and (eventually) in the emergent consensus that, despite appearances, it did conform after all. Schneider's work represents an advanced stage of this process, which culminated in the early nineteenth century in Boeckh's interpretation of the odes. Boeckh's method was founded on the premiss (anticipated in eighteenth-century criticism, but not applied so systematically) that apparent digressions were to be understood as commenting by implication on the victor's personal or political circumstances, which the interpreter may conjecturally reconstruct. But each poem's presentation of this 'objective' content was in turn

---

[24] From the 'Preface to Albion and Albinus' (1685); Dryden 1961, i. 272.
[25] Masenius 1661–4, ii. 331.
[26] See, e.g., Clarke 1981, 106–55 on Homer in the *querelle*.
[27] Perrault 1688, ii. 235.

intended to subserve a unifying moral purpose, the presentation of the poem's single *Grundgedanke*. We shall return to Boeckh's theory when we have considered some aspects of the history of dramatic criticism.[28]

If modern critics were asked to select two of Euripides' plays for special commendation few, I suspect, would nominate *Hecuba* and *Heracles*, plays frequently disparaged in modern times as broken-backed and lacking in unity; but these were the two plays singled out for praise by the sixteenth-century scholar Caspar Stiblinus in his edition of Euripides. *Hecuba* was traditionally the first play in the Euripidean corpus, and Stiblinus claims that it merits that honour:

> This play, both because of the variety and because of the exceptionally tragic grimness of its plot [propter argumenti tum varietatem, tum plusquam tragicam atrocitatem], rightfully takes first place; for it contains the captivity of Hecuba, the sacrifice of Polyxena, Polydorus' cruel murder, the blinding of Polymestor, and the pitiful stabbing and slaughter of his children.

Of *Heracles* he says that it is 'inferior to none of the preceding plays, whether one considers the economy of its composition, or the seriousness and variety of its plot, or the dire and grim reversals of fortune, of the kind that tragedies claim as peculiarly their own'.[29] The contrast between the complaints of 'disunity' so common in modern criticism of these two plays and Stiblinus' admiration for their *varietas* is striking and revealing. I confess that I have come to have more sympathy with the Renaissance scholar's view; and it is surely closer to the Greek attitudes surveyed in this book.

In addition to the occasional aesthetic evaluation, Stiblinus in his introduction to each play summarizes the plot and comments on the *scopus* (intent) or use of the play; that is, he indicates briefly the moral lessons to be learnt from it—as *Medea*, for example, is designed to

---

[28] In what follows I draw on the more detailed and better documented study of the history of Euripides' *Hecuba* in Heath 1987c. (In that paper I passed over Euripidean criticism in the nineteenth and early twentieth centuries, for which see now Michelini 1987, 3–51, and the colloquium published in *Greek, Roman and Byzantine Studies* 27(1986), 325–430.)

[29] Stiblinus 1546, 38, 626; he also admires Seneca's adaptation of *Heracles* for the elegance of its Latin, and for the skill with which he has adapted the 'economy' ('summo ingenio, ac summa arte'). The one play on which he passes an adverse judgement is *Electra* (its economy is 'in part rather frigid, and insufficiently coherent', 659); he regards its authenticity as doubtful. (This edition contains, in addition to a Greek text, Stiblinus' Latin translation, introduction and commentary to each play, together with Brodaeus' textual notes and two essays by Myconius.)

deter us, by means of a horrifying exemplum, from 'immoderate
loves and dishonourable lusts' (168), or *Bacchae* to promote piety
(475). I cannot deny that I am rather less in sympathy with his
approach to the plays in this respect; but it is not the adequacy of this
moralizing on which I wish to concentrate here, so much as its
implications for our investigation of changing concepts of unity.
Scopus is a term which we met in connection with the strictly
centripetal Neoplatonist approach to interpretation (Chapter 9); but
those centripetal implications are not present in Stiblinus.[30] His moral
exegesis stands in a continuous tradition with that of the ancient
scholia, and indeed with the moralizing view taken (for example) in
Aristophanes' *Frogs*.[31] In this tradition a text is not understood as an
integrated exposition of some single moral theme; rather, its narrative
unity provides a platform on which a plurality of moral lessons (as of
diverse emotional and ancillary effects) can be built. So Stiblinus
discerns in *Hippolytus*, in addition to the 'outstanding exemplum of
innocence and chastity' provided by the hero (who testifies in
particular to the morally beneficial effects of a vigorous outdoor life),
diverse moral counterexamples in the other characters; the critic
points out useful models and maxims without worrying about
thematic integration or the determination of a single overarching
scopus in the Neoplatonic sense.

This position, characteristic of sixteenth-century criticism, was
abandoned by stages. The first step was the exclusion by seventeenth-
century critics of digression. Daniel Heinsius, in his essay on tragedy,
still accepted the conventional distinction (which we have seen
already in connection with epic) between plot, every part of which
must be causally integral, and 'episodes' added to 'amplify' or
decorate the play.[32] André Dacier, by contrast, will admit 'episodes'
only if they are 'proper to the Subject, and drawn from the ground of
the Fable; ... so join'd with the Principle Act, that one is the
necessary Consequence of the other, either truly or probably';[33] the

[30] *Scopus* is a topos of Greek philosophical and rhetorical prolegomena; its Latin
equivalent *intentio* appears in the list of seven expository topics in Servius' introduction
to the *Aeneid* (Vergil's *intentio* was 'to imitate Homer and praise Augustus from his
ancestors'), and in due course passed into the medieval *accessus ad auctores* (Klopsch
1980, 48–64, Quain 1945), and into early modern hermeneutic theory.
[31] References and discussion in Heath 1987a, 2. 2 and (for the 'platform' image
below) 3. 2.
[32] See Heinsius 1643, 92 (first published 1611).
[33] Dacier 1705, 134 (first published 1692).

episode was now, in the words of an English contemporary, 'a necessary Part of an Action extended by probable Circumstances'.[34] Dacier reflects also the growing demand for a single 'chief character' in each play: if two characters 'had both been Heroes, so equal, that the part of one had not been subordinate to the other, there had been no unity of action' (47). This requirement was formulated most explicitly by La Motte, who argued that 'unity of interest' is in fact more fundamental to drama than unity of action.[35] This trend anticipates the intense concern which critics of the later eighteenth and nineteenth centuries had with the character and subjectivity of individual 'dramatis personae'. At this time, too, we find that older ideas of the moral utility of tragedy gave way to a philosophically more ambitious vision of tragedy as the embodiment of an 'idea'. This point could be illustrated from Hegel, if Hegel lent himself to concise quotation; instead, we shall return to Boeckh.

We have already mentioned August Boeckh's theory of literary unity in connection with Pindar—and that is perhaps its best known, and certainly most influential, application. But it was in fact a general theory of much wider application.[36] The first level of unity in Boeckh's theory is that of objective unity; in the case of a tragedy, this would be the unity of action. The subjective unity is the purpose beyond itself to which the exposition of the plot is subservient. Taken together, these two determine the material unity of the play, the functional subordination of objective to subjective content ensuring that the two, taken together, are unified. This is distinguished from its formal unity, the logically and rhetorically apt disposition of its parts in the service of the material unity. The purpose which constitutes the subjective unity is, for Boeckh, the expression of a unitary thought (*Gedankeneinheit*: 132): 'the whole dramatic action is simply the embodiment of a *Grundgedanke*, the presentation of which is therefore the play's overall purpose (*Gesammtzweck*)' (146); 'The essence of drama is the presentation of an action, but the inner kernel of the action, its soul, is an idea, which discloses itself there' (90). This 'idea' may be moral; for example, *Antigone* embodies the thought that moderation is best and should be observed—on pain of disaster— even in just endeavours.[37] This approach to the plays does not differ

[34] Dennis 1939–43, i. 58 (from 'Remarks on Prince Arthur', 1696).

[35] See La Motte 1859, 455 (from 'Discours à l'Occasion des Machabées', 1730).

[36] Boeckh 1886, 131–3, 144–7; here too I draw on and develop the discussion in Heath 1986b and 1987c.

[37] Boeckh 1886, 90; cf. the detailed discussion in Boeckh 1884, 125, 130–47.

significantly from the moralizing exegesis of the sixteenth century—
except in the strenuous insistence on the *unity* of the moral lesson, on
the thematic integration of each text; and Boeckh explicitly relates
this requirement to the Neoplatonist theory of unique *skopos* (citing
Proclus on *Republic*), in the belief (mistaken, as we have seen) that this
accurately reflects both Plato's, and the general ancient, aesthetic.[38]

I suggested in Chapter 1 that the intellectualising and centripetal
tendencies of recent exegesis stand squarely in the tradition of
Boeckh. It would not, of course, be fair to say that recent critics have
adhered to a theory of unified *skopos* or of *Grundgedanke* in quite the
systematic and uncompromising way of Boeckh or the Neoplatonists;
but it would be fair to speak of an analogous tendency.[39] Our remoter
forebears, the classical scholars of the Renaissance, took (or took over
from the ancient rhetoricians) a view of literary structure essentially
the same as that which I have been attributing to the Greeks; but we
have inherited the concept of unity from more recent predecessors
who were deeply hostile to thematic proliferation and digression, and
we remain deeply suspicious of such practices ourselves. If one's
techniques of exegesis are sufficiently powerful, it will always be
possible to reconcile any text with any set of aesthetic norms that one
chooses; so we need come to no overt grief if we insist on applying to
the products of a centrifugal literary culture the exegetical techniques
of our own centripetal criticism. But misunderstandings which do not
advertise themselves as such are the most dangerous kind.

[38] Boeckh 1886, 133, with 1872, 439–40 (first published 1835).

[39] This is true, in a sense, even of poststructuralist interpretation, despite its radically
centrifugal outcome; the deconstructive 'aporia' is typically generated by pressing the
common insistence on thematic integration to a point at which the coherence sought
breaks down into apparently irresolvable perplexities. When the sweeping claims
which poststructuralists like to make about 'reading' and 'textuality' are reinterpreted
as claims about certain historically contingent things that we have learnt to do with
some kinds of text, they become more plausible, but somewhat less exciting.

I I

Conclusion

In Chapter 1 we saw that unity or coherence is one of the qualities we expect in a well-formed text, and that we interpret texts on the (defeasible) assumption that they will possess it. But it is also a cultural variable: what counts as coherence differs from one time or people to another. In view of the difficulty which modern criticism has had with texts such as Euripides' *Suppliants*, it is tempting to conjecture that a cultural difference of this kind is impeding our approach to Greek literature. We read on the assumption that these texts will be well-formed according to our—broadly, 'centripetal'— notion of coherence; but there is reason to suspect that a more 'centrifugal' conception of literary unity would be more appropriate to them. The question which this book set out to raise, therefore, was whether ancient secondary poetics supported that conjecture. The answer to which the preceding chapters point is—yes; where the characteristic tendency of modern criticism is to seek coherence in thematic unity, the characteristic tendency of ancient criticism was to seek coherence in thematic plurality ordered primarily at a *formal* level.

We began by looking at Plato. In the *Phaedrus* Plato formulates a principle of appropriate order; this proved to be a teleological notion—appropriateness must be judged by reference to the end or ends of a given genre. In the case of a philosophical dialogue the end is to promote philosophical understanding or moral virtue through discussion; texts of this kind, therefore, unfold as the participants follow the lead of their argument (or are distracted from it by their own character and interests), subject to the constraint of philosophical utility, but not of thematic unity. Nor did Plato in practice feel constrained to pursue integration at the thematic level.

In fourth-century rhetorical theory the notion of *kairos*, when applied to questions of structure, corresponds to Plato's notion of appropriate order. Here, too, genre is decisive. Forensic oratory, a strictly utilitarian genre, eschews digression and is obliged to concentrate on the point at issue; there is a task in hand, and everything is subordinated to that task. But in epideictic oratory these constraints do not apply, and digression is in order; Isocrates can be seen to have to composed in this way, and Aristotle recommends the principle.

Aristotle seems at first sight to take a more stringent view of unity in his theory of narrative genres—primarily, epic and drama; but this is due to a shift in the level on which he is working. He is not concerned, as Plato was, with the organization of the literary text as such, but with the underlying structure of its plot. He argues that a unifed plot (a closed causal sequence of events) is a condition of appropriate order in a tragedy; but this does not exclude digression and other centrifugal techniques in the text which realizes that plot, and his commendation of *epeisodia* in epic shows that he saw a place for such techniques.

Aristotle seems to have regarded chronological closure as the equivalent in history to the unified action of epic and drama, the structural *sine qua non* of good order. Later rhetorical theory does not follow him in this. Dionysius discusses the choice of subject-matter and its delimitation in terms not of unity but of such qualities as attractiveness and instructiveness; even Polybius, who notes the peculiarly unified nature of the events of the period with which he is concerned, does not seek to impose chronological or causal closure on historiography in general. Unity enters the discussion when the text is in question, and designates a text that is lucidly and interestingly achieved. Herodotus' subject-matter is not unified, but his text is; an extreme case, perhaps, but in general diversity inherent in the subject is desirable, and over and above this opportunities to digress from the subject are sought since (used in due measure) they help to make the text lucid and interesting by relaxing and refreshing the reader.

The scope for diversification in history and the legitimacy of the techniques by which this can be achieved depend on the view taken of historiography's function; the more emphasis is placed on its aesthetic dimension, the more diversification is desired. This is parallel to the distinction in rhetorical theory between forensic and epideictic oratory, which can be traced also in Hellenistic and later rhetoric. Theorists took a restrictive view of digression in forensic speaking, although most allowed it limited scope as a way of holding attention and so achieving the genre's functional ends; in oratory designed for ornament and display digression was more freely available—historiography and poetry being classed as genres of this kind. The organization of the text—the making of a lucid and interesting text

out of a possible plurality of themes together with such digressions as
may be included—is the level at which the organic analogy (which
has a wide range of other uses) makes significant contact with
concepts of unity.

Since poetry as well as history was classed with epideictic oratory,
we would expect the same kinds of analysis to be applied in poetic
criticism. This is confirmed by the Homeric scholia, which are deeply
interested in *poikilia*, and note digressions and episodes approvingly.
The flexible treatment of similes in the scholia suggests that this kind
of analysis could be very effective in practice; and we saw that there is
evidence in the Homeric texts themselves to support the scholiasts'
view of digression. There is no doubt that later epic, especially in the
Callimachean tradition, made deliberate use of digressive techniques.
The scholia differ from Aristotle in taking a more historiographical
view of the epic hypothesis—they see it as a broad field of events
rather than as a single action; they use the order of exposition to
distinguish epic from history, epic being inverted, historiography
direct. However, this leads to a result similar to Aristotle's analysis of
Homeric episodes.

The sole significant exception to the generally centrifugal approach in ancient criticism is the Neoplatonist theory of unified
skopos, mistakenly believed by its proponents to have been Plato's
theory. It is in fact a novelty; a much more Platonic approach is to be
found in Dio, while in the rhetorical tradition the standard concepts
of refreshment and relaxation were freely applied to the dramatic
elements of Plato's dialogues. The Neoplatonists were aware that
they were diverging from this tradition; and we can in fact trace the
emergence of their theory—Porphyry was not an adherent, Iamblichus was.

In the last Chapter we surveyed briefly the history of unity in post-
classical criticism. In the criticism of epic the multiple action which
romance inherited from medieval poetics clashed in the Renaissance
with classicizing demands for a single action; but there was at this
stage no exclusion of digression even on the part of the classicists—on
the contrary, epic's digressive potential was part of the case against
romance. The exclusion of digression was a subsequent development.
This is true also of dramatic criticism. In the early Renaissance a
single action was demanded; but this action could be extended and
diverse, and admitted digression. That tolerant attitude gave way to
increasingly centripetal requirements; digression was excluded, the

single action was defined restrictively and unity of personal focus was expected, and in due course thematic unity was also required. Similarly in Pindaric criticism the acceptance, based on ancient rhetoric, of digression and plurality of theme eventually gave way first to a condemnation of it, and then to a thematically integrated reinterpretation. We have inherited prejudices, of which this history traces the origins.

Can we derive a general theory from this summary?[1] It may be helpful if we continue to distinguish between two levels of analysis—those of hypothesis and text.

(i) At the level of the hypothesis (the underlying subject-matter of a text), the criteria of selection and delimitation differ according to genre. They *may* include conditions related to unity—for example, continuity and closure of plot in epic or drama. But this is not inevitable; the functions of a genre may render these irrelevant and promote other considerations, as in history or philosophy. Even when unity is imposed as a condition at this level, it is only a minimal condition; the plot of a tragedy may be unified without being *good*. The criteria for an optimal plot must be defined in relation to the genre's end—in tragedy, the excitation of certain kinds of pleasurable emotion.

(ii) Whether or not criteria of unity are imposed at the level of hypothesis, unity is always an issue at the level of text (the way the hypothesis is realized). There are two dimensions, to consider: the individual segments of text, and the whole text as an ordered

---

[1] In Heath 1987a, 3. 2, I proposed four criteria by which to judge the 'unity' of a Greek tragedy. Two of these criteria, closure (completeness) and continuity, were derived from Aristotle's analysis of the tragic plot. A third, diversity, governed the treatment of material within the framework established by the plot; this reflected the emphasis in ancient criticism on *poikilia*. The fourth, coherence, was seen as imposing a necessary constraint on the pursuit of diversity; a tragedy's diversity should be so ordered as to afford an aesthetically satisfying sequence of primary and ancillary effects. A fifth consideration, I suggested, was that of quality; the components of a play ought to achieve effects appropriate to tragedy, and ought to do so without infringing the other norms (such as dignity) of tragic poetics. This consideration, though clearly connected in some way to coherence, was distinct from and more fundamental than the four structural criteria. In the case of Sophocles' *Ajax*, for example, what exercised ancient commentators was not the play's 'unity' (which has troubled some modern critics), but the quality of its closing scenes—did they dissipate its emotional effect (πάθος) and sink to the undignified level of comedy (see Σ S. *Aj.* 1123, 1127, with Heath 1987a, 5. 42, 5. 63)? This scheme still seems to me broadly correct, but the relation between its elements could have been developed more perspicuously; the text attempts a more satisfactory formulation.

sequence of segments. We are concerned at this level, therefore, both with the intrinsic quality of each part of the text, and with the quality of their conjoint effect—that is, with their coherence: a text must achieve generically appropriate ends in a lucid and interesting way.

(iii) Diversity is one constituent of coherence; for a lack of diversity, if it produces fatigue (κόρος), necessarily precludes coherence. It may be inherent in the hypothesis—for example, an extended action in tragedy, or one with potential for suprise effects.[2] But it may also be achieved by digression from the hypothesis. This does *not* mean that an author may wander from his hypothesis at whim; although (by definition) not part of the exposition of the hypothesis, a digression is—or ought to be—a calculated enhancement of a particular text at a particular point, rather than a random divagation (it is not, therefore, open to the criticisms which Aristotle makes of ἐμβόλιμα). A digression must be smoothly articulated with the surrounding text, so as to seem a natural elaboration of the text rather than an arbitrary excrescence, emerging from and returning us to the hypothesis by some intelligible train of thought; and it must fulfil, or contribute to the fulfilment of, some function appropriate to the genre (ornamentation is a function, and is appropriate in different degrees to different genres).

(iv) It should be stressed that we are concerned not only with the relatively formal issue of smooth articulation, but also in every instance with the characteristic end or ends of each genre; one must ask whether a segment of text, or a sequence of such segments, achieves the (primary or ancillary) effects appropriate to a text of that genre, subject to any constraints imposed by that genre. This means that the assessment of a text's appropriate construction always involves questions of content: are the functions of the genre fulfilled? Giving precedence to criteria at the level of the text over those concerned with subject-matter in a discussion of unity is therefore not a 'formalist' move; it is simply to maintain that we are ultimately concerned not with the structure of a hypothesis in the abstract, but with its concrete embodiment as text.

This, then, is something like a general theory of unity in Greek poetics—derived from secondary sources, but I would argue also faithful to the primary poetics of Greek literary production and

---

[2] Cf. *Σ* BT *Il.* 21. 34 (ch. 8 n. 20 above) on the *poikilia* of suprise.

reception. What follows? It certainly does not follow that Greek literature *cannot* be interpreted in other terms; the history of the reception of Greek literature in modern times proves that it can. But the fact that a text *can* be interpreted in a particular way does not mean that it is *rightly* so interpreted. To answer that question, I have argued, it is necessary to be critical of our own preconceptions and attempt to reconstruct the conventions of literary practice current in the texts' culture (or cultures) of origin; in which case the conclusions reached in this book suggest that Greek texts are not rightly so interpreted. A centripetal aesthetic was not, until a late and anomalous stage, influential in the Greek world; tolerance of digressive and centrifugal techniques of composition was standard. Consequently, centripetal assumptions are quite unacceptable as premises in the interpretation of Greek texts; and interpretations of particular Greek texts that try to coerce them into conformity with the centripetal aesthetic deserve to be treated with caution. This is not, of course, to deny that some Greek texts are amenable to such treatment: centripetal options were always in principle available to Greek authors *within* their centrifugal aesthetic;[3] but they were not prescriptive.

A qualification is necessary. To speak of texts being 'rightly' interpreted presupposes a normative standard of interpretation, a criterion of meaning; and no such criterion can lay claim to exclusive validity. The aptness of an answer depends on the question asked. The questions I have been asking in this study are literary-historical ones: what did ancient authors mean, and how did ancient readers understand them? I do not deny that other questions may legitimately be asked. I have therefore been arguing conditionally: if one adopts a certain norm, what exegetical consequences follow? Were the texts meant for centripetal reception? Were they designed to be so understood? My conclusion is that they were not; but that is a challenge to the use of centripetal assumptions in interpretation only in so far as it purports (expressly or by implication) to be something other than the forceful imposition of alien preconceptions on ancient literature. I have offered no arguments against interpretations that make no claim to historical validity of that kind; in other contexts, and for other purposes, I would not necessarily reject them.

---

[3] Cf. ch. 1 n. 18 above, on Heliodorus. Pindar is an obvious case: some of his victory odes present no problem, even *prima facie*, to thematically integrated interpretation, while others are recalcitrant; we should not feel obliged, or indeed licensed, to force the latter into the same mould as the former.

Appendix A
Epeisodion before Aristotle

A FRAGMENT of a commentary on *Iliad* 21 attributes to Protagoras the following view of the fight between Achilles and the river: this *epeisodion* exists to interrupt (διαλαβεῖν) the battle and make a transition to the theomachy.[1] By the criteria we have derived from Aristotle, the battle with the river and the theomachy (which follows from it) are not necessitated by what has gone before, and have no consequences in the plot. We seem here, therefore, to have an analysis and terminology very similar to that found in Aristotle. We cannot, of course, be sure how far the coincidence is due to the commentator's paraphrase of Protagoras' otherwise unattested remark; the terminology is suspiciously similar to that of a much later period (see Chapter 8 above).

Two fragments of late fifth-century comedy contain the term. Cratinus' *Putine* ('Wine-Flask', performed in 423) began with Comedy's attempt to divorce the alcoholic poet on grounds of neglect and ill-treatment; in fr. 195 Kock (= 208 Kassel–Austin) one character seems to be advising another on the composition of a play: 'Don't talk nonsense; put him in an *epeisodion*; Cleisthenes will look ridiculous playing dice ...'.[2] In a fragment, presumably from the parabasis, of Metagenes' *Philothutes* (undated, but Metagenes is known to have been active active in the last decade of the fifth century), we find: 'I vary my text κατ' ἐπεισόδιον, so that I give the audience a rich feast of novel delicacies' (fr. 14 Kock). Kock remarks on these fragments that he can see no reason why *epeisodion* should not mean in comedy just what it means in tragedy, a part of the play included between choral odes; but this merely shows that he has not given sufficiently careful

---

[1] POxy. 221 = Pap. XII, xii 19–24 Erbse; Protagoras 80 A 30 DK. The note is to *Il.* 21. 240.

[2] Kock (following Pierson) transfers ἐν ἐπεισοδίῳ from the fragment to the context of the citation; Zielinski's acid words ('quis enim umquam antiquus scriptor, cum poetae scenici verba efferet, ea ut ex episodio petita insignivit! Videlicet ne a stasimo deprompti viderentur tetrametri iambici') are sufficient reply. (See Zielinski 1931, 87–90; but he is wrong to apply the term to the 'episodic' scenes which typically follow the parabasis; see Norwood 1930, 218.)

158 *Appendix A*

thought to the differences between the formal structure of tragedy and comedy. Kock's view was one which Meineke had already rejected. Quoting Plut. *Mor.* 1065d–6e Meineke argued that an *epeisodion* in comedy is a brief digression, a joke inserted to raise a laugh but having no necessary connection with the rest of the action.[3] He was mistaken in thinking that this passage equates ἐπεισόδιον and ἐπίγραμμα, although it is still true that the sense of digressiveness is essential to Plutarch's argument; but Plutarch's use of the term is not at issue, for fifth-century usage may have differed. Norwood argues that Metagenes' remark would be pointless if digression were not implied; the argument is weak, for Metagenes might well say that his rivals flog the same jokes in scene after scene, but that he is always introducing fresh ideas. Rather more persuasive is his observation that the word which I rendered by 'delicacy' (παροψίς) is strictly a side-dish, an extra, not part of the main menu, and therefore digressive.[4] It could be argued that the context in which Athenaeus quotes the fragment (459c) gives no support to this interpretation; Athenaeus is indicating a change of subject in the next book, and no digression is in view. But Athenaeus' interest in the lines is unlikely to have been concentrated, like ours, on the occurrence of *epeisodion*: the motif of variation (μεταβάλλω τὸν λόγον) is of more signficance for him, and the context should therefore not be pressed for clues as to the sense of our term. (In a sense, everything in Athenaeus is, being conversation accompanying dinner, a kind of side-dish;[5] this metaphor, too, is of more interest to him than the term *epeisodion*—which by his time, in any case, had certainly come to connote digression.) On balance, the evidence seems to point to a digressive implication; but the evidence is scanty, and the question can hardly be settled.

It may be worth adding that the fourth-century tragedian Astydamas used the same metaphor as Metagenes in his satyric *Heracles*, and connected it with *poikilia*: the wise poet should provide his audience with a 'varied feast' (ποικίλην εὐωχίαν: fr. 4 Snell).

[3] Cf. the definition in Bekker *Anecd. Gr.* 253. 19–20: '*epeisodion*: properly, in comedy that which is introduced into the drama for comic effect outside the subject-matter (γέλωτος χάριν ἔξω τῆς ὑποθέσεως).'

[4] G.Norwood 1920, 221.

[5] Cf. Plut. *Quaest. Conv.* 629c, which distinguishes between the essential components of a dinner (food, drink, tables etc.) and the *epeisodia* added 'for pleasure' (ἡδονῆς ἕνεκα)—various entertainments. Plutarch includes a comedian (γελωτοποιός): e.g. Philip at Xen. *Symp.* 1. 11 and *passim*; cf. Plut. *Quaest. Conv.* 710d: Xenophon and Plato both used *epeisodia* to diversify (διαποικίλλειν) their symposia, and did not have unrelieved discussion.

Appendix B
Other Poetic Scholia

THE Homeric scholia have been discussed at length in Chapter 8; the Latin commentaries on Vergil take a similar approach: see Servius on *G.* 2. 195 ('ne uniformis narratio sit'), 3. 72, 4. 136, 336 ('ne continuatio nominum posset creare fastidium'), *Aen.* 3. 24, 126, 432, 5. 154, 6. 773, 7. 732, 8. 185, 12. 90, 581; Donatus on *Aen.* 1. 546, 4. 153, 6. 562, 854 ('ne una et continua narratio taediosa sit'), 9. 416, 702, 10. 315 ('propter descriptionum varietatem et fastidium legentis mittuntur fabulae non necessariae descriptioni belli'), 575 ('ut continuatio interrupta narrantis legentis taedium relevet removeatque ex varietate fastidium'), 11. 11, 411, 605, 646, 12. 139, 340.[1] For narrative 'by inversion' see Servius' preface to the *Aeneid* (4. 16–5. 5 Thilo-Hagen): '. . . hanc esse artem poeticam, ut a mediis incipientes per narrationem prima reddamus et nonnunquam futura praeoccupemus, ut per vaticinationem: quod etiam Horatius praecipit . . . [*AP* 43f.]'; Donatus, in his preface to Terence's *Andria* (2. 2), says that the tragedians, comedians, Homer and Vergil all follow this principle.[2] Similes are treated in much the same way as in the Homeric scholia; Donatus on *Aen.* 12. 856: 'interponitur parabola, qua orationis continuatio rumperetur, ut interiectio media taedium legentis excludat'; they are used for ornament (7. 462, 10. 728, 11. 492, 721) and αὔξησις (12. 587, 'propter addendum splendorem'). Servius on *Aen.* 1. 497 attests criticism of a partial simile ('ad hoc tantum sequens pertinet comparatio, quam vituperant multi')—but this criticism he rejects as ill-informed ('nescientes . . . comparationes adsumptas non semper usquequaque congruere, sed interdum omni parte, interdum aliqua convenire'). One commentator on Apollonius of Rhodes (his hallmark is the term ὑγιής, 'sound'; this is used very frequently in the Homeric scholia in discussions of textual criticism and in evaluating

---

[1] Macrobius *Sat.* 5. 15. 14–18: Vergil varies expression in the catalogue more than Homer; 5. 16. 1–4: both insert stories for variety in catalogues; 5. 16. 5: likewise in each book of the *Georgics*.

[2] See Mühmelt 1965, 115–16.

rival interpretations, but its insistent use here in literary critical evaluation seems to be distinctive) is committed to global correspondence: approval in notes to 1. 1003–5, 1201–5, 1243–5, 1265–72 (also, without ὑγιής, 1. 307, 781); disapproval for partial correspondence on 1. 879–93 (οὐχ ὑγιὴς οὐδὲ εἰς πάντα ἁρμόζει); another, more orthodox, note to the same passage replies that part of the image is for illustrative clarity (σαφήνεια), part for descriptive beauty (πρὸς κάλλος μόνον καὶ ἔκφρασιν).[3]

There is much less relevant material in the tragic scholia; I note *PV* 631: the interlacing of Io's and Prometheus' stories is 'to refresh (νεαροποιῆσαι) the audience'; A. *Eu.* 94: *poikilia* of the opening scenes of the play; S. *Aj.* 38, 295, 784: avoidance of tedium (τὸ προσκορές); *Aj.* 719: *poikilia* of the *dramatis personae* (cf. S. *El.* 328, 632, on the juxtaposition of contrasting characters ἕνεκα τοῦ διαποικίλλειν; the hypothesis to E. *Ph.* praises the play as πολυπρόσωπον);[4] S. *Life* 20 remarks on his *poikilia*, E. *Life* on the *poikilia* of his style; the hypothesis to E. *Ph.* is unusually hostile to digression: the play is 'padded out (παραπληρωματικόν)', the *teikhoskopia* not being 'part of the play' and Polyneices' appearance being 'pointless'.

Donatus on Terence has a number of references to stylistic variety: *An.* 549, *Eun.* 322, *Ad.* 2, 993 (using the Greek term *poikilia*), *Phorm.* 65.

The scholia on Pindar should also be mentioned. When Lefkowitz attributes to these commentators 'the remarkable notion that allusions to myth are "digressions" or "excursions" rather than integral and inevitable facets of a victory ode', she is taking for granted an opposition foreign to the critical tradition in which the scholia originated;[5] as we have seen, digression is regarded in ancient rhetoric precisely as 'integral and inevitable'. The Pindaric scholia share this view. They are not worried by digression as such, but by those digressions the rationale of which is opaque; they complain only when a digression seems 'irrational' (ἄλογος: *P.* 10. 46b Drachmann) or 'inopportune' (ἄκαιρος: *P.* 11. 23b, 58ab, cf. *N.* 1. 49bc). In the special case of *Pythian* 4, they feel that the digression is of a kind inappropriate to the genre; it is 'historical' (*P.* 4 Inscr. a) or 'diegematic' (*P.* 5 Inscr.). Its narrative technique is indeed untypical

---

[3] Mühmelt 1965, 121.
[4] But according to Dion. Hal. *Imit.* 6. 2. 10 (ii 206. 7–8) Aeschylus is 'more varied' (ποικιλώτερος) than Sophocles and Euripides in introducing characters.
[5] Lefkowitz 1985, 274–5.

of epinician lyric; the conflation of this expansive and linear style of narrative with the more intricate narrative order of the first part of the poem seems to be an experiment in generic contamination—and the poem is exceptional in other respects also. See further on *P.* 8. 40, 43a, 10. 79b, *N.* 3. 45c, 114b, 4. 53a, 60b (and on Simonides also Cic. *de Or.* 2. 86 = *PMG* 510), 6. 94a, 8. 32a, 10. 35. Eustathius observes (iii 287. 16–288. 10 Drachmann) that sometimes the digression, a πάρεργον, has more space than the ἔργον of the ode, so that it is as if the song's body is pot-bellied; but this is not, he says, a mistake, but a deliberate technique: Pindar took pleasure in the greater scope which it allowed him, so that he could display his breadth of learning and his literary powers. Some digressions, he continues, have a connection with the victor and contribute to his praise; others are not so connected, although the victor is even so elevated by sharing the ode with a hero. Later (292. 27–293. 4) he says that some of Pindar's myths have a paradigmatic function, some support gnomes, and most are encomia of the victor's ancestors or country, though some have no apparent connection with their poems at all; and sometimes, he concedes, Pindar may exceed due measure.

Bibliography

Ackrill, J. L., 1974, 'Aristotle on *Eudaimonia*', *PBA* 60, 339-59 (= A. O. Rorty, ed., *Essays on Aristotle's Ethics*, Berkeley 1980, 15-34)

Atkins, J. W. H., 1943, *English Literary Criticism: The Medieval Phase* (Cambridge)

Austin, Norman, 1966, 'The function of digressions in the *Iliad*', *GRBS* 7, 295-312

Barker, Andrew, 1976, 'The digression in the *Theaetetus*', *Journal of the History of Philosophy* 14, 457-62

Barwick, K., 1928, 'Die Gliederung der Narratio in der rhetorischen Theorie und ihre Bedeutung für die Geschichte des antiken Romans', *Hermes* 63, 261-87

van der Ben, N., 1987, 'Aristotle's *Poetics*, ch. 8: a reaction', *Mnemosyne* 40, 143-8

Bielmeier, A., 1930, *Die neuplatonische Phaidrosinterpretationen* (Paderborn)

Boeckh, August, 1872, *Kleine Schriften*, vii (Leipzig)

——, 1884, *Sophokles, Antigone* (revised edn., Leipzig)

——, 1886, *Encyclopädie und Methodologie der philologischen Wissenschaften* (2nd edn., Leipzig)

Bowie, E. L., 1986, 'Early Greek elegy, symposium, and public festival', *JHS* 106, 13-35

Bramble, J., 1970, 'Structure and ambiguity in Catullus 64', *PCPS* 16, 22-41

Brink, C. O., 1963, *Horace on Poetry, I: Prolegomena to the Literary Epistles* (Cambridge)

——, 1971, *Horace on Poetry, II: The Ars Poetica* (Cambridge)

Brinkmann, A., 1906, 'Phoibammon *peri mimēseōs*', *RhM* 61, 117-34

Buchheit, V., 1960, *Untersuchungen zur Genos Epideiktikon von Gorgias bis Aristoteles* (Munich)

Buchner, E., 1956, review of F. Zucker, *Isokrates' Panathenaikos* (Berlin 1954), *Gnomon* 28, 350-3

Bundy, E. L., 1972, 'The epilogue of Kallimachos' *Hymn to Apollo*', *UCSCA* 5, 39-94

Burgess, T. C., 1902, 'Epideictic Literature', *Chicago Studies in Classical Philology* 3, 89-261

Burian, P., 1985, '*Logos* and *pathos*: the politics of the *Suppliant Women*', *Directions in Euripidean Criticism* ed. P. Burian (Durham), 129-55

Canter, H. V., 1931, '*Digressio* in the orations of Cicero', *AJP* 52, 351-61

Cantieni, Räto, 1942, *Die Nestorerzählung im XI Gesang der Ilias* (Diss. Zurich)

Castelvetro, Lodovico, 1576, *Poetica d' Aristotele vulgarizzata et sposta* (Basel)

Cave, Terence, 1979, *The Cornucopian Text* (Oxford)

Clarke, H., 1981, *Homer's Readers* (London)

Clausing, A., 1913, *Kritik und Exegese der homerischen Gleichnisse im Altertum* (Diss. Freiburg)

Cobet, J., 1971, *Herodots Exkurse und die Frage der Einheit seines Werkes* (*Historia* Einzelschriften 17, Wiesbaden)

Coleman, R., 1971, 'Structure and intention in the *Metamorphoses*', *CQ* 21, 461–77

Combellack, F. M., 1978, review of Moulton 1977, *AJP* 99, 127–9

Coulter, J. A., 1967, '*Phaedrus* 279a: the praise of Isocrates', *GRBS* 8, 225–36

——, 1976, *The Literary Microcosm* (*Columbia Studies in the Classical Tradition* 2, Leiden)

Curtius, E., 1953, *European Literature and the Latin Middle Ages* (London)

Dacier, André, 1705, *Aristotle's Art of Poetry* (London)

Dahlmann, H., 1953, 'Varros Schrift De Poematis und die hellenistisch-römische Poetik' (*Abhandlungen der Akademie . . . Mainz*, 1953 no. 3, 89–152)

Davies, J. C., 1968, 'Reditus ad rem aptus et concinnus esse debebit: Some comments on Cicero's use of *digressio*', *Latomus* 27, 894–903

Davison, J. A., 1965, 'Thucydides, Homer and the "Achaean Wall"', *GRBS* 6, 5–28

Dee, J. H., 1982, 'Catullus 64 and the heroic age: a reply', *ICS* 7, 97–109

Dennis, John, 1939–43, *Critical Works*, ed. E. N. Hooker (Baltimore)

Deubner, L., 1921, 'Ein Stilprinzip Hellenisticher Dichtung', *NJb* 42, 361–78

Dilke, O. A. W., 1954, *Statius, Achilleid* (Cambridge)

Downing, E., 1984, 'οἷον ψυχή: an essay on Aristotle's *muthos*', *Classical Antiquity* 3, 164–78

Drews, R., 1973, *The Greek Accounts of Eastern History* (Washington)

——, 1975, review of Cobet 1971, *Gnomon* 47, 329–34

Dryden, John, 1961, *Essays of John Dryden*, ed. W. P. Ker (2 vols., New York)

van der Eijk, P. J., 1987, 'Aristotle and the wounding of Odysseus', *Menmosyne* 40, 140–3

Else, G., 1963, *Aristotle's Poetics: The Argument* (Cambridge, Mass.)

Eucken, C., 1982, 'Leitende Gedanken im isokratischen Panathenaikos', *MH* 39, 43–70

——, 1983, *Isokrates* (Berlin)

Faral, E., 1923, *Les Arts Poétiques du XIIe et du XIIIe Siècle* (*Bibliothèque de l'École des Hautes Études* 283, Paris)

Fenik, Bernard, 1974, *Studies in the* Odyssey (*Hermes Einzelschriften* 30, Wiesbaden)

Fitton, J. W., 1961, 'The *Suppliant Women* and the *Herakleidai* of Euripides', *Hermes* 89, 430–61

Forcione, A. K., 1970, *Cervantes, Aristotle and the Persiles* (Princeton)

Friedl, A. J., 1936, *Die Homer-Interpretation des Neuplatonikers Proklos* (Diss. Würzburg)

Friedrich, R., 1975, *Stilwandel im Homerischen Epos* (Heidelberg)

——, 1983, '*Epeisodion* in drama and epic' *Hermes* 111, 34–52

Gamble, R. B., 1970, 'Euripides' *Suppliant Women*: decision and ambiguity', *Hermes* 98, 385–405

van Gelder, G. J. H., 1982, *Beyond the Line: Classical Arabic Literary Critics on the Coherence and Unity of the Poem* (Leiden)

Giangrande, G., 1972, 'Das Epyllion Catulls', *AC* 41, 123–47

——, 1981, 'Catullus 64: basic questions of method', *MPhL* 4, 19–23

Gilbert, A. H., 1940, *Literary Criticism: Plato to Dryden* (New York)

Gilbert, C. D., 1976, 'Ovid, *Met.* 1. 4', *CQ* 26, 111–2

Giraldi Cintio, G. B., 1554, *Discorsi intorno al comporre dei romanzi, delle commedie, e della tragedia* (Venice)

Goold, G. P., 1977, 'The nature of Homeric composition', *ICS* 2, 1–34

Gräbener, H. J., 1965, *Gervasius von Melkeley: Ars Poetica* (*Forschungen zur Romanischen Philologie* 17, Munster)

Griesinger, R., 1907, *Die ästhetischen Anschauungen der alten Homererklärer* (Diss. Tübingen)

Griffin, J., 1976, 'Homeric pathos and objectivity', *CQ* 26, 161–85

——, 1980, *Homer on Life and Death* (Oxford)

——, 1981, 'Haec super arvorum cultu', *CR* 31, 23–37

——, 1985, *Latin Poets and Roman Life* (London)

Gunn, A. M. F., 1952, *The Mirror of Love* (Lubbock, Texas)

Guthrie, W. K. C., 1975, *Plato, the Man and his Dialogues* = *A History of Greek Philosophy*, iv (Cambridge)

Hackforth, R., 1952, *Plato's* Phaedrus (Cambridge)

Hägg, T., 1971, *Narrative Technique in Ancient Greek Romances* (Stockholm)

Hainsworth, J. B., 1970, 'The criticism of an oral Homer' *JHS* 90, 90–8

Halliwell, Stephen, 1986, *Aristotle's* Poetics (London)

Heath, M. F., 1986a, 'Thucydides 1. 23. 5–6', *LCM* 11, 104–5

——, 1986b, 'The origins of modern Pindaric criticism', *JHS* 106, 85–98

——, 1987a, *The Poetics of Greek Tragedy* (London)

——, 1987b, *Political Comedy in Aristophanes* (*Hypomnemata* 87, Göttingen)

——, 1987c, '"Iure principem locum tenet": Euripides' *Hecuba*', *BICS* 34, 40–68

——, 1989, 'The unity of Plato's *Phaedrus*', *Oxford Studies in Ancient Philosophy* 7 (forthcoming)

Heilbrunn, G., 1977, 'The composition of Isocrates' *Helen*', *TAPA* 107, 147–59

Heinsius, Daniel, 1643, *De Tragoediae Constitutione* (2nd edn., Leiden)

Herrick, Marvin T., 1946, *The Fusion of Horatian and Aristotelian Literary Criticism, 1531–55* (*Illinois Studies in Language and Literature* 32. 1, Urbana)

Hoerber, R. G., 1957, 'Thrasyllus' canon and the double titles', *Phronesis* 2, 2–10

Hollis, A. S., 1978, 'Callimachus, *Aetia* fr. 1. 9–12', *CQ* 28, 402–6

Hunger, H., 1978, *Die hochsprachliche profane Literatur der Byzantiner* (*Handbuch der Altertumswissenschaften* xii. 5, 2 vols, Munich)

Immerwahr, H. R., 1966, *Form and Thought in Herodotus* (Cleveland)

Janko, R., 1982, *Homer, Hesiod and the Hymns* (Cambridge)

——, 1984, *Aristotle on Comedy* (London)

Jenkyns, R., 1982, *Three Classical Poets* (London)

de Jong, I. J. F., 1985, 'Eurykleia and Odysseus' scar: *Odyssey* 19. 393–466', *CQ* 35, 517–8

Kakridis, J. T., 1949, *Homeric Researches* (Lund)

Kames, Henry Home, Lord, 1785, *Elements of Criticism* (6th edn., 2 vols., Edinburgh)

Kelly, D. C., 1966, 'The scope and treatment of composition in the twelfth- and thirteenth-century Arts of Poetry', *Speculum* 41, 261 – 78

——, 1969, 'Theory of composition in medieval narrative poetry and Geoffrey of Vinsauf', *Medieval Studies* 31, 117–48

Kennedy, G. A., 1958, 'Isocrates' *Encomium of Helen*: a Panhellenic Document', *TAPA* 89, 77–83

1983, *Greek Rhetoric under Christian Emperors* (Princeton)

Kenney, E. J., 1976, 'Ovidius prooemians', *PCPS* 22, 46–53

Kirk, G. S., 1962, *The Songs of Homer* (Cambridge)

——, 1976, *Homer and the Oral Tradition* (Cambridge)

——, 1985, The Iliad: *a commentary, I: Books 1–4* (Cambridge)

Kitto, H. D. F., 1961, *Greek Tragedy* (3rd edn., London)

Klingner, F., 1964, *Studien zur griechischen und römischen Literatur* (Zurich)

Klopsch, P., 1980, *Einführung in die Dichtungslehren des lateinischen Mittelalters* (Darmstadt)

Köhnken, A., 1981, 'Apollo's retort to Envy's criticism', *AJP* 102, 411–22

Koster, S., 1970, *Antike Epostheorien* (*Palingenesia* 5, Wiesbaden)

Kovacs, David, 1987, 'Ovid, *Metamorphoses* 1.1–4', *CQ* 37, 458–65.

Kustas, G. L., 1973, *Studies in Byzantine Rhetoric* (Thessalonica)

Lamberton, Robert, 1986, *Homer the Theologian* (Berkeley)

de La Motte, A. Houdart, 1859, *Les Paradoxes Littéraires de La Motte*, ed. B. Jullien (Paris)

Larsen, B. Dalsgaard, 1972, *Iamblique de Chalcis: Exégète et Philosophe* (Aarhus)

Lawall, G., 1966, 'Apollonius' *Argonautica*: Jason as anti-hero', *YCS* 19, 119–70

Lawler, T., 1974, *The* Parisiana Poetria *of John of Garland* (New Haven)

Lefkowitz, M. R., 1980, 'The quarrel between Callimachus and Apollonius', *ZPE* 40, 1–19

——, 1985, 'The Pindaric scholia', *AJP* 106, 269–82

Lewis, C. S., 1936, *The Allegory of Love* (Oxford)
——, 1953, review of Gunn 1952, *Medium Aevum* 22, 27–31
Little, D., 1970, 'The speech of Pythagoras in *Metamorphoses* 15 and the structure of the *Metamorphoses*', *Hermes* 98, 340–60
——, 1972, 'The non-Augustanism of Ovid's *Metamorphoses*', *Mnemosyne* 25, 389–401
Lloyd-Jones, H., 1984, 'A Hellenistic miscellany', *SIFC* 2, 52–72
Lloyd-Jones, H. and Rea, J., 1967, 'Callimachus, Fragments 260–1', *HSCP* 72, 125–45
Lowth, Robert, 1753, *De Sacra Poesi Hebraeorum* (Oxford)
Lyne, R. O. A. M., 1978, 'The neoteric poets', *CQ* 28, 167–87
McCall, Marsh H., 1969, *Ancient Rhetorical Theories of Simile and Comparison* (Cambridge, Mass.)
MacDowell, J., 1973, *Plato*, Theaetetus (Oxford)
Macleod, C. W., 1982, *Iliad Book xxiv* (Cambridge)
Marquardt, J. and Mau, A., 1886, *Privatleben der Römer* (2nd edn., Leipzig)
Marti, B. M., 1958, *Arnulfi Aurelianensis glosule super Lucanum* (*American Academy in Rome, Papers and Monographs* 18, Rome)
Masenius, J., 1661–4, *Palaestra eloquentiae ligatae* (3 vols., Cologne)
Michelini, A. N., 1987, *Euripides and the Tragic Tradition* (Madison)
Miller, A. M., 1983, '*N*. 4. 33–43 and the defence of digressive leisure', *CJ* 78, 202–20
Moles, J., 1979, 'Notes on Aristotle, *Poetics* 13 and 14', *CQ* 29, 77–94
Moulton, C., 1977, *Similes in the Homeric Poems* (*Hypomnemata* 49, Göttingen)
Mühmelt, M., 1965, *Griechische Grammatik in der Vergilerklärung* (*Zetemata* 37, Munich)
Murphy, J. J., 1974, *Rhetoric in the Middle Ages* (Berkeley)
Nickau, K., 1966, 'Epeisodion und Episode', *MH* 23, 155–71
Nisbet, R. G. M., & Hubbard, M., 1970, *A Commentary on Horace, Odes Book I* (Oxford)
Norwood, G., 1930, '"Episodes" in Old Comedy', *CPh* 25, 217–29
Notopoulos, J. A., 1949, 'Parataxis in Homer: a new approach to Homeric literary criticism', *TAPA* 80, 1–23
Orsini, G. N. G., 1975, *Organic Unity in Ancient and Later Poetics* (Carbondale)
Page, D. L., 1955, *The Homeric* Odyssey (Oxford)
Parson, P., 1977, 'Callimachus: *Victoria Berenices*', *ZPE* 25, 1–50
Pedrick, Victoria, 1983, 'The paradigmatic nature of Nestor's speech in *Iliad* 11', *TAPA* 113, 55–68
Pépin, J., 1965, 'Porphyre: exégète d'Homère', *Entretiens sur l'Antiquité Classique* 12, 229–66
——, 1974, '*Merikōteron-epoptikōteron* (Proclus, *In Tim.*, i, 204, 24–27). Deux attitudes exégétiques dans le néoplatonisme', *Mélanges d' histoire des religions offerts a H.-C. Puech* (Paris), 323–30

Perrault, C., 1688, *Parallele des Anciens et des Modernes* (Paris)

Pfeiffer, R., 1968, *History of Classical Scholarship, 1: From the beginnings to the end of the Hellenistic Age* (Oxford)

Poliakoff, M., 1980, 'Nectar, springs, and the sea: Critical terminology in Pindar and Callimachus', *ZPE* 39, 41–7

Pontanus, J., 1597, *Poeticarum Institutionum Libri iii* (ed. 2, Ingolstadt)

Praechter, K., 1910, 'Richtungen und Schulen im Neuplatonismus', *Genethliakon C. Robert* (Berlin), 105–56 = *Kleine Schriften* (Hildesheim 1973), 165–216

——, 1912, 'Hermeias', *RE* 8: 732–5

Putnam, M. C. J., 1961, 'The art of Catullus 64', *HSCP* 65, 165-205

Quadlbauer, F., 1982, 'Zur Theorie der Komposition in der mittelalterlichen Rhetorik und Poetik', *Rhetoric Revalued*, ed. B. Vickers (New York), 115–31

Quain, E. A., 1945, 'The medieval *accessus ad auctores*', *Traditio* 3, 215–64

Race, W. H., 1978, '*Panathenaicus* 74–90: the rhetoric of Isocrates' digression on Agamemnon', *TAPA* 108, 175–85

——, 1980, 'Some digressions and returns in Greek authors', *CJ* 76, 1–8

Richardson, N. J., 1980, 'Literary criticism in the exegetical scholia to the *Iliad*', *CQ* 30, 265–87

——, 1983, 'Recognition scenes in the *Odyssey* and ancient literary criticism', *PLLS* 4, 219–36

——, 1985, 'Pindar and later criticism in antiquity', *PLLS* 5, 383–401

Rowe, C. J., 1986, 'The argument and structure of Plato's *Phaedrus*', *PCPS* 32, 106–25

——, 1987, *Plato*, Phaedrus (Warminster)

Russell, D. A., 1978, 'The pseudo-Dionysian *Exetasis* and *Mistakes*', *Entretiens sur l' Antiquité Classique* 25, 113–34

Russell, D. A. and Wilson, N. G., 1981, *Menander Rhetor* (Oxford)

Sacks, K. S., 1983, 'Historiography in the rhetorical works of Dionysius of Halicarnassus', *Athenaeum* 60, 65–87

Scheller, P., 1911, *De Hellenistica Historiae Conscribendae Arte* (Leipzig)

Schlunk, Robin R., 1974, *The Homeric Scholia and the Aeneid* (Ann Arbor)

Schmidt, M., 1976, *Die Erklärungen zum Weltbild Homers und zur Kultur der Heroenzeit in den bT-Scholien zur Ilias* (*Zetemata* 62, Munich)

Schneider, J. G., 1774, *Versuch über Pindars Leben und Schriften* (Strasburg)

Shaw, M. H., 1982, 'The ethos of Theseus in *The Suppliant Women*', *Hermes* 110, 3–19

Sheppard, A. D. R., 1980, *Studies in the Fifth and Sixth Essays of Proculus' Commentary on the* Republic (*Hypomnemata* 61, Göttingen)

Sicking, C. M. J., 1963, 'Organische Komposition und Verwandtes', *Mnemosyne* 16, 225–42

Smith, W. D., 1966, 'Expressive form in Euripides' *Suppliants*', *HSCP* 71, 151–70

Spingarn, J. E., 1908, *A History of Literary Criticism in the Renaissance* (2nd edn., New York)

Steiner, Grundy, 1958, 'Ovid's carmen perpetuum', *TAPA* 89, 218–36

Stevens, P. T., 1971, *Euripides*, Andromache (Oxford)

Stiblinus, Gaspar, 1562, *Euripides Poeta, Tragicorum Princeps* (Basel)

Süss, W., 1910, *Ethos: Studien zur älteren Griechischen Rhetorik* (Leipzig)

Taplin, O., 1976, 'χοροῦ and the structure of post-classical tragedy', *LCM* 1, 47–50

——, 1977, *The Stagecraft of Aeschylus* (Oxford)

——, 1980, review of Moulton 1977, *CR* 30, 183–4

Tarrant, H., 1983, 'The date of Anon. In *Theaetetum*', *CQ* 33, 161–87

Tasso, Torquato, 1594, *Discorsi del Poema Eroico* (Naples)

——, 1973, *Discourses on the Heroic Poem*, tr. M. Cavalchini and I. Samuel (Oxford)

Tigerstedt, E.N., 1977, *Interpreting Plato* (*Stockholm Studies in History of Literature*, 17)

Toechterle, K., 1980, 'Die μεγάλη γυνή des Mimnermos bei Kallimachos', *RM* 123, 225–34

Tsagarakis, O., 1973, 'κατάχρησις of the Aristotelian term ἐπεισόδιον as applied to Homer', *REG* 86, 294–307

——, 1982, 'The Teichoskopia cannot belong to the beginning of the Trojan War', *QUCC* 12, 61–72

van der Valk, M., 1963, *Researches on the Text and Scholia of the* Iliad (2 vols., Leiden)

Verdenius, W. J., 1983, 'The principles of Greek literary criticism', *Mnemosyne* 36, 14–59

Vessey, D., 1973, *Statius and the* Thebaid (Cambridge)

Vickers, Brian, 1988, *In Defence of Rhetoric* (Oxford)

Vinaver, E., 1967, *The Works of Sir Thomas Malory* (2nd edn., 3 vols., Oxford)

Viperanus, J. A., 1987, *On Poetry*, tr. P. Rollinson (London)

Walbank, F. W., 1957–79, *A Historical Comentary on Polybius* (3 vols., Oxford)

——, 1972, *Polybius* (Berkeley)

Walcot, Peter, 1978, *Envy and the Greeks* (Warminster)

Wardman, A. E., 1960, 'Myth in Greek historiography', *Historia* 9, 403–13

Warton, Thomas, 1762, *Observations on the* Faerie Queene *of Spenser* (2 vols., London)

Weinberg, Bernard, 1961, *A History of Literary Criticism in the Italian Renaissance* (2 vols., Chicago)

West, S. R., 1967, *The Ptolemaic Payri of the* Iliad (*Papyrologica Coloniensia* 3, Cologne)

Westlake, H. D., 1969, *Essays on the Greek Historians and Greek History* (Manchester)

Wilson, N. G., 1983, 'Scoliasti e commentatori', *SCO* 33, 83–112

Wiseman, T. P., 1979, *Clio's Cosmetics* (Leicester)

Woodman, A. J., 1988, *Rhetoric in Classical Historiography* (London)

Young, David, 1970, 'Pindaric criticism', *Pindaros und Bakchylides*, ed. W. M. Calder and J. Stern (*Wege der Forschung* 134, Darmstadt) 1–95

——, 1983, 'Pindar, Aristotle and Homer: a study in ancient criticism', *Classical Antiquity* 2, 156–70

Zanker, G., 1977, 'Callimachus' *Hecale*: a new kind of epic hero?', *Antichthon* 11, 68–77

——, 1987, *Realism in Alexandrian Poetry* (London)

Ziegler, K., 1966, *Das hellenistische Epos* (2nd edn., Leipzig)

Zielinski, T., 1931, *Iresione, I* (*Eus Supplementa* 2), 87–90

Zuntz, G., 1955, *The Political Plays of Euripides* (Manchester)

General Index

Index of Greek Words

Index of Passages Cited